CAMBRIDGE STUDIES IN PHILOSOPHY

Paradoxes

A study in form and predication

CAMBRIDGE STUDIES IN PHILOSOPHY

General editor D. H. MELLOR

Advisory editors J. E. J. ALTHAM, SIMON BLACKBURN,
MARTIN HOLLIS, FRANK JACKSON, T. J. SMILEY, BARRY STROUD

Paradoxes

A study in form and predication

James Cargile

Corcoran Department of Philosophy, University of Virginia, USA

Cambridge University Press

CAMBRIDGE

LONDON · NEW YORK · MELBOURNE

CAMBRIDGE UNIVERSITY PRESS
Cambridge, New York, Melbourne, Madrid, Cape Town, Singapore, São Paulo, Delhi

Cambridge University Press
The Edinburgh Building, Cambridge CB2 8RU, UK

Published in the United States of America by Cambridge University Press, New York

www.cambridge.org
Information on this title: www.cambridge.org/9780521109635

First published 1979
This digitally printed version 2009

A catalogue record for this publication is available from the British Library

Library of Congress Cataloguing in Publication data
Cargile, James.
Paradoxes, a study in form and predication.
(Cambridge studies in philosophy)
Includes bibliographical references and index.
1. Paradox. 2. Predicate (Logic) 3. Form (Logic)
4. Reference (Philosophy) I. Title. II. Series.
BC199.P2C38   165   78–67299

ISBN 978-0-521-22475-8 hardback
ISBN 978-0-521-10963-5 paperback

Contents

THIS BOOK IS DEDICATED
TO THE MEMORY OF MY MOTHER
MARTHA ELIZABETH CARGILE

A Summary of the Argument

Chapter 2 Mill's theory of names

12 Mill's theory of names – criticized by Frege for discussing meaning of a name outside the context of a proposition – ambiguity of 'meaning' – Frege's complaint is unclear – based on the idea of meaning as a proposition or a constituent of one – examples only show that there may be more than one candidate for 'meaning' of a term, not that meaning can never be assigned to a term independently of a proposition.

13 Mill's threefold subdivision of names mixes logical, grammatical and metaphysical questions – leads to obscurities in the distinctions – such as that between abstract and concrete.

14 Mill's distinction between general and singular names conflicts with his claim that proper names have no connotation – his answer to this difficulty is fallacious – Wolterstorff's version of Mill's distinction in terms of 'import'.

15 Mill's distinction between connotative and non-connotative, in terms of 'implying an attribute' involves the distinction in the 'paradoxes of strict implication'.

16 Lockwood sees Mill's distinction between connotative and non-connotative as similar to Donnellan's distinction between attributive and referential – Lockwood's version of this distinction – a related view of Geach – difference from Donnellan.

17 The notion of a referential use of a term to make a statement confuses statements with predications – this mistake makes it impossible to adequately say what the statement is that is allegedly made in the case of a referential use – an act of predication can be performed using an inaccurate description to refer.

18 The historical view that beliefs about physical objects are never direct goes against the doctrine that some assertions about them can be purely referential.

19 In the primary case, an assertion is the verbal expression of a belief – but even in that case, asserting of, or predicating of, is not the same as believing of – rather than 'purely referential uses of terms to make statements' we should speak of uses of terms to perform acts of predication.

20 Mill says all names are associated with mental items, which is inconsistent with his denial that proper names have connotation.

21 Whether a proper name implies attributes may be partly a matter

of conventional choices among attributes figuring in the belief expressed by the statement using the name.

22 It cannot be said what in general must be believed in using a name in an atomic statement – the 'disguised description theory' is treated as a vain attempt to do this – the 'causal theory' is a complaint about certain versions of the disguised description theory which is incorrectly called a theory – the complaint is correct, but it is no account of the relation between a name and its bearer.

23 The notion of connection between name and bearer must be distinguished from the notion of unconditioned apprehension – the causal theorists misconstrue the role of the conditions associated with a name.

24 The principal objection to the disguised description theory, that it assigns necessary consequences to uses of proper names, can be turned to the theory's advantage, as a basis for determining which among the variety of conditions a user associates with a name are the ones connected with it in a given assertion – Donnellan's 'rule for negative existence statements' is not incompatible with the disguised description theory, but only with certain choices of descriptions.

25 Though he is called a disguised description theorist, Frege's position about reference failure and existential implications is thoroughly referentialist – his inability to admit the equivalence of a 'subject-predicate' and an 'existential' version of a claim is due to his unfortunate view about 'the parts of a thought'.

Chapter 3 Platonism

26 Lockwood criticizes Mill for failing to see that an account of what is said should not include claims about the words used to say it – the predications the assertion is principally concerned to make may not be about the words – the act of abstract predication may be concerned only with properties – still, even the abstract predication is not what is said – the question whether assertions may be about the words used to make them remains.

27 Frege's view of how properties and thoughts are apprehended is circular.

28 The pure doctrine of universals is simply a consequence of the objectivity of truth – Dummett's criticism of Mill – Mill equates the connotation with properties, which is right – but he does

imply that connotation is mixed up with determining the application of a term in a way it isn't – vagueness is not in the connotation of a term, but in our own lack of knowledge.

29 The pure doctrine of universals must be distinguished from other doctrines of rationalist metaphysics.

30 Platonism and Meinongianism must be distinguished.

31 The universality of natural language celebrated – Quine's claim that the concept of objectivity is a provincial feature of our culture.

32 Quine's claim that philosophical analysis is not concerned with ordinary language – all language has ontological features which do not disappear merely by constructing a technical language which does not include the means for describing the features.

33 Platonism is misrepresented as based on a craving to make all possible existence assumptions.

34 Reasons for assuming the existence of propositions as abstract entities.

35 The complaint that properties and propositions lack satisfactory criteria of identity and individuation – Quine's formula for identity for physical objects.

36 Vagueness is not a logical matter, but an epistemological one – the distinction between subjective and objective – even a radically subjective property is a perfectly objective relation – objectivity is a sufficient basis for the pure doctrine of universals.

37 Attempts to reduce propositions to properties tend to cause worries about how 'the parts of thought' hold together – if ontological economies are needed it is classes that should go – the 'no-class' theory is not 'idle' – identity criteria for some classes are not good – there is no empty set, at least not if sets are extensional – a no-class theory could reinstate 'every property determines a class' – the principle that things can be collected into a class is a referential tautology – the 'iterative' notion of set should not be regarded as making sense of the idea that sets are human creations.

38 'One can believe that "Oxen ruminate" is true without believing that oxen ruminate' – this can be interpreted so as to be true, but it is not the only possible interpretation – the variety of possible 'states of mind' of someone who assertively intones 'Oxen ruminate' might lead us to ignore these 'states of mind' and focus on the words.

sense and saying something about the referent exclude one
another.

50 Quine advocates a view similar to the foregoing one of Frege and
Mill – rules such as exportation and substitution can be explained
for modal contexts, but not so as to make their application a
mechanical matter – my view of sense leaves it useful in answering the paradox of analysis, for which Frege's notion of sense is
not helpful.

51 A singular term is associated with the thought that a condition
is uniquely satisfied, the general term is simply associated with a
condition – but this distinction depends on adequately distinguishing denoting and connoting.

52 Mill sometimes says a term denotes a class, sometimes that it
denotes its members – he probably had a 'no-class' theory – his
claim that denotation is 'direct' and 'connotation' indirect is
undermined by the fact that denoting can be easily defined in
terms of connoting and not conversely.

53 Mill attempts to distinguish between denoting and connoting by
appeal to the fact that a term is true of what it denotes, not what
it connotes, but this is not always true – being true of, just is
denoting.

54 Various associations with a term could be called 'connotation' –
reasons for preferring one association over others.

55 On this account, the question what holds the parts of a thought
together does not arise – there is an infinite series of instantiation
relations – but this is not due to any problem about attaching a
property to a thing to which it is attributed or to an instance of
it.

56 Anything can be predicated of anything – on this point Ramsey
is right, though he mistakenly runs this together with the false
view that there is no difference between subject and predicate
position – Geach's 'absolute distinction between names and
predicables' does not count against this.

Chapter 5 Meinongianism

57 Formal and functional singularity.

58 Failure of reference occurs in the existential 'version' of 'The
King of France is wise' just as much as in the original – this raises
a difficulty for both Russell and Strawson – substitutional
quantification does not solve Russell's problem.

70 Attributing a predicate and holding it to be satisfied are distinct but not mutually exclusive – belief-ascribing a predicate must be distinguished from assertion-ascribing – singular belief is more fundamental than singular assertion, but quantified assertion is more fundamental than quantified belief – English readings of universal generalizations may use the pronoun in a sham reference – this 'reference' can be 'carried on' in a separate general statement – in natural language, we might say that the same quantifier can govern separate statements.

71 The formal distinction between subject-predicate and existential does not apply to propositions – the natural functional distinction involves considerations of emphasis which may be brought into the style of description of the thought so that two descriptions of the same thought have different emphasis – functionally the 'bare existence' claim can be classed as a type of subject-predicate claim.

72 A popular argument for the view that statements about future individuals must be general is a typical example of the idea that using the term 'subject' so that a term does not qualify as 'subject' guarantees that the term therefore does not refer, or that if a sentence contains no term which qualifies as referring, the statement it conveys cannot be about anything.

73 Distinctions between general and singular statements are not as important as attending to the bases they can have, and recognizing that they do not mark epistemological distinctions – modern quantification theory based on the singular, traditional theory based on the general – the four categorical forms – Mill's account of the universal affirmative ignores distinction between grammatical singular and plural.

74 Russell's view that 'man' and 'all men' denote 'the class of all men' suggests the 'class subsumption' analysis of (A) propositions – which is not a very satisfactory formal classification.

75 The 'class membership' analysis extends more naturally to the other categorical forms – whether this makes the (A) proposition an ontologically singular subject-predicate one depends on what is the predicate – the distributive predication version does not apply well to all categoricals, especially in the case of 'some' – the alternative is to count the quantifiers as part of the predicate.

76 Distributive predication more plausible for 'every', but the case

of 'some' is still odd – it would not be if Hilbert's epsilon operator were a genuine referential device – but it isn't.

77 Even if a radical view which rejects my claim that statements are never individuated by reference to physical objects is accepted, my criticism of referentialism stands – a condition's being uniquely satisfied is always the basis of reference.

78 Kinds of predication.

79 Asserting is predicating truth and conversely – types of predication and assertion – the distinction between assessable and non-assessable asserting is crucial to the semantic paradoxes.

Chapter 7 Semantic paradoxes

80 The semantic paradoxes are sentences such that the traditional style of stating what they say leads to contradiction.

81 Paradoxes involving other propositional attitudes than saying by a sentence or a person can be dealt with separately.

82 The adequacy of a description of what is said depends on the purpose for which the description is required – what a sentence by itself says has to do with what people take it to say, but this does not make it a simple matter of people *deciding* what to take it to say.

83 Our formulation of semantic paradoxes is incompatible with nominalism, but everything is – there are some paradoxes that could be put in nominalist terms.

84 What it means to rule that a sentence says nothing – this 'cross out' approach is incompatible with the ideal of 'straightforward' assessment of meaning – but does not limit what can be said – it is only unsatisfactory because of what it leaves unexplained.

85 Tarski's doctrine that the notions of the theory of reference and meaning are relative to a language doesn't apply well to a natural language.

86 Tarski's use of 'semantically closed language' is ambiguous between merely being a language (such as English) which includes its own semantic terms and being such a language *and* having all the so-called 'T sentences' as theorems – Tarski holds that there could be semantically closed languages in the latter sense.

87 Russell's attitude towards stratification differs from Tarski's because he does not think there are languages that violate it – but

Preface

This book has grown out of a chapter of my PhD dissertation (Cambridge, 1965) and I am glad to have the opportunity to again thank Jonathan Bennett for having been such an inspiring dissertation advisor. Time to finally finish the book was made available by a Sesquicentennial grant from the University of Virginia and a grant from the American Council of Learned Societies. The University also provided a grant to cover the cost of typing the manuscript, which was ably done by Mrs Beverly W. Fox. Our department secretary, Mrs Eusebia Shifflet, has been a great help in the preparation of the manuscript, and David Holt worked on the index. I am especially grateful to Timothy Smiley for reading through the penultimate draft and offering many helpful comments. W. E. ('Ted') Morris has been a regular source of encouragement. Most of all, my wife, Jean, has encouraged this work.

Introduction

Historically, the semantic paradoxes were thought to undermine the rationalist metaphysics of Plato and the Stoic ideal of the life based on reason. Epictetus told his followers that while he could not give them an answer to the Liar paradox, they should have faith that an answer would be found. I hope in this work to justify that admirable faith.

In modern times, the theory of sets which was shown to be inconsistent by the paradoxes of Cantor, Russell, and others, has been called 'absolute platonism'. I will argue that this is a misnomer. I believe that a platonistic ontology is correct, and that reasonable objections to certain confusions in platonistic epistemology have unfortunately been taken to count as well against the ontology. I have made no attempt to establish the objectivity, the mind-independence, of truth, or the absolute generality of the laws of classical logic. My concern has been to show that this basic doctrine of rationalism is free of inconsistency.

Besides the semantic paradoxes in the narrow sense, which are cases in which the traditional assumptions about what is said or conveyed by pieces of language lead to contradictions, there are paradoxes such as the Sorites, or the arguments for treating cases of reference failure as exceptions to the laws of classical logic, which I have also tried to answer. In the course of this I have devoted considerable space to explaining and justifying the traditional semantics of connotation and denotation. However, I realize that I have not adequately answered those who favor the 'naturalization' of epistemology. My plan is to take up questions of knowledge and perception in a separate work. Again, my concern here is to show that there is no good reason to reject the laws of classical logic or their universal applicability. The semantic paradoxes are not due to anything wrong with classical assumptions about truth or to an ontology including propositions and properties, but to mistakes in describing what propositions and properties are expressed by given sentences or other linguistic expressions. Furthermore, an essentially platonistic theory of predication not only avoids the paradoxes, but provides the basis for a natural and convincing answer to them which calls for no restrictions on generality.

I

Subject-predicate form

1 It is common, in traditional grammar, to say that the subject
of a sentence is the word or group of words that denotes the thing
or things of which the predicate is predicated. It is also commonly
said that virtually all sentences have a subject and predicate, or are
compounds of sentences which do. (This is usually applied not only
to declarative sentences, but to others as well.) A third standard idea
of traditional grammar is that a sentence is a word or group of
words that expresses a complete thought.

Each of these three ideas is in apparent conflict with things many
philosophers and logicians have said about the terms 'subject' and
'sentence'. Many philosophers have said that in many sentences the
grammatical subject does not denote anything at all. Furthermore,
it is common to say that many sentences are not of subject-predicate
form, and do not have subjects. And finally, with regard to the third
idea, it is common to say that many sentences, considered apart from
their use to make a statement, do not express a complete thought.
For example, it is said that the sentence 'He is sick', though it can be
used to make many distinct statements, does not, by itself, express a
complete thought.

Philosophical criticism of the grammatical definition of 'sentence'
is reasonably well-founded. 'He hit him' is clearly a sentence, but
does not obviously express a complete thought. However, 'expresses
a complete thought' is very vague, and it is probably vague enough
to make it unjustifiable to say that the grammatical definition was
simply mistaken.

Similarly, the philosophical criticism of the grammatical definition
of 'subject' is fairly sound. It is almost as clear that 'He' is the
subject of 'He hit him' as it is that this latter is a sentence. And it is
also quite clear that 'He' in this sentence, taken by itself, does not
denote anything.

However, the situation is much less clear with respect to the
grammatical idea that virtually all sentences have subjects. For here

everything depends on what is meant by 'subject'. And having shown cause for setting aside the grammatical definition, philosophers have used the term 'subject' without offering any adequate definition for the term.

It may be replied that a term can be used quite precisely without benefit of a definition. This is true. The terms 'grammatical subject' and 'sentence' may even serve as good examples of this, since most educated persons can apply them very accurately. But as philosophers use 'subject' there are disputes about its application. And even to begin to settle these disputes would require knowing precisely what the parties to the dispute mean by 'subject'.

There is a tension here between reforming the grammatical definition, on the one hand, and restricting its application, on the other. In this connection, the following remarks of Miss Anscombe's are worth considering:

> I am not opposing the practice of grammarians and linguists for whom the expression 'direct object' is defined as an expression for a phrase; they use that as I use the expression 'direct-object phrase'. But ... the question 'What does the sentence say John gave?' is fundamental for understanding either 'direct object' or 'direct-object phrase' as I am using those expressions; and hence for understanding 'direct object' when it is used for a phrase. And though the question is answered (like many questions) by uttering a phrase – in this case 'a book' – the phrase has *a special use* in answer to that question 'What does the sentence say John gave?' It can name neither a piece of language, nor anything that the piece of language names or otherwise relates to, nor indeed anything else. The interest of the question and answer is the rather special interest of getting grammatical understanding.
>
> (Anscombe 1965, p. 165)

Now consider the sentences 'John gave Mary no consideration whatever' and 'John gave Mary nothing'. The 'direct-object phrase' in the first is 'no consideration whatever', in the second, 'nothing'. But is 'grammatical understanding' enhanced by asking 'What does the sentence say John gave?'? This question might just confuse the student and make teaching him to identify direct-object phrases more difficult. You would have to explain that sometimes it helps to ask that sort of question, but even when the sentence plainly doesn't say John gave anything at all, the verb 'gave' may have a direct object.

The same is true of 'Nothing suits him' or 'At most one person is a King of France'. 'What does the sentence say suits him (or is a King of France)?' is not likely to help a student understand what the grammatical subject is.

At this point, we could go two ways. We could stay with the spirit of the grammatical definition of 'subject', and hold that it has been misapplied, or we could stay with the grammatical application of the term, and say that it has not been correctly represented by the definition. That is, we could either revise the definition, or correct its application.

Some philosophers use the notion of 'logical form' in a way that tends to take over the grammatical definitions and correct their application. We might say that when a sentence really does express a complete thought, and has a term which really does stand for something of which the predicate is predicated, then it is of logically subject-predicate form. Then the notion that virtually all English sentences are of this form would be clearly false. Similarly, we might define logical, as opposed to grammatical, direct and indirect objects, and so on.

However, to begin to speak in this way (and it is only a beginning) immediately raises questions about the 'logical' in 'logical form'. For it would seem that, on this account, 'The positive rational root of four is even' would be of logical subject-predicate form, while 'The positive rational root of two is even' would not. But the difference between the status of these sentences appears to be a matter of mathematics, not of logic. A similar point can be made with the examples 'The present Queen of England is married' and 'The present Queen of France is married'. Should their difference be a logical matter? Russell, for example, assumes not, and takes it as obvious that these sentences are of the same logical form. And yet he also assumes that logical subject-predicate form always involves a thing being denoted by the subject. This will be a matter for further discussion.

2   The grammatical definition of a sentence applies better to statements, or 'cognitively meaningful sentences', or 'propositions' on one use of this ambiguous term.

The principal interpretations of 'proposition' are, on the one side, a sentence which expresses a complete thought, and on the other the complete thought expressed by the sentence, viewed as an entity itself, separate from language, which can be expressed by different sentences, in different languages. These two ways of interpreting 'proposition', one as a term for a sentence that expresses a complete thought, the other as a term for the thought itself, are associated with a long-standing philosophical controversy. On one side there are those who hold that propositions are sentences and that it is a mistake to think there are such things as thoughts, as abstract entities, expressed by sentences. On the other side are those who insist that there are such entities, so that even if 'proposition' is used for sentences expressing complete thoughts, a term will still be needed for the thoughts themselves.

As is common in philosophy, this distinction between two possible ontological views, one for, and one against, propositions as abstract entities, is almost as apt to create misunderstanding as it is to help, in the classification of the views of individual philosophers. I propose to call the sentence which expresses a complete thought the 'Russellian proposition', and the thought itself, as an abstract entity, the 'Fregean proposition'. But in addition to justifying this usage I must warn against the idea that the views of these two thinkers can be neatly classified on this ontological question.

This is especially true of Russell. In *The Principles of Mathematics* (1903) he says that 'a proposition is anything that is true or that is false'. Someone who (like me) accepts the idea that such a sentence as 'Man is a rational animal' expresses the thought that man is a rational animal, and that this latter is a thing separate from the sentence and also expressed by the Latin sentence 'Rationale enim animal est homo', would naturally take this claim of Russell's to require that both the sentence 'Man is a rational animal' and the thought it expresses be called propositions. For the thought is true, and by virtue of expressing it, the sentence is true.

Russell never did deny that there is something besides the sentence which must be associated with it if the sentence is to count as true or false. This idea is a great source of confusion. Sometimes it is held that a sentence that expresses a complete thought will be associated with mental images, which are what distinguish the sentence from one that hasn't been given sufficient 'meaning' to have a truth value. Whatever merit this sort of idea has, it is unfortunate if the Fregean proposition, the thought expressed by a sentence, is attached to a sentence for the purpose of giving it a meaning. The doctrine that mental images associated with a sentence provide it with 'meaning' is at least not circular. But the situation is very different with Fregean propositions. To say that the difference between a sentence meaning nothing to a given person and another sentence meaning something to him is a matter of his being stimulated to mental images by the one and not by the other, for all its deficiencies, is a substantive claim. To say that the difference is that one expresses a proposition or thought to him while the other does not just begs the question. Thus it is important to be conscious of the different interpretations that can be given to the claim that a certain entity connected with a sentence is its meaning.

Russell says:

> The phrase which expresses a proposition is what we call an 'incomplete' symbol; it does not have meaning in itself, but requires some supplementation in order to acquire a complete meaning. This fact is somewhat concealed by the circumstance that judgement in itself makes no *verbal* addition to the proposition. Thus 'the proposition "Socrates is human"' uses 'Socrates is human' in a way which requires a supplement of some kind before it acquires a complete meaning; but when I judge 'Socrates is human', the meaning is completed by the act of judging, and we no longer have an incomplete symbol. The fact that propositions are 'incomplete symbols' is important philosophically, and is relevant at certain points in symbolic logic.
>
> (Whitehead and Russell 1913, p. 44)

These remarks show that it would not be fair to charge Russell with failing to distinguish between a sentence and a use of a sentence to make a statement. It is in the use to make a statement that the sentence receives the necessary 'supplementation'.

Russell says that the proposition is an incomplete symbol, and also that the phrase which expresses it is an incomplete symbol. Since it is a sentence which is the incomplete symbol, this is to identify the proposition first as something expressed by the sentence, and second as the sentence itself, provided that it is suitably supplemented.

However, I do not think Russell meant to have the proposition play the role of supplement to the sentence. What he did mean is not clear. In his *Inquiry into Meaning and Truth* (1940), he said that the proposition is a class of synonymous sentences. This was his attempt to account for the idea that the same proposition can be asserted in different languages, and a bad attempt it was, since to call a class of sentences true or false or to say that someone, in asserting a proposition, is asserting a class of sentences, calls for explanations which are not worth giving. But the attempt does show that Russell was sensitive to the idea that the same proposition can be asserted in different languages. He was sensitive to considerations in favor of the proposition as an entity distinct from a sentence, but he earlier tried to resist giving the proposition this status.

Russell also says:

> a judgement does not have a single object, the proposition, but has several related objects . . . when we judge (say) 'This is red', what occurs is a relation of three terms, the mind, and 'this', and red . . . It follows from the above theory that a 'proposition', in the sense in which a proposition is supposed to be *the* object of a judgement, is a false abstraction, because a judgement has several objects, not one.   (Whitehead and Russell 1913, p. 44)

What this suggests to me is the view that the supplementation of a sentence is provided by things which are not propositions. However, what Russell calls the 'judgement' is either true or false, and so this would qualify as a proposition, according to the standard put forward in Russell (1903), which has it that anything which is true or false is a proposition. And the 'judgement' (as Russell uses the term) is such a thing as a person's judging a thing to have a property. But when he talks of the form of propositions, Russell never considers any such entity. What he usually considers, and needs to be interpreted as considering, is just the 'supplemented' sentence. And this is what I am going to mean by the 'Russellian proposition'. Russell does speak of the constituents of a proposition in a way that best makes sense in reference to the proposition as the 'judging complex'. But this doesn't square with his calling 'the proposition as object of judgement' a 'false abstraction'. He could, I suppose, have said that the judging complex is not the object of judgement, but is still a proposition, but he did not say this. His remarks about constituents of propositions are certainly important features of his work, but in my opinion his claims about form are more important, and they call for taking the proposition to be the supplemented sentence.

On the other hand, by the 'Fregean proposition', I mean the thought expressed by a 'supplemented' sentence treated as an entity distinct from it. ('Distinct from it' is a redundancy, except that it is common to use expressions such as 'the thought expressed by the sentence' while denying 'ontological commitment' to such entities, and then otherwise redundant phrases such as 'distinct entity' come to be accepted as signals of 'ontological intent', whatever that may be.)

Russell's notion of 'supplementation' and the corresponding notion of 'expressing a complete thought' are very unclear. He says that the act of judging supplies the needed supplementation. But complete sentences may occur as disjuncts or antecedents or consequents in judgements and clearly express complete thoughts without being 'judged' or asserted themselves. Furthermore, the notion of judging itself is open to debate in a way similar to the terms it is used to explain. Thus there could be dispute over whether 'The Absolute is red' expresses a complete thought, which would not be resolved by looking into whether someone employs the sentence in an 'act of judgement'. For someone may think he is judging something in assertively intoning 'The Absolute is red', while others may hold he is talking nonsense. To decide whether a judgement has been made amounts to the same task as deciding whether the sentence expresses a complete thought.

When we speak of form, it is the Russellian proposition that should be the bearer of form. The Fregean proposition can only be said to have form in a derivative way, since it is not a concrete thing. It might be asked whether the Russellian proposition is really a concrete thing. Russell never bothers with the trouble it would be if the proposition were a supplemented sentence token. For example, he freely engages in repeating a sentence written earlier as if it were the same proposition. The mere publishing of several copies of a manuscript complicates matters for an author who wishes to speak of the proposition as a supplemented sentence token. But strictly speaking, it is with such concrete things that talk of forms should start. The extension to more natural ways of speaking is plain enough to be taken for granted.

3 It may be worth explaining the notion of 'a form' as it is used here. A *linguistic form* is one or more blanks plus some linguistic expressions, strung out in the way appropriate for expressions of

that language. For example, the following are linguistic forms for English:

(i) _____
(ii) _____struck_____
(iii) _____'s is a _____and a_____
(iv) s_____a_____o_____and_____ebc_____

A sentence is *of* a given form if it can be derived from that form by making substitutions in its blank places.

A *restricted linguistic form* is a linguistic form accompanied by requirements which must be met by an expression in order for it to qualify as a correct substitution in a blank of the form. Sometimes these restrictions can be written in parentheses in the blanks. For example:

(i) (subject) _____ (predicate) _____
(ii) (five-letter word) ___ (obscene word) ___ (three-word phrase) ___
(iii) ('Yes' if Fermat's conjecture is true, otherwise 'No') _____

These examples may show that all sorts of considerations may be relevant to deciding whether a given sentence is of a given restricted form. It may even be impossible to decide whether a sentence is of a given restricted form. Furthermore the question whether a sentence is of a given form may be absolutely devoid of interest.

In the case of our 'subject-predicate' example, it is left unanswered what it is to be a subject. This is part of the topic of this book.

The question of logical form is very obscure. That is, there is a substantial usage built up around the term 'logical form', and this usage is very obscure. It may be that logical form, as some philosophers use the term, is no more a matter of form than a decoy duck is a duck. But I prefer to treat the notion as dealing with linguistic forms, so that some subclass of linguistic forms would qualify as logical forms. However, it is difficult to make clear what makes a form a logical form. One notion that naturally suggests itself is formal validity. In logic, claims are made to the effect that all arguments of a given form are valid. This fits the present account of form quite nicely. But an indication of logical form may be concerned with other things than formulating generalizations about validity, and the notion of logical form is as important in metaphysics as it is in logic. At any rate, even if my notion of logical form is too austerely tied to the notion of linguistic blank forms to capture some metaphysical uses of 'logical form', those uses may be clearer by comparing them with my notion.

4 It should be clear, on this account of form, why Russell's notion of a proposition is better suited to talk of form than the abstract notion of a proposition or a statement. For in this latter sense, the same proposition is conveyed by the sentences 'McGovern opposes Nixon' and 'Nixon is opposed by McGovern'. But this means that the question of the order in which Nixon and McGovern are mentioned in the proposition cannot arise. The abstract proposition is thus totally dissimilar from a sentence, and the notion of form applicable to sentences is not applicable to such propositions in any direct way.

Frege employed the notion of a proposition or thought in the abstract sense, according to which sentences of very different forms and in different languages may express the same proposition. This notion has been criticized from an ontological standpoint for assuming the existence of abstract entities. I have no quarrel with the ontological assumption. But Frege did not recognize clearly that propositions do not have form in the way sentences do. Frege was forced to reject the idea that 'Socrates is wise' and 'Wisdom is a characteristic of Socrates' express the same proposition. To acknowledge that they do would require giving up the attempt to treat abstract propositions as having form in the same way sentences do.

This distinction between the Russellian proposition and the abstract, Fregean proposition would have helped the discussion of the question whether truth is a property of statements. Austin (1950) and Strawson (1950a) had a well-known disagreement on this question, with Strawson holding that truth is not a property at all, and Austin holding that truth is a property possessed by statements by virtue of correspondence with facts. Both these philosophers regarded ascribing truth to sentences, rather than statements, to be a serious mistake. But they do not seem to mean the same thing by 'statement'. For Strawson, the statement is like the Fregean proposition; for Austin, it is like the Russellian proposition. Thinking in terms of the Russellian proposition, 'The statement "Socrates is wise" is true' can be viewed as a claim about the Russellian proposition 'Socrates is wise' which involves in part the idea that the parts of this expression and their structural arrangement correspond with a state of affairs. On the other hand, thinking in terms of the Fregean proposition, 'It is true that Socrates is wise' can be regarded as adding nothing to the assertion that Socrates is wise. And the notion of correspondence has no clear application to a thing which has no formal structure at all.

When we say, with respect to the *sentence* 'Socrates is wise', that the thing denoted by the subject is in the class denoted by the predicate, we may be saying that the thing denoted by 'Socrates' is in the class denoted by 'wise', and this is usually to say a very different thing from what is said in saying 'Socrates is wise'. On the other hand, if we try to do something similar in expressing the truth conditions of the Fregean *proposition* that Socrates is wise, we will say something to the effect that the thing which satisfies the condition of being Socrates is an instance of the property of being wise, and this is to say nothing but what is said in saying that Socrates is wise. If this were taken to be the condition of the truth of the proposition, on analogy with the condition for the truth of the sentence, then stating the truth conditions of the proposition and asserting that they are satisfied would amount to nothing more than asserting the proposition. This provides a natural basis for Strawson's idea that predicating truth is empty. Austin's idea to the contrary finds a basis when the object of the predication is the interpreted sentence, or Russellian proposition.

5   One popular conception of logical form is the idea that the logical form of a sentence is the form of its translation into the standard symbolism of predicate logic. This idea ignores the basis of formal classification. To say, for example, that 'Socrates is wise' is of subject-predicate form because it is symbolized by '*Fa*', is to overlook the question why '*Fa*' itself is said to be of subject-predicate form. This is not just a matter of arbitrary stipulation. It has to do with the semantic rules for interpreting '*Fa*'. And once this is recognized it should also be recognized that there were semantic rules applying to 'Socrates is wise' long before there were any for '*Fa*'.

This is not to say that the apparatus of quantification theory does not provide a useful tool for evaluating the validity of arguments. It is just that when this apparatus is applied to an argument in English, the assessment of the argument will not be a purely formal one. On a given interpretation, '*Fa*' will say that a certain thing, which is denoted by '*a*', belongs to a certain class, denoted by '*F*'. On such an interpretation '*Fa*' has the form '(term denoting a class) (term denoting a thing)'. Such a form is extremely unusual in English. But English sentences of many forms may be regarded as conveying this same information. Thus 'George is deficient in iron' and 'George is suffering from an iron deficiency' might both be represented by '*Fa*' where '*a*' denotes George and '*F*' denotes the class of iron-deficient people. This representation ignores many complexities, and yet, for the purpose of assessing some arguments in which George's illness is premised, this simplification will leave out nothing of importance to the validity of the argument. But the simplification does involve translating the premise into an equivalent one of another form. And this is a highly informal procedure. Being of a certain form is one thing; being representable for certain purposes by something of that form is another.

Rather than interpreting such a formula as '*Fa*' by having '*a*' and '*F*' *denote* things, they are sometimes related to things in a different way. For example, '*a*' might be made to symbolize 'Socrates' and '*F–*' to symbolize '——— is wise'; and '*Fa*', the result of putting '*a*' into the blank of '*F–*', would thus represent 'Socrates is wise'. The rules for interpreting the standard symbolism in this way are not nearly as clear and simple as they are for the previously discussed sort of interpretation. Furthermore, it would be a mistake to assume that an abbreviation for 'Socrates is wise' would automatically have the same form as the original, in the sense of being also of every form the original is an instance of. For example, the abbreviation has the order reversed. It represents the original order, of course, but not by copying it. Thus, on this interpretation, a claim about the form of '*Fa*' would not necessarily apply as well to 'Socrates is wise'. But insofar as claims about the forms of symbolic formulae are merely a way of expressing claims about natural language sentences there is no conflict with my approach.

6 The requirements placed on a restricted form are usually not formal. For example, whether a term *denotes* is not a formal question about it. But the question may arise in deciding whether the term satisfies the condition placed on the blank in some restricted form. For that matter, a restricted form may arise by placing restrictions on the entirety of some less restricted form.

Consider for example the form 'All *A*'s are *B*'s' or the form 'All

S is *P*', which are two versions of 'the' categorical universal affirmative in traditional logic. One traditional question about this form was whether it has existential import; that is, whether something of the form 'All *A*'s are *B*'s' entails a corresponding thing of the form 'Some *A*'s are *B*'s'. Taking the entailment to hold gives the existential interpretation of the universal affirmative, rejecting it gives the hypothetical interpretation. It is possible to make the entailment into a restriction on a form which had left this question unspecified. Then, if something which was otherwise of the universal affirmative form did not have the required entailment, it would not, for that reason, be of this new restricted form.

Overlooking the possibility of this sort of restricted form may lead to confusing a preference for one sort of formal classification over another with a substantive disagreement as to the logical powers of a form. The question 'Does every statement of the form "All *A*'s are *B*'s" entail the corresponding statement of the form "Some *A*'s are *B*'s"?' cannot be answered without a careful account of what is involved in being of the form 'All *A*'s are *B*'s'. The notion 'being of the form "All *A*'s are *B*'s"' may well be ambiguous.

The statement 'All Iranians with IQs over 180 are educationally underprivileged' might be made on the basis of a survey of Iranians with IQs over 180, or it might be based solely on a study of the Iranian educational system which did not enquire whether there were any such Iranians. A statement made on the latter basis might naturally be treated hypothetically, while a statement with the former basis might be treated existentially. Whether or not one agrees with these two treatments, it would be incorrect to hold that both cannot be right on the grounds that the two statements under study are exactly the same or at least the same in form.

The fact that the logical powers of a statement may be necessary conditions for its qualifying for a certain formal classification must not be confused with the idea that the logical powers could be sufficient conditions. This is not true. Formally different statements may have the same logical powers. And except for trivial exceptions (such as the trivially general form '——' restricted solely in terms of logical consequences), mere identity of consequences is never enough to guarantee identity of form.

If a sentence form is restricted in terms of the logical powers of the sentence, then such a formal classification will not help in determining the logical powers of the sentence. If some sentences of the form

'All *A*'s are *B*'s (for a suitably unrestrictive version of the form) have existential import and others do not, then it would be nice to have a general account of the difference. This might not be possible merely in terms of the functioning of the parts of the sentences, if, say, it was a matter of the joint functioning of the parts being affected by features of the context of utterance, or some such. But anyway, a formal analysis based on a form restricted to sentences having existential import would obviously be of no use at all in such an enquiry. However, that is no reason for denying that such restricted forms are forms. Equating the notion of form with that of interesting or useful form is a bad practice. The fact that there are uninteresting forms may itself be interesting, and even if it isn't, it is still a fact.

It might seem that if the notion of form is flexible enough to allow for the possibility of treating existential import as a formal feature, then it is flexible enough to allow translation into symbolic form to serve as a test of form. Now, for one thing, the fact that existential import may be a feature required for being of a certain form does not make it a formal feature. A formal feature arises as a result of combining a number of functional units by putting them into a given form. Existential import is not a matter of combination of parts, but of other considerations external to the sentence. (Or rather, that is how it is with 'All *A*'s are *B*'s' – it might be a matter of combination in some other case.) But it may be important, in a system of formal classification, to keep track of the fact that among statements of the form 'All *A*'s are *B*'s' some have existential import and some do not. Whether we do this by adding existential import as a requirement to obtain a further restricted form, or instead, merely use the common form and remind ourselves of the two different classes, is not important. It is only important to be aware that it is possible to proceed in the former way, so as to avoid needless argument and misunderstanding. Existential import can be made to belong to a system of formal classification without being a formal matter.

The same could be done with translations into symbolic logic. But it would be pointless and apt to mislead. We might say that 'Socrates is wise' is of subject-predicate form because it can be obtained by substitution from '(sentence a properly taught student would symbolize as "Fa")'. To be precise, this would call for explaining how the proper teaching works. But it would make a formal classification.

The trouble with this is that it would be an absurdly circuitous way to get at the notion of subject and predicate. And that is the principal defect in the idea that translation into symbolic logic reveals logical form. My requirement, that the claim that a sentence is of a given form should be established by actually exhibiting the sentence as a substitution instance of that form, will only serve to initially bring out the inadequacy of the translation notion of form. For people who talk about logical form in terms of translation into symbolic logic never even think about meeting this requirement. But the requirement could be met in a trivial way. The more important defect is that by moving the question of the form of one sentence over to the question of the form of some other sentence in a symbolic notation, one is not any closer to the concepts of subject and predicate. These concepts *have to do with forms*, but that does not mean they are purely formal.

With respect to many classificatory terms, the question whether they are formal or functional needs to be raised. For example, consider the notion of being a conditional, or, for the sake of simplifying the discussion, the notion of being a material (truth-functional) conditional. It might be said that the following is a conditional form: '(name of a proposition) materially implies (name of a proposition)'. But why is it called 'conditional'? We could of course say that this is merely the arbitrarily assigned name for that form; but no one thinks that reflects the truth about the use of the term 'conditional'. We might explain in terms of what the relation of material implication is. But that relation, which holds between p and q if the substitution of a name for p in the first blank and a name for q in the second yields a true sentence, also holds in the same way with respect to: 'Either (name of a proposition) is not the case or (name of a proposition) is the case.' And this latter is clearly a different form. The function of asserting that one proposition materially implies another can be accomplished equally well by either of these two distinct forms. A third form for the same purpose, '(name of a proposition) is implied by (name of a proposition)' differs from the first only in explicitly referring to the converse of the relation referred to by the first and requiring a different order.

The first of these forms could correctly be called *the* form of a material conditional, reflecting the fact that it explicitly mentions the relation of material implication and puts the terms related in a standard order. But then, to say that a statement does not have the form of a material conditional does not entail that it does not perform the function of conveying a material conditional assertion. The idea of *purely* formal validity is a confusion. *Modus ponens*, for example, can be called a formal rule, but the forms used to express it will contain parts which function to represent a certain relation. There is of course the idea of a 'purely formal system' with syntactic rules for manipulating expressions to which no interpretation is assigned. But to call a certain relation determined by such rules 'validity' is either just arbitrary, or else derives plausibility from the 'coincidence' that these 'arguments' ascribed 'formal validity', though viewed as uninterpreted, do have interpretations which make them genuinely valid (that is, truth-preserving).

The laws of logic are thus not purely formal, and it is misleading to call them 'laws of thought'. For they are the laws they are because of ideas they express, and these ideas cannot regulate themselves, or determine their own limits of application. And such concepts as negation or implication are not formal concepts in the sense that they are somehow derived from or even adequately explainable in terms of their relation to statements of certain forms. Rather, that those statements have the forms they do is determined by their involving those concepts.

7   A superficial defect of the idea that logical form is translation into symbolic notation is the fact that the translation process is not precisely described. One alternative conception of logical form which remedies this defect, is offered by Katz (1965). His account gives accurate instructions for performing the translations, not from the sentence into a symbolic notation, but from 'underlying phrase markers' to the sentence.

Katz defines 'logical form' as follows: 'The logical form of a sentence is the set of its semantically interpreted underlying phrase markers; the grammatical form of a sentence is its superficial phrase marker with its phonetic representation' (1965, p. 600).

Katz would say that the sentences (i) 'John is easy to leave' and (ii) 'John is eager to leave' have the same grammatical form, but that this grammatical analysis fails to bring out 'the logical difference that in (i) "John" is the object of the verb "leave" whereas in (ii) "John" is its subject'. He says:

The logical difference between (i) and (ii) noted above can be indicated with the underlying phrase markers:

(I) ((((it) ((one)$_{np}$ ((leaves)$_v$(John)$_{np}$) $_{vp}$)$_s$)$_{np}$ ((is) (easy) $_a$) $_{vp}$)$_s$

(II) ((John) $_{np}$ ((is) ((eager) $_a$ ((John) $_{np}$ (leaves) $_{vp}$)$_s$)$_a$)$_{vp}$)$_s$

The grammatical relations *subject of* and *object of* are defined in syntactic theory in terms of subconfigurations of symbols in underlying phrase markers as follows:

Given a configuration of the form

$$((X)\,_{np}\,(Y)\,_{vp})_s \text{ or } ((X)\,_{np}\,((Y)\,_v\,(Z)\,_{np})_{vp})_s$$

X is the subject of the verb Y and Z is the object of the verb Y. By this definition, 'John' in (i) is marked as the object of the verb 'leaves' because it occupies the Z-position and 'leaves' occupies the Y-position in the appropriate subconfiguration of (I), and 'John' in (ii) is marked as the subject of 'leaves' because it occupies the X-position and 'leaves' occupies the Y-configuration in the appropriate subconfiguration of (II).   (1965, p. 596)

We could indicate that 'John' is subject of the verb 'leave' in (ii) and object in (i) by adding to a grammatical form which both (i) and (ii) have in common, such as

$$((NP) ((is) (Adjective) (V)) VP)\,_s$$

a further restriction on the adjective place in the form – the restriction that the adjective be one which has the effect of making the NP the subject of the V (or the object) in the resulting sentence. This will give two distinct forms which exhibit the difference between (i) and (ii).

Katz's procedure is more formidable, and probably has great merit in linguistics, though I am in no position to say. But it does not go any further towards explaining what it is to be an object or subject of a verb (or what it is to be a verb). To be subject or object of a verb is not primarily a matter of form. To present the ideas that leaving John is easy or that leaving is something John is eager to do, are functions that can be accomplished in language in a great variety of ways. We might say that when X is the subject of the verb Y we will mark this fact with the symbolic expression ($(X)\,_{np}\,(Y)\,_{vp})_s$, but then the only defining done here is the verbal business of introducing a symbol for the undefined idea of being a subject of a verb.

Katz says, 'By this definition, "John" in (i) is marked as the object of the verb "leaves" because it occupies the Z-position and leaves

occupies the Y-position in the appropriate configuration of (I)'
(1965, p. 587). But if this is so, then 'object' is not a logical classification. The question as to what is the object of the verb arises in (I) as
much as in (i).

As has already been observed, my elementary requirement for
logical form, or any linguistic form (namely, that of exhibiting the
sentence as a substitution instance of the alleged form), can be
satisfied in trivial ways, so that satisfying the requirement is no
guarantee of being a non-trivial formal classification. That discussion was concerned with the requirement as a necessary condition.
It would seem that the requirement would make a very straightforward sufficient condition. But this raises difficult questions.

8   Perhaps the most obscure employment of the notion of logical
form is involved not so much in positive claims as in denials that a
given sentence is of a given form. The classic example is Russell's
denial that 'The King of England in 1905 is bald' is really, or logically, of subject-predicate form.

In 'On Denoting' (1905), Russell says that the phrase 'the present
King of England' denotes a certain man, namely the man who was at
that time King of England. Thus the sentence 'The King of England
is bald' is, on Russell's own acknowledgement, of the form '(term
denoting a thing) (predicate)'. Thus it would seem that if my
requirement is a sufficient condition, the above sentence would
qualify as of subject-predicate form. Russell could argue (would
argue) that being of the above form is not enough to qualify as
being of subject-predicate form, but his primary argumentative
device is to say that the sentence is not of subject-predicate form
because it is merely an abbreviation for something of another form.
If my formal test is a sufficient condition (and I think it should be)
this style of argument is incorrect.

Russell says:

If we say, 'the King of England is bald', that is, it would seem,
not a statement about the complex *meaning* 'the King of England',
but about the actual man denoted by the meaning. But now consider 'the King of France is bald'. By parity of form, this also
ought to be about the denotation of the phrase 'the King of
France'. But this phrase, though it has a *meaning* provided 'the
King of England' has a meaning, has certainly no denotation, at

least in any obvious sense. Hence one would suppose that 'the King of France is bald' ought to be nonsense; but it is not nonsense, since it is plainly false.   (1905, p. 46)

Russell then goes on to say:

> we must either provide a denotation in cases in which it is at first sight absent, or we must abandon the view that the denotation is what is concerned in propositions which contain denoting phrases. The latter is the course that I advocate. The former course may be taken as by Meinong, by admitting objects which do not subsist, and denying that they obey the law of contradiction; this, however, is to be avoided if possible.   (1905, p. 47)

We might begin by asking just what form it is these statements have in common. All Russell provides is that both 'The King of France' and 'The King of England' are 'denoting phrases'. He says:

> By a 'denoting phrase' I mean a phrase such as any one of the following: a man, some man, any man, every man, all men, the present King of England, the present King of France, the centre of mass of the solar system at the first instant of the twentieth century, the revolution of the earth round the sun, the revolution of the sun round the earth. Thus a phrase is denoting solely in virtue of its *form*.   (1905, p. 41)

Russell's use of 'form' here is very casual. He has done nothing but cite examples, assuming we will know how to generalize. A natural generalization would be to say that by 'denoting phrase', Russell means the same as 'grammatical substantive', whatever that means. However, in his earlier chapter on denoting in *The Principles of Mathematics* (1903), Russell says, with respect to the six words 'all', 'every', 'any', 'some', 'a', and 'the', that 'It is plain, to begin with, that a phrase containing one of the above six words always denotes.' This doctrine is rejected in 'On Denoting' (1905), along with the theory of denoting which includes it. But perhaps Russell retained the idea that to be a denoting *phrase* was a matter of beginning with one of those six words even if it didn't guarantee denoting. This would be a start towards a formal classification, whether useful or not. But the term 'phrase' would still need explaining. Russell obviously does not mean that a denoting phrase has the form '(one of the six key words) (some string of words)', but if a phrase is not a string of words then what is it?

We might answer that the phrase must be a 'noun phrase'. This would give a formal classification based on the undefined idea of a noun phrase, or perhaps on the idea of a noun and its modifiers. Taking these ideas for granted would not be satisfactory, in view of the stress Russell places on the distinction between these grammatical notions and the notion of a genuine logical substantive.

At any rate, if we assume that both 'The King of England is bald' and 'The King of France is bald' are of the form '(denoting phrase) (predicate)' we still do not have any justification for Russell's conclusion that since the two sentences are of the same form and the second is not 'concerned with' or 'about' a denotation, the first is not either. For one thing, 'All Iranians with IQs over 180 are educationally underprivileged' is also of this form. But even if there are no such Iranians, and thus that sentence is not 'concerned with' its denotation, that is not a reason for thinking the same must apply to 'The King of England is bald'.

If the focus is narrowed from denoting phrases generally to definite descriptions, the argument from 'parity of form' is still obscure. (Furthermore, there is difficulty in characterizing 'definite description' that starts even before the difficulty of defining 'noun phrase', since it is not clear whether Russell wants to count 'The whale is a mammal' as involving a description to which his theory does not apply or rather, to somehow disqualify it as a description.) If someone says, in 1905, 'The King of England is bald', a certain person would, in Russell's terms, be denoted by the phrase 'The King of England', but the statement would not be about, or concerned with, that person. Whatever meaning this may have is not brought out merely by observing that 'The King of France' is also a denoting phrase, or also a definite description.

It is here that the burden of argument falls on Russell's famous *analysis* of 'The King of England is bald'. This analysis is not stated correctly in 'On Denoting' (1905) and the correct version calls for some separate discussion, but for the present we may consider a popular version of Russell's analysis which Russell himself used, even though it is quite different logically from the intended analysis. It is 'At least one person is a King of England; at most one person is a King of England; and any person who is King of England is bald.'

This analysis consists of three separable assertions. With respect to each one of them, taken by itself, it is quite natural to say that it is not about or concerned with any individual. To say 'At least one person is a King of England' leaves open the possibility that many are Kings of England and does not purport to single out any one of them. To say 'At most one person is a King of England' leaves open the possibility that no one is, and to say 'Any person who is King of England is bald' is speaking hypothetically, with no concern whether there is a King.

If we accept the principle that if each of a series of assertions is not about an individual, then the series as a whole isn't either, then it would be quite plausible to say that the popular version of Russell's analysis of 'The King of England is bald' is not concerned with, or about, the individual who was King of England at that time. This is not to suggest that I endorse that principle. I think it is false. Nor is it clear that Russell endorses it. He should not argue from the popular version of his analysis, anyway. But the popular version shares with the real version the feature that it is at least possible to see what someone is thinking when he says it is not concerned with or about the denotation of 'The King of England'. Thus Russell's argument turns on denying that 'The King of England is bald' is concerned with the denotation of its grammatical subject term, on the ground that this statement is in some sense equivalent to a statement which is not so concerned. The parity of form between 'The King of England is bald' and 'The King of France is bald' is not what establishes the paradoxical claim about aboutness. It is the parity of form with the Russellian analysis that does. And it is with regard to this alleged formal parity that my requirement for a formal analysis is violated. For Russell would not suggest that both 'The King of England is bald' and his analysis can be derived by substitution from some underlying form. He would say, rather, that his analysis is the right way of making the statement because it brings out what one is really concerned with or thinking about. But even if this were true, it would not establish any kind of formal similarity between the statement and the analysis.

Against the fact that both 'The King of England is bald' and 'The King of France is bald' are of the form (*denoting phrase*) (*predicate*), we can balance the fact that the former is of the form (*denoting phrase which denotes*) (*predicate*) while the latter is not. Why should not this disparity of form be just as impressive as the parity with respect to another form? The answer is, again, that everything depends on Russell's attributing the form of his analysis to the statement of which it is an analysis. Thus I think Russell's notion of 'logical form' is not really a formal notion after all.

9 Russell presents his theory as if it were the only alternative to two other theories, those of Meinong and Frege. Both these theories 'provide a denotation in cases in which it is at first sight absent'. Meinong (1961) would say that the phrase 'the King of France (in 1905)' stands for an object which does not exist. Frege's approach is very different. For strictly mathematical purposes, Frege (1952, 'On sense and Reference') arranges his logical system so that a definite description 'the F' denotes the class of F's in cases where there is not exactly one F. This rule has 'the King of France in 1905' denoting the null set. Frege himself pointed out that this was only a technical device, and he would probably have accepted Russell's complaint that this device 'is plainly artificial, and does not give an exact analysis of the matter'.

Frege did have a view about what actually happens, which is a very interesting alternative view. He held that when a sentence which expresses a complete thought has a subject term which does not denote, the sentence is then neither true nor false. This suggests that a system of logic adequate to deal with all language would not satisfy the principle of bivalence.

That some things are neither true nor false is quite obvious. The vast majority of sticks, stones, bodies of water, celebrations, and such like, are neither true nor false. But classical logic holds that 'propositions', in one or another sense of this term, or 'statements' or 'cognitively meaningful sentences' are either true or false. This amounts to the doctrine that whatever could appear in an argument as premise or conclusion is either true or false. This principle is obviously important in formulating semantic generalizations about arguments. Matters would be more complicated if some genuine arguments contained premises or conclusion which lacked a truth value.

Frege's attitude about this seems to be that natural languages are undesirable for scientific purposes because they do allow non-referring singular terms to be used, and this leads to a breakdown of classical logical principles. He would thus probably have regarded his artificial device for eliminating non-referring singular terms as an improvement.

Russell's attitude is commendably different. He wants to know the true principles of logic applicable to argument in any language whatever. For this enterprise, pragmatic appeals to scientific utility carry no weight, unless of course one espouses philosophical pragmatism and presents that as the truth of the matter, or all there is to truth itself.

Many philosophers seem to think, as Frege seemed to think, that the true logical principles applicable to natural languages are quite messy or at least not the principles of classical logic. Russell tends to regard this as obviously wrong, a mistake due to the fact that natural languages really are misleading and confusing, so that they give the superficial impression of not conforming to principles of logic. The language really fits the principles, but the misleading appearances need to be corrected to ensure scientific accuracy.

We have here two very different motives for replacing part or all of a natural language with an eye to greater logical precision. One would do so to make logical principles applicable. The other would do so to make their applicability more perspicacious.

Those who adopt the former attitude may not do so with respect to all principles. It is quite common (though in my opinion, quite mistaken) to think that the law of non-contradiction is more fundamental than the law of excluded middle. So apparent conflicts with the law of non-contradiction (as when we hedge by saying 'It is and it isn't') are dismissed as mere appearance while the law of excluded middle is not treated so generously. (In fact, I have heard philosophers cite 'It is and it isn't' as a counter-example to the law of excluded middle!) Again, in ordinary English, the statement 'Johnny just isn't behaving at all' is equivalent to 'Johnny is behaving badly', and no one treats this as a proof that, in English, contradictories can be true at once.

The fact that the laws of classical logic are absolutely and universally applicable has profound consequences for metaphysics. As will be brought out later, even Russell was not successful in acknowledging this full universality in his system. But on the present topic, I can only endorse his assumption that an exact account of the topic of reference will conform to classical logic.

Russell's view and the views he sees as alternatives can be related by considering the following three assumptions, which form an inconsistent triad:

(1) A sentence with a genuine, non-referring subject term cannot be either a true proposition or a false proposition.

(2) The sentence 'The King of France is bald', as understood by many English speakers with reference to 1905, is a true or false proposition.

(3) The sentence 'The King of France is bald', so understood, has a genuine subject term which does not refer.

Frege's view as to the truth of the matter is the one advocated later by Strawson (1950), according to which it is (2) that must be rejected. But Frege's technical device would avoid this by pretending that it is (3) that is false. And this corresponds to the course taken by Russell and by Meinong as well. Thus Russell considers only three alternatives to his view, and the two he mentions as serious alternatives are two different ways of rejecting (3).

If Russell's survey of the competition is accepted, his view must seem irresistible. For when someone sincerely asserts 'The King of France in 1905 is bald' (in a case in which he believes there is a king, and not some ingeniously devised irrelevant example), it is perfectly ridiculous to suggest that he has unwittingly ascribed baldness to the null class or to some non-existent entity. Meinong's theory acquires a superficial appearance of plausibility in connection with terms such as 'Santa Claus', where there is a common temptation to regard the term as standing for a non-existent. But in a case of a sincere error as to what exists, as when I say 'The man who set this fire deserves to be punished' when in fact the fire was set by lightning, it is absurd to suggest that I have, unbeknownst to me, ascribed a predicate to a non-existent, so that the question whether I am right will now depend on whether a certain non-existent entity has that predicate, so that whether I am right will then be quite a mystery.

It is striking that in his canvass of alternatives, Russell does not even mention the possibility of rejecting premise (1). He rejects the idea that 'The King of France (in 1905) is bald' is neither true nor false, but he does not even consider the idea that this proposition is false *precisely because* it has a subject term which does not refer. He holds that the proposition is false, and concludes that it cannot be the case that it has a genuine non-referring subject term. His answer is that it does not have a genuine subject term at all. So he sees the competition as views that hold the proposition to have a referring subject term after all, and those views are no competition.

One philosopher who has suggested marking sentences which

are not logically compound as false if they contain non-referring terms is Quine (1953, 'Meaning and Existential Inference'). However his reasons are pragmatic. If one insists on a formal system which allows non-referring terms, then that is a way to arrange the semantics conveniently. Thus the proposal is just an alternative to Frege's technical device of avoiding reference failure, with the guiding idea being that it is technically convenient to preserve bivalence in a system of logic meant for use in doing science. The assumption that premise (1) still tells the truth of the matter for natural language is left unchallenged.

My view is that premise (1) is false, and that when a sentence expressing a complete thought, which is not logically compound, contains a non-referring singular term, then the sentence is false. This doctrine has important philosophical consequences which can only be brought out by analysing crucial terms in premise (1). Russell could say that my denial is vacuously true because no sentence with a genuinely non-referring term can express a complete thought. To show that this isn't so requires some further clarification of, among other things, what reference failure is.

10 I propose to give a definition of a logically subject-predicate sentence which is implicit in Russell's writing. The definition is no explanation but it will help organize an explanation and provide a basis for contrast with such a notion as grammatical subject-predicate form.

From the traditional grammatical definition we may retain this much: a logical singular term is a term which denotes (or stands for or refers to) exactly one thing. A sentence is of logically subject-predicate form if it expresses a complete thought; has just one logical singular term other than the predicate term or phrase; has just one predicate term or phrase, which is in some suitable way related to a predicate, which is thereby predicated of the denotation of the logical singular term which is the logical subject term; and is not a compound sentence. To extend this definition to cover the case of logically n-place relational sentences would be easy enough if we accepted the practice of regarding relations as predicates of ordered n-tuples. This practice is all right mathematically, but misleading ontologically. We should, strictly speaking, not say that the relation $Rx_1 \ldots x_n$ is predicated of the n-tuple $a_1 \ldots a_n$ but rather that it is predicated of $a_1 \ldots a_n$ respectively.

This approach has the consequence that predicating a relation is not simply a matter of predicating an *n*-place predicate of a thing (an *n*-tuple), which makes the transaction straightforwardly analogous to the subject-predicate case (where $n=1$). Rather, a relation is predicated of more than one thing, and is predicated of them in an order. This means that the predication of relations is not really just a trivial generalization of the subject-predicate case.

This definition of logical subject-predicate form takes for granted the idea of a sentence expressing a complete thought, the idea of a predicate term (it is left open whether a predicate term is a logical singular term – this must be discussed later), the idea of a compound sentence, and the idea of a word or group of words denoting, standing for, or referring to, exactly one thing. Each of these notions is such that disagreement has arisen over its range of application.

One might avoid reference to the notion of a compound sentence by saying that a logically subject-predicate sentence has just one logical subject and one predicate and nothing else. But without introducing a definition to restrict the vagueness of 'predicate', which I do not choose to do at this point, this would be no gain in precision. For one thing, the question whether there is a copula, in addition to the subject and predicate, should not be dismissed without discussion. And further, does a sentence such as 'John is blond and blue-eyed' (when used in reference to some person) have just one predicate ('is blond and blue-eyed' or 'blond and blue-eyed') or two ('blond' and 'blue-eyed')? This question is just the same as the question whether this sentence is compound or not (assuming 'John' to be a logically singular term in this case).

One of the simplest 'compounders', negation, raises the most difficulties. Does 'John is not blond' qualify as a logically singular subject-predicate sentence on a 'regular' occasion of use? Not if it is the *negation* of 'John is blond', because both these statements would be false if, due perhaps to a group hallucination, 'John' failed to refer. (That is, they would on the basis of the doctrine I am opposing to premise (1)). And a statement and its negation cannot both be false, by the definition of 'negation' (or even the common part of various competing definitions). The presence of grammatical negatives is not enough by itself to determine whether a statement is compound. If a statement is really the negation of a subject-predicate statement, it must be true if the subject term fails to refer.

This can give rise to puzzlement. For if I say 'John is not blond' or even 'It is not the case that John is blond' in a situation in which it is perfectly obvious that there is such a person as John, it is natural to think that I have ascribed to John, predicated of him, not being blond, or equally well, denied being blond of him.

This shows that in natural language we cannot attach too much weight merely to the words of a statement. A genuine negation may not attribute a predicate. But in the above case, it is equivalent to 'Either there is no such person as John or John lacks the property of being blond'. The second disjunct would, if asserted, attribute a predicate. And the obvious falsity of the first disjunct leads us to take the assertion as an enthymeme, so we can in this way correctly regard someone who says 'It is not the case that John is blond' as having denied blondness of John.

However, we must not attach too little weight to the words of a statement either. With natural languages we have a delicate balance to achieve.

When we analyse the symbolism of predicate logic, such questions are much easier to handle. The standard semantics for this symbolism does not allow subject terms to fail to refer. Before any question of truth, falsity, or lack of truth value is raised for Fa, a must be assigned a reference. The question what should be done if the rules are changed and we raise questions about truth value without having to have assigned a a reference can at least be discussed without encountering difficulties as to the range of applicability of the resultant rulings. We can ask 'If names are not assigned referents, how should we evaluate atomic formulae containing them?' Then we can go on as usual to determine how this ruling for atomic formulae effects other formulae, such as negations and other compounds.

In English, there is no such clear notion of an atomic or non-compound subject-predicate sentence. When we decide about evaluating Fa with a non-referring, we can turn to $\sim Fa$ recognizing that we have a different kind of formula, so that the effect on the truth value of $\sim Fa$, of a's non-referring, may be different from the effect on Fa. But in English, there is intuitive basis for the feeling that reference failure means different things in different sentences, but the terminology for distinguishing sentences into classes in order to formulate general rules about the effects of non-referring is not well developed.

On the other hand, the great classificatory clarity of symbolic logic is achieved by means that tend to deprive the results of significance for natural language. Suppose we wonder about the significance of reference failure. In symbolic logic claims about the consequences of reference failure can be made with great precision. But then the 'reference failure' in symbolic logic is nothing but a matter of arbitrary stipulation. The generalizations arrived at may nonetheless be of logical interest. But the application to real languages may bring back the problems that appeared to be avoidable thanks to the greater precision of the formal language.

One question about reference that is avoidable in a formalized language is the question as to what fails to refer. We can say that if in *Fa*, *a* is not assigned a referent, *a* fails to refer. The fact that *we* are the ones who failed to assign *a* a referent is irrelevant to the enquiry as to how the semantic rules should be constructed and what their formal consequences are. The matter is not so simple with respect to reference in a natural language.

11   Philosophers are generally well aware nowadays that referring and failing to refer are things done by people. It may even be said that they are done by people and *not* by pieces of language, or *primarily* by people and only *secondarily* by pieces of language.

It is plausible to say that no piece of language could refer apart from being understood and used by minds. It might be said that apart from minds, nothing could even be a piece of language. There could be a dead language, such that no minds now understand it. And it would seem to be possible that the wind could trace out in the sand a 'dead language' no one had ever used; say it traced out English, and explained the 'dead language' in terms of it, or even used no other language to explain, but did so with arrows and gestures. Perhaps then we would insist on the mentality of the wind. But this is an unnecessary airy question. The present point is that even if language needs users, users also need language, in a way that makes claims of primariness unclear.

When someone uses an expression to refer to a thing, it is not obvious that the claim that that expression refers to that thing is always secondary and derivative from the person's using the expression to refer to the thing. Sometimes the person's success in referring to the thing may be thanks to the expression's referring to it. This is particularly true of general terms. Our thinking about things that are not present to the senses is facilitated by language in a way that makes it natural to say that it is thanks to the terms' having the reference they do that speakers make the reference they do. If I say something about all Iranians, my reference to Iranians will be due to the terms I use. If I were talking about my writing desk, I could achieve the referring function without using language for the purpose, or even by using language not meant for the purpose, say, by insisting on referring to my writing desk as 'that table'. But when I assert that absolutely every citizen of Iran is a Caucasian, I ascribe being a Caucasian to people I can only refer to thanks to the pre-arranged working of the term 'Iranian', among others.

It is a common doctrine (though of course not a universal one) that 'Iranian' is a general term such that every Iranian is denoted, or referred to, by this term. By contrast, the phrase 'that table' would be called a singular term. It might be said to be compounded of the general term 'table' and 'that', but this is not clearly applicable to my example, in which the reference of 'that table' was something which is in fact not a table, but a writing desk.

At any rate, while it is a common doctrine that both general terms such as 'Iranian' and singular terms such as 'that table' refer or denote, there are important differences in the account of reference or denotation for these two sorts of terms. There are also serious obscurities in the distinction between them. And if we are to adequately assess the assumption that reference failure entails lack of truth value, we must examine this famous subdivision of the kinds of referring expression. Doing so will help to answer a basic question raised by our definition of a logically subject-predicate sentence: does it apply to sentences such as 'All men are mortal', 'Every man is mortal', 'Some men are not mortal', and the like? The grammatical definition, which ours resembles, of course does apply to these examples. But to determine whether they contain the logically singular term required by our definition will be easier if the distinction between singular and general is clarified.

The examples given of singular and general happen to also be grammatically singular ('this table') and plural ('Iranians'). However, not all terms classed as general are grammatically plural. The meaning of the grammatical distinction between singular and plural is rather doubtful. 'Every Iranian is a Caucasian' is singular, 'All Iranians are Caucasians' is plural. Traditionally the difference between singular and plural is the difference between speaking of 'one' or 'more than one'. But the two foregoing examples are equivalent statements. To say we are speaking of more than one Iranian with 'all' and of only one with 'every' can't be right. We might say that we are proceeding 'one at a time' with 'every', and with 'all at once' with 'all'. This is suggestive for explaining the difference between 'There is one toilet for every family' or 'There is one toilet for each family' on the one hand, and 'There is one toilet for all families' on the other. But it is best to consider the logical classifications of general and singular before the grammatical ones of singular and plural.

2

Mill's theory of names

12 The distinction between general and singular terms or 'names' is taken up in Mill's famous theory of names. In his theorizing, Mill does not consider the question being followed here about the significance of failing to refer. This is just one of the questions that bothered Frege and Russell and other more recent writers about which Mill is not sensitive. But his theory provides an excellent basis for introducing these questions.

Mill explains why he is interested in names. He says:

> every proposition consists of two names, and every proposition affirms or denies one of these names, of the other. Now what we do, what passes in our mind, when we affirm or deny two names of one another, must depend on what they are names of; since it is with reference to that, and not to the mere names themselves, that we make the affirmation or denial. Here, therefore, we find a new reason why the signification of names, and the relation generally between names and the things signified by them, must occupy the preliminary stage of the enquiry we are engaged in. (1.1.3)[1]

Thus an interest in 'what passes in our minds' should lead us to study names. Names are the constituents of propositions, and 'Whatever can be an object of belief, or even of disbelief, must, when put into words, assume the form of a proposition.'

This use of 'proposition' appears to be the same as the one we have called 'Russellian'. The proposition is a sentence given a certain understanding. The proposition is the object of belief, provided that the belief is 'put into words'. It seems that Mill allows the possibility of beliefs that are not put into words, and so does Russell. The proposition, Mill says, may be adequately defined as *'discourse, in which something is affirmed or denied of something'* (1.1.3). Thus Mill holds that all belief, when put into words, is an affirmation or denial of something of another thing, and this affirma-

---

[1] All references to Mill are to book, chapter and section of *A System of Logic* (1843).

tion or denial is dependent on what the names in the proposition are names of. It would seem, on Mill's account, that affirming a proposition would be affirming an affirmation. Perhaps it would be better to speak of 'endorsing' or 'agreeing with' propositions.

On this account, it appears that it is a name that determines what is the subject of the proposition. One might get the impression that Mill proceeds by examining a name by itself, apart from propositions, finding out what is its reference, and then using this information in the analysis of propositions in which the name occurs.

Mill does regularly discuss examples of names without setting them in a propositional context, but this is not proof that he regarded the above principle as a generally sound one. At any rate, it has been much criticized. A famous source of such criticism is Frege, who says:

> In the enquiry that follows, I have kept to three fundamental principles:
>   always to separate sharply the psychological from the logical, the subjective from the objective;
>   never to ask for the meaning of a word in isolation, but only in the context of a proposition;
>   never to lose sight of the distinction between concept and object.
>   In compliance with the first principle, I have used the word 'idea' always in the psychological sense, and have distinguished ideas from concepts and objects. If the second principle is not observed, one is almost forced to take as the meanings of words mental pictures or acts of the individual mind, and so to offend against the first principle as well. As to the third point, it is a mere illusion to suppose that a concept can be made an object without altering it.   (1968, introduction)

There is much to discuss in this quotation, but for the present, it is difficult to see why, asking about the meaning of a word taken in isolation, one should be 'almost forced to take as the meanings of words mental pictures or acts of the individual mind'. It does seem that Mill did both these things – ask about the word outside a proposition, take as its meaning acts of the individual mind – though one reason it seems this way is that these two descriptions are so vague as to allow considerable latitude in their application. But it is difficult to see that they are connected, or that Mill was forced to the latter procedure by the former. Someone holding the naïve view that the meaning of a word is its dictionary entry would be an example of taking the meaning of the word in isolation without making the meaning anything subjective or psychological.

Our man who believes meaning to be given by dictionary entries is not relevant to Frege's claim about meaning because Frege was concerned with 'meaning' as something that differentiates assertions. It is perfectly natural to say that when 'That man is ill' is used to make different assertions, perhaps differing in truth value, the 'meaning' of the sentence doesn't change. But Frege was concerned with the content (*Inhalt*) of the different assertions, the 'thoughts' or 'propositions' expressed on the different occasions; and by the 'meaning' of the words in the sentence he meant things which were constituents of these thoughts or propositions, and if the propositions differ, some of their constituents would have to differ.

When the theory of meaning is taken as the theory of the nature of the 'thought' and its constituents, as it is by Frege, then this sort of 'semantics' cannot be contrasted with 'pragmatics'. It is obvious that a natural use of such a sentence as 'That is a petunia' will not express a correct identification of a certain flower merely because of a 'meaning' possessed by the word 'that' in every context. Perhaps one could enquire how context-independent features of the word 'that' work, so that in a situation in which my hearer and I are directing our attention to the same flower and know we are, my uttering 'That is a petunia' will inform the hearer. This might be thought of as an elementary bit of 'semantics and pragmatics'. But it is not a corrective to Frege-style semantics, filling in something left out.

When I say 'That is a petunia', a thought is expressed, which might equally well be expressed, on this occasion, by my nodding and saying 'a petunia'. Thus 'that' would seem to be relatively unimportant in the expression of the thought. But I could perhaps have said 'That . . .', pausing a moment, and my hearer would know I meant a certain flower. That is not to say the flower would be the meaning of 'that'. It would be its denotation. Mill would say 'that' in this case had no meaning – no connotation. But this is a weak point in Mill's theory, for he would have to say that 'that' in this case was a 'mark for ideas' since he says all names are, and he would have to call 'that' a name in this case. At any rate, if I went on to complete the statement with '. . . is a petunia', it could be said that

'that' was connected with a constituent of the thought expressed in a way which did not require looking first at the whole sentence.

In other writings Frege makes clear that in this case he would think 'that' had the meaning of a definite description such as 'The flower we are now looking at' would have. I do not particularly agree with this, but anyway, the meaning of 'that' in this case would be possessed by it thanks to our success in communication, rather than our success in communication being thanks to the meaning of 'that'. (This is provided we mean by 'meaning' the propositional constituent and not something else.) On the other hand 'petunia' contributes its meaning in a less context-dependent way. Even with it, though, my hearer might have known that a petunia is a kind of flower only thanks to our situation.

These contributions of 'context' aren't what Frege means in speaking of the 'context of a proposition'. He means the context provided by the proposition, not the context in which the proposition is expressed. This latter sort of context is not fallaciously overlooked, it is just taken for granted. A complex range of factors are involved in a sentence's expressing a proposition. Frege thought the proposition had parts, to which the parts of the sentence corresponded. Some such sentence parts might be said to contribute their meanings to the proposition. With 'that', 'contribution' would be too strong a term – mere 'correlation' would be better. Either way, correlation or contribution, the question can be raised whether this association between a part of a sentence and a part of a proposition can exist apart from the sentence and proposition. This need not mean 'apart from context' – only apart from the particular sort of context provided by the complete sentence.

If we recognize, then, that our (translated) Frege was not using 'meaning' in the usual way, and we are concerned with the 'meaning' of, say, the word 'man' only insofar as its 'meaning' is a constituent of the 'meaning' of the sentence, 'That man is ill', on a particular occasion of the use of this sentence to express (not necessarily to assert) a particular proposition, then we can see Frege's view as one to the effect that the contribution made by that word to the expressing of the proposition can only be assessed by looking at the word in the context of the sentence expressing that proposition in which it makes its contribution.

This characterization of Frege's view brings in the notion of 'proposition'. But it need not involve all of Frege's doctrines about the proposition, such as the doctrine that propositions are not mental entities. What is involved is the idea that paralleling a sentence there is a proposition with parts that parallel the parts of the sentence.

Mill sometimes writes as if he shared this latter view, though he certainly did not explicitly accept it. For example, he says that in asserting 'All men are mortal' the assertion is that 'Whatever has the attributes connotated by the subject, has also those connoted by the predicate' (1.iv.3). The connotations are mental items of some sort, distinct from the words that express them. If there were also distinct apparatus for connecting them in the assertion, we would get a whole separate item from the sentence just as with Frege, though it would not be an abstract entity but a concrete mental entity existing in the mind of the individual making the assertion (and perhaps, one hopes, being 'matched' by similar entities in the minds of hearers of the assertion).

This idea is not true to Mill's intentions, but neither is Mill. There is at least a tendency to the idea in his writing. There is a similar tendency in Russell.

Russell explicitly rejected Frege's theory of meaning and denotation, according to which a description such as 'The King of England in 1905' has a meaning and a denotation which is determined by the meaning. But this rejection is ambiguous because it might only be concerned with Frege's idea of meaning as an abstract entity. Russell, like many others, would hold that the words *in isolation* do not denote anything. But taken up in a judgement they may. And Russell was by no means clear about what being taken up in a judgement does for the words to make them denote. Mill held that some psychological entities are associated with words in a meaningful judgement. Furthermore he said that at least in some cases, when the associated entities are the connotation of the word, they are also the word's *meaning*. This style of contrasting meaning and denotation, as opposed to Frege's, is not clearly rejected by Russell. To say that Russell rejects a theory of meaning and denotation is misleading unless it is stressed that it is Frege's theory he rejects.

If we assume that Mill had enough of a tendency to suppose that a particular asserted (or otherwise 'supplemented') sentence was paralleled by another entity of similar structure whose parts are paired with parts of the sentence, then we could ask whether Mill goes against Frege's doctrine that words do not have meanings in isolation rather than merely ignoring the presuppositions of the doctrine.

To go directly, rather than obliquely, against the doctrine calls for granting that there are proposition-parallels to asserted sentences. Mill does not directly affirm this. But setting that aside, one must then hold that the contribution a word makes to the proposition expressed by a sentence is something the word *brings* to the sentence rather than something arising only in the interaction of that word with the other words of the sentence in the particular structural arrangement of that sentence.

When I say 'contribution a word makes' I mean 'contribution of a constituent'. For surely there is something about the word by itself which makes it suitable for expressing the constituent it expresses (if any), and that feature of the word might be called its 'contribution' to the proposition. It might be called its meaning. And surely Frege was not out to reject all such suggestions. 'Meaning' is a slippery term. The question is whether a word that contributes a constituent of a proposition has that constituent associated with it independently of the sentence. It isn't a question of whether it has something else associated with it which contributes to the functioning of the sentence on the particular occasion. It would be very strange if this latter weren't true. This is not to say that it must be true that a word is related to an entity which somehow causes it to contribute a part of a proposition when it occurs in the right sort of sentence. That view contains many questionable presuppositions. It is just that there are surely facts about words which do not involve specific reference to all sentences the word belongs to, which facts explain how the word contributes to the functioning of sentences in which it occurs. And this might be treated as part of a theory of 'meaning', but it would not be what is involved in Frege's doctrine, which is concerned with meanings as propositional constituents.

The question whether there are propositions and propositional constituents overshadows the question whether such constituents are expressed by words outside the context of a sentence. From my point of view, there is nothing wrong with the idea of the proposition as an abstract entity, but the idea of a propositional constituent is a major source of confusion. The notions of part and constituent have such thoroughly concrete applications that they bring confusing associations when applied to abstract entities. In this work there will be more than one occasion to deplore Frege's tendency to think of propositions as having form and being made up of parts. This is not to say that, for example, the proposition that there is a wise King of France does not 'include' the proposition that there is a King of France. It is just that this inclusion is completely different from any concrete, physical inclusion.

Mill did not hold that all words express propositional constituents, but he did hold that 'names' express something, usually 'connotation' which might be regarded as suitable for being a propositional constituent. Furthermore, he discusses what he calls 'singular names' (which Frege called 'proper names', a term Mill reserved for only a subclass of his 'singular names') as if they had either a 'connotation' or a 'signification' and a denotation independently of their occurrence in a sentence. And if we restrict ourselves to these cases (ignoring the fact that such terms as 'singular name' still need explanation) we may ask whether this is a mistake.

Discussing a singular name in isolation from a sentence is not the same 'isolation' that Russell meant when he said that even a sentence has no meaning 'in isolation'. The name is not 'isolated' from a language or speakers of the language or from possible occurrences in sentences. What then is the trouble?

This could be a very difficult question, if it were to involve a survey of possible reasons for Frege's doctrine. In later writing, such as his essay 'On Concept and Object' (1952), Frege said some very obscure things about the nature of the parts of propositions and their connection. He said that some propositions consist of a 'holding together' of the sense (meaning) of a grammatical subject-phrase with something else, a concept, expressed by the remainder of the sentence. The concept, he said, is not an object, not an entity or thing, and cannot even be referred to. Perhaps in my account I seem to be referring to concepts, at least in a general way? Frege had similar troubles expressing himself. Though usually both precise and extremely severe with imprecision, he asks the reader not to begrudge him a 'pinch of salt'!

Frege says that concepts are 'incomplete'. Whatever this means, it is possible to see in it a reason for thinking that some parts of a proposition 'cannot stand alone'. And this might be a reason for thinking that the parts or aspect of a sentence that expresses such concepts cannot stand alone either, or cannot perform their expressive function apart from the rest of a complete sentence.

It is never wise for a philosopher to ridicule obscurity, since it is one of his own major professional hazards. He ought always to conduct himself so as to deserve tolerance in times of need. But we can at least avoid giving ourselves over to this particular tangle. I mention it only to suggest that it might have been involved in the Fregean doctrine that the meaning of a word cannot be determined apart from a sentence.

While the interpretation of 'isolation from a sentence' can lead into obscurities, there is also a very simple way of interpreting it, suggested by another theory of Frege's. He held that 'Hesperus' in 'Bill knows Hesperus is identical with Phosphorus' does not denote a planet (1952, 'On Sense and Reference'). Rather, it denotes the sense of the word 'Hesperus' as it occurs in 'Hesperus is identical with Phosphorus'. Furthermore, in the first sentence its sense is also different.

Thus, on this theory, one could not say that 'Hesperus' by itself had a definite sense (meaning), because it would mean different things in different sentences. This is rather like warning someone who thinks that the meaning of a word is its dictionary entry that some words have more than one dictionary entry.

There are less 'theory-laden' examples for this point. In 'If Elizabeth had died in childhood, Princess Margaret would have been the Queen of England in 1960', it seems natural to deny that the description has the same denotation as in 'The Queen of England in 1960 was married to Phillip of Macedon'. This plausible denial with respect to denotation could naturally be extended to apply to meaning as well, provided we accept Frege's idea that meaning is what determines denotation – an idea that we must examine later.

For another kind of example, there is Geach's 'the woman every Englishman loves best' which could be the subject for either ' . . . is his Queen' or ' . . . is his wife'. Here again, the idea that we can simply ask what the description denotes without looking at the rest of the sentence, looks wrong, and the example can again be stretched to apply to meaning as well.

If this sort of example were all Frege had in mind (which is doubtful) he should not have stopped at warning to look beyond the word to the sentence, since there can be ambiguity at that level too which is resolved by facts about the context in which the sentence is asserted.

For example, suppose that people at a party are sitting down, and someone says 'The chair John is sitting in is very comfortable', meaning to make a remark about a certain chair. Someone telephones and asks what is going on at the party, and is told that they are all sitting. He says, 'Well, one thing I'm sure of – the chair John is sitting in is very comfortable.' The caller need not be taken to refer to a specific chair. He might just as well have said, 'Whatever chair John is in, it (the chair John is sitting in) is very comfortable.' Or again, on being told over the telephone that the chair John is sitting in is very comfortable, the caller might reply 'The chair John is sitting in is always comfortable'. It is natural not to class this as a reference to the chair John is sitting in at that moment. So even in a setting in which it is clear who John is, and that he is sitting in a chair, a speaker using the phrase, 'The chair John is sitting in' may not be correctly describable as employing this expression to make a reference to a certain chair.

These examples provide a clear basis for Frege's doctrine, but not for regarding violating it as a mistake liable to vitiate a theory such as Mill's, or for thinking that violating it inevitably leads (or should lead) to a mentalistic account of meaning. Mill does do such things as discuss compound names like 'the Queen of England' as if it always brings the same ingredients, namely, its connotation and denotation, to every sentence in which it occurs. But he does not assert that this is so, and there is no reason to think it should be important to his theory of connotation and denotation that it be so. For these examples only show that we can't be sure there is 'the meaning', not that there isn't 'a meaning' which is common to a very large number of supplemented sentences. Nor do they show that a meaning for a term only arises when it is combined with words to form a sentence.

The naïve view that a child first learns 'meanings' for words and then learns how to combine them into propositions (*via* sentences) cannot be refuted merely by examples which show some words or phrases to have a variety of meanings. For then we only need to modify the view so that the child picks out one of these meanings and goes ahead as before. No doubt Frege had in mind something more than this, but at any rate, the readily available examples do not yield a version of his doctrine that counts seriously against Mill's approach to meaning.

13 Mill's theory of names is a mixture of three different kinds of

enquiry – grammar, formal logic, and the theory of the mind and its operations and objects, which I will call metaphysics.

Prominent in Mill's theory is his threefold subdivision of names into abstract–concrete, general–singular, and connotative–non-connotative. None of these divisions is well defined, and each involves an uneasy mixture of grammatical, logical, and metaphysical considerations. It is almost as if the three subdivisions were chosen for special emphasis for that reason. According to Mill, some names connote, and others do not. He also says that some names denote, while others do not, but he does not divide names into the denotative and the non-denotative, or the denoting and non-denoting. And one difference is that being deno*tative* is rather a characteristic of names generally, while being deno*ting* is of logical and metaphysical, but not grammatical, significance. There should be no grammatical difference between 'the Queen of England in 1975' and 'the Queen of France in 1975'. (The traditional grammatical definition with which this discussion began does suggest a difference, but that is a defect in this definition.) But there are grammatical differences between the names Mill regards as connotative, and those he does not – grammatical differences mixed with logical and metaphysical differences as well.

Mill says, 'A concrete name is a name which stands for a thing; an abstract name is a name which stands for an attribute of a thing' (I.II.4). In the next paragraph he says, 'By *abstract*, then, I shall always, in logic proper, mean the opposite of *concrete*; by an abstract name, the name of an attribute; by a concrete name, the name of an object.' Thus he commits himself to a view that sounds like Frege's previously mentioned view that concepts aren't objects. Attributes are not things or objects. At the least, this needs some explaining. There is also the fact that Mill's definition makes it implausible to class 'the number seven' or 'the set of integers' as abstract terms. Again there is no explanation.

One reason for the half-heartedness of this definition may be brought out by considering something Mill says later in setting forth his 'substitute for the Categories of Aristotle considered as a classification of Existences'. First, there are 'feelings', second, 'minds' and third,

> The bodies, or external objects which excite certain of those feelings, together with the powers or properties whereby they excite

them; these latter (at least) being included rather in compliance with common opinion, and because their existence is taken for granted in the common language from which I cannot prudently deviate, than because the recognition of such powers or properties as real existences appears to be warranted by a sound philosophy.   (1.III.14)

Thus 'a sound philosophy' would not have any abstract things (if I may use for convenience a phrase which Mill's definition would class as contradictory). Of course it does not follow that 'abstract' would therefore be either meaningless or indefinable, but it might not seem worth troubling over. For Mill's 'sound philosophy' would have it that we all know what 'states of consciousness' are, by direct acquaintance, so there is no need for a definition of that term. And whatever *abstracta* are, if they are something other than states of consciousness, it does not require a definition to show there are no such things in Mill's scheme of things. To grant, then, as Mill explicitly does, that there are names which stand for attributes is to go straight against his 'sound philosophy', according to which there really are no attributes.

It seems that Mill might have replied that his definition was merely a concession to grammar (and perhaps formal logic). But that is no way to proceed in grammar or anywhere else. It is just like putting up with the previously mentioned definition of 'subject' from traditional grammar. A grammatical doctrine can't be saved from being bad metaphysics merely by not being metaphysics at all, but grammar. If they don't fit together, something is wrong somewhere.

14   Mill's notion of connotation is employed before it is introduced, notably in his distinction between general and singular names. The well-known definitions are: 'A general name is, familiarly defined, a name which is capable of being truly affirmed, in the same sense, of each of an indefinite number of things. An individual or singular name is a name which is only capable of being affirmed, in the same sense, of one thing' (1.II.3). 'Sense' here means the same as 'connotation'.

Nicholas Wolterstorff (1970) accepts Mill's definitions with two changes. Instead of 'capable of being affirmed of an indefinite number of things' he makes it a matter of being affirmable of more than one thing. And he substitutes 'import' for 'sense', a step which we shall be evaluating. He points out that the definitions have the consequence that 'prime number between 4 and 7' is a singular name, while 'prime number between 4 and 8' is a general name (p. 52). Mill did not consider this, but he might not have found it as congenial as Wolterstorff does. It certainly does not fit well with grammatical usage. Wolterstorff also adds a further subdivision of 'terms' (I assume 'term' to be interchangeable with Mill's 'name'), the 'contradictory term' which 'cannot be true of anything', to cover such terms as 'prime number between 8 and 10'.

Wolterstorff defines a 'term' as a word or phrase which can be applied to or affirmed of a thing. Perhaps I should not say 'define'. He offers this in answer to the question 'What is a term?' but indicates it can be misunderstood. I do not mention it, though, to quibble with it, but to contrast it with the definition Mill accepts for a name: 'a word (or set of words) serving the double purpose of a mark to recall to ourselves the likeness of a former thought and a sign to make it known to others' (1.11.1). He adds that 'Names, indeed, do much more than this, but whatever else they do grows out of and is the result of this.'

Mill would certainly accept Wolterstorff's definition as a truth about names. His division of general and singular names is in terms of how many things they can be affirmed of. But his own definition, the one he accepts from Hobbes, lays the basis for a metaphysical project – that of explaining what is involved in affirming a name of a thing, how this is achieved. And this project gets entangled with grammatical and logical considerations.

To define names in terms of marks and signs may sound circular. But a metaphysical theory of marks and signs is available in Mill's associationist psychology. The notion of connotation has a central and puzzling role in this account. For connotative names, the connotation is what the name is a mark of. But non-connotative names are also marks, and how what they are marks of differ from connotations is a difficult question.

Mill says, 'Logic, according to the conception here formed of it, has no concern with the nature of the act of judging or believing; the consideration of that act, as a phenomenon of the mind, belongs to another science.' Thus the definition of 'name' is aimed at an enquiry Mill places outside the boundaries of logic. It may be all right to draw the boundaries of logic as one wishes, but this will be no excuse for any actual conflict between the doctrines of logic and those of 'another science'.

Mill's doctrine that some singular names do not have connotation or sense, conflicts badly with his definition of 'singular name'. He recognizes the conflict, and makes the following attempt to deal with it:

> *John* is only capable of being truly affirmed of one single person, at least in the same sense. For, though there are many persons who bear that name, it is not conferred upon them to indicate any qualities or any thing which belongs to them in common, and cannot be said to be affirmed of them in any *sense* at all, consequently not in the same sense.   (I.II.3)

This argument is thoroughly fallacious. Granting that 'John' has no sense does keep it from qualifying as a general name, but it does nothing to square the claim that it is a singular name with the definition. 'John' can be applied truly to more than one thing. The only way this can be compatible with classing it as a singular name is if each affirmation is in a different sense. Not having any sense eliminates this essential feature and leaves the name neither singular nor general.

Wolterstorff's notion of 'import' is meant to solve this difficulty. He says that while 'John' does not have sense, it does have 'import'. Unfortunately, he does not define 'import', merely saying it is 'analogous to sense'. And he does not say in what way it is analogous.

Wolterstorff points out that 'That is John' can be used to make different statements about the same person. At the playground, I may point to a distant child and say 'That is John', meaning my son, John. Another father, on the other side of the playground may say, with reference to the same child, 'That is John', meaning his son, John. Even if the child is named John, one of us must be mistaken. This is Wolterstorff's basis for concluding that 'John' must have different import in the two statements.

This is not a very convincing argument. It is, strictly, an argument for the existence of such a thing as import, analogous to sense, but different. Even if we grant that for two statements about the same subject to differ, some parts must differ, we cannot draw from this such a strong conclusion. After all, 'John' has a different denotation in the two statements. Wolterstorff has not shown that this is not a sufficient basis for explaining the difference between the two statements. More importantly for our discussion of Mill, he has not shown that 'import' is different from 'sense', so the conflict between Mill's doctrine that some singular names have no sense or connotation and his definition of 'singular name' remains unresolved.

15 Mill says: 'A non-connotative term is one which signifies a subject only, or an attribute only. A connotative term is one which denotes a subject and implies an attribute' (1.11.5). (I will assume that Mill did not mean to rule out the possibility that at least some compound connotative terms have no denotation.)

The notion of 'implying an attribute' is an important source of obscurity, not only in Mill's writing, but more generally as well. Mill would say that the term 'bachelor' connotes the property of being unmarried. But it is the statement that, say, Nixon is a bachelor, that logically implies the statement that Nixon is unmarried. The relation of implication holds between statements, not between terms such as 'bachelor' and other things.

The fact that 'That is a bachelor' implies 'That is unmarried' can be used to define the saying that the term 'bachelor' implies or connotes being unmarried, and this is a common practice. As will be seen, it is not adequate to explain Mill's own usage of 'connote'.

One minor difficulty with this definition arises in connection with the so-called paradoxes of logical implication – that is, the fact that a contradictory statement logically implies any other statement and a logically necessary statement is logically implied by any other. These facts about implication have the consequence that, say, 'ruler and compass construction of a square equal in area to a given circle' would, in Mill's terminology, be a compound general name (a contradictory one) which connotes all properties, such as, for example, being a man. Also, being a thing which is not such a construction would be connoted by all general names, including 'man'. These consequences might have disturbed Mill. But then again, they might not have. That they are consequences of explaining connoting in terms of logical implication is only something worth noting in passing.

16 Michael Lockwood (1975) sees Mill's distinction between 'connotative' and 'non-connotative' as like Donnellan's distinction between 'attributive' and 'referential' (1966). I think this is an

important mistake. Mill may well have had in mind a distinction like Donnellan's, but he attaches to the term 'connote' a theory that makes it quite incorrect to compare 'connotative' with 'attributive' uses of names, as Lockwood does. And this is a point of more than historical interest, since this complication of Mill's notion over Donnellan's reflects an important distinction in the kind of project a theory of names can be.

Lockwood presents his own account of the notion of 'a referential use of a term', warning that his notion 'does not exactly correspond either to Donnellan's notion or to Kripke's concept of rigid designation':

> Let $S(t)$ be a sentence, containing a definite singular term t. In offering this sentence, by way of making an assertion, a person will (in my sense) be making referential use of the term t if and only if there is an object x such that
> (i) it is a necessary and sufficient condition of the truth of what $S(t)$ is being used to assert that x satisfy the predicate expressed by the context $S()$;
> (ii) it is a necessary condition of anyone's knowing what $S(t)$ is being used to assert that he know, of x, that it satisfies clause (i);
> (iii) $S(t)$ is uttered with the intention that conditions (i) and (ii) are satisfied.

This is probably not quite watertight as it stands. But the motivation behind it should be fairly clear. Consider once again the sentence (a) 'Her husband is a lucky man'. Now I take it that if any individual is to stand to 'her husband' in the relation that clause (i) requires, if this phrase is to be construed referentially, it will be the man who is actually married to the girl under discussion. (This incidentally is the point on which I differ from Donnellan.) So let us suppose that her husband is in fact one Jacob Jones. Then for 'her husband' to be serving a purely referential function, the truth conditions of the statement which (a) is being used to express must be: that Jacob Jones is a lucky man. Such will not be the case where 'her husband' is being used attributively. There the truth conditions of the statement which (a) is intended to express are, rather: that *someone* is both (the only person) married to the girl and a lucky man. Jacob Jones's being a lucky man is not, by itself, either a necessary or a sufficient condition for the truth of *this* statement. It is not sufficient, since he could be lucky without being the girl's husband; and it is not necessary, since the statement would also be true if (contrary to fact) Harry Cohen were married to the girl instead, and *he* were a lucky man. There can in this case be no one individual such that *his* being lucky is either necessary or sufficient for the truth of (a); and clause (i) accordingly fails. Note that, where 'her husband' is functioning referentially (so as to designate Jacob Jones) Jacob Jones's being married to the girl in question is on this view a necessary condition, not of the truth of the *statement* which (a) expresses, but merely of (a)'s being used to express that statement. (Donnellan would deny that even this much is true.)

(Lockwood 1975, pp. 485–7)

Lockwood's difference with Donnellan is not over his clauses (i) (ii) and (iii), but over the question whether, say, 'Her husband is a lucky man' can be used in accordance with established usage to convey a true statement even if, say, the girl under discussion is unmarried. Donnellan points out that a description may be used to refer to something which does not 'satisfy' the description. I may say 'That table is covered with books' and the fact that it isn't a table, but a television set with a cloth over it, might be treated as irrelevant to assessing my statement. That is, Donnellan would treat it so, while Lockwood would hold that in that case what the speaker *means* to say may be true, but he does not succeed in saying it. He says

> a speaker may, in Grice's sense, be said to *mean*, by his utterance of S(t), that a is P; and I would even allow that there is *a* sense of 'refer' in which the speaker would be said to be referring here to the object a. But I do not think it follows from this that the speaker, in uttering S(t), has actually *asserted* that a is P; nor that he has referred to a, in the sense of 'refer' in which it functions as what Ryle calls a 'success verb'. (Lockwood 1975, p. 486 n. 21)

Lockwood's position in this disagreement with Donnellan is similar to a position taken by Geach.

Geach says:

> Personal reference – i.e. reference corresponding to the verb 'refer' as predicated of persons rather than expressions – is of negligible importance for logic; and I mention it only to get it out of the way. Let me take an example: Smith says indignantly to his

wife, 'The fat old humbug we saw yesterday has just been made a full professor!'. His wife may know whom he refers to, and will consider herself misinformed if and only if that person has not been made a full professor. But the actual expression 'The fat old humbug we saw yesterday' will refer to somebody only if Mr. and Mrs. Smith did meet someone rightly describable as a fat old humbug on the day before Smith's indignant remark; if this is not so, then Smith's actual words will not have conveyed true information, even if what Mrs. Smith gathered from them was true.

(1962, p. 8)

Geach's distinction between reference by a person and reference by an expression does not correspond to the 'referential' – 'attributive' distinction, but his treatment of Smith's performance is similar to what Lockwood recommends. He holds that Smith's words don't convey true information, where Lockwood would say that Smith has not made a true assertion. On the other hand, it seems that Donnellan would hold that Smith might have made a true statement or assertion.

17   I think the truth of the matter is that Smith has made a true predication, but not a true assertion (of a proposition) or statement. A predication, unlike a proposition or statement, is an act. One important type of predication is that in which something is singled out, made known, to some people, as the thing to which the predicate is being attributed. (This is not the only kind of predication.) This singling out may be accomplished by acts of predication, sometimes by acts of false predication. For example, someone may say 'That miserable syphilitic is trying to seduce Mary' and succeed in referring to an unhealthy person who does appear syphilitic though he is not, and who does indeed have designs on Mary. Here the speaker may have, in passing, predicated being syphilitic of the person, and his doing so may have been instrumental to his success in singling out that person. But he has also truly predicated having designs on Mary of that person. And this latter act of true predication is separate from the act of false predication which made it possible.

With 'The table is covered with books' the case is not so clear because it is not so clear that the speaker means to call the television a table. We might say that the speaker doesn't predicate being a table, but rather presumes it. However, the difference is probably only one of emphasis. That it is a table is as much a part of this belief as the man's being a syphilitic is part of the other – it is just that the speaker has no interest in the thought that it's a table while he is impressed by the idea that the man is syphilitic.

Donnellan is mistaken in holding that in cases such as my 'That syphilitic is trying to seduce Mary' the fact that the speaker succeeds in identifying a person and correctly attributes to him designs on Mary may be enough to qualify the speaker as making a true statement, in spite of the fact that the person who has been identified is not a syphilitic. He is mistaking an act of predication for a statement.

(Actually, Donnellan (1966) displays awareness of the distinction between statements and acts of predication. But he advocates a theory which does not allow him to consistently attend to the distinction. For purposes of criticizing Strawson, he is content to say that Strawson is wrong in thinking that 'If someone asserts that the Φ is Ψ he has not made a true or false statement if there is no Φ'. This implies that on the contrary, someone might, in such a case, if he were using 'the Φ' referentially, have made a true *statement*. Thus, for the sake of neatness in criticizing Strawson, Donnellan commits himself to a claim over which he hesitates elsewhere.)

However, Lockwood makes the same mistake in the cases where it happens that the expression used to make the reference really does apply truly to the thing referred to. For he holds that in such cases, if the use of the referring expression is purely referential, then a statement is made such that its truth conditions do not include any contributed by the referring expression. And this again is not a fact about a statement, but about an act of predication.

Lockwood says that with a referential use of a description as in 'Her husband is a lucky man', there will be a person such that it is a necessary and sufficient condition of the truth of what the sentence is being used to assert that that person is a lucky man. But what is it that the sentence, on this referential use, is being used to assert? Surely not that her husband is a lucky man, since that is presumably a correct account for the attributive use, which is supposed to exclude the referential use.

Lockwood only says: 'So let us suppose that her husband is in fact one Jacob Jones. Then for "her husband" to be serving a purely referential function, the truth conditions of the statement which (a) is being used to express must be: that Jacob Jones is a lucky man' (1975, pp. 485–6). But in order that Jacob Jones should be a lucky man there has to be someone who is Jacob Jones. Does Lockwood really mean to include that in 'the truth conditions of the statement which (a) is being used to express'? If so, then it would seem that someone who knew only that the man standing next to the woman is her husband without knowing his name, could not know that the statement is true or even what would be required for it to be true.

It might be replied that someone could know that Jacob Jones is a lucky man without knowing the lucky one to be Jacob Jones. This could be said, but it needs explaining in terms of knowing that a certain act of predication would be correct, not in terms of knowing the truth of a statement.

What it is to be Jacob Jones, or more realistically (if that is the right word), Richard Nixon, is not a matter of general agreement. It is perfectly natural to suppose that being named 'Richard Nixon' is a requirement. It is natural to think that while Richard Nixon might not have been named 'Richard Nixon' he would then not have been Richard Nixon. He could have been the same person, and had the same career, but still would not have been Richard Nixon. Some hold that our name 'Richard Nixon' designates the same person in all 'possible worlds' in which he is to be found, even those in which he is not so named in that world. But that does not show that he is Richard Nixon in such 'possible worlds' any more than his being hirsute in this world precludes his being bald in a possible world. To say that it is not necessarily true that Richard Nixon is Richard Nixon is ambiguous. The statement that Richard Nixon is Richard Nixon is necessarily true relative to the premise that there is such a person as Richard Nixon. But the act of predication which involves attributing being Richard Nixon, and which, when performed with respect to Richard Nixon, is true, is nonetheless never necessarily true. Making a statement may accomplish this act, but it always involves something more.

In reply to this, it is reasonable to think that someone might nod in the direction of Jacob Jones and say 'that's a lucky man', producing a statement which really does exactly parallel an act of predication. 'This', 'that' and 'it' were once Russell's candidates for English-language examples of 'logically proper names'.

This raises difficult questions, but before embarking on them we may try to characterize the issue between Lockwood and Donnellan in terms of the idea that what is said in a referential use is the sort of simple statement made using 'that' as in the above paragraph. This seems to be the best hope for an answer to the request for a report of what is said in a referential use that differentiates it from what would be said in an attributive use. The idea would then be that when someone utters 'Her husband is a lucky man' making a referential use of 'her husband', he says merely that that is a lucky man, where 'that' refers to her husband.

If this is right, then Donnellan's view that a referential use may be made and yield a true statement, even if the referring expression is not true of the thing referred to by it, seems reasonable. If we ignore the descriptive content of the referring expression in determining what is said, then why demand that the descriptive content should determine whether anything *is* said?

One reason might be that there is a lingering trace of sensitivity to a traditional problem about referring – that of explaining, in the case of reference to, or thought about, something, *what is thought*. Rather than merely talking about referring to some woman's husband, we might ask what thought this involves. And Lockwood's opposition to Donnellan reflects the idea that this referential success involves employing an attribute – being married to a certain previously identified woman – which the thing referred to uniquely satisfies.

However, I think this is the wrong place for this traditional concern to be manifested, if that is what is behind Lockwood's reservations to Donnellan's view. For the traditional problem concerns the referential-attributive distinction in a much more fundamental way.

18 Historically, knowledge, perception or reference with respect to physical objects has been made out to be indirect in one way or another. In Russell's terms, it was alleged that we never have knowledge by acquaintance of a physical object or person other than our self. Russell's distinction between knowledge by acquaintance and knowledge by description led him to a distinction between atomic and non-atomic statements which resembles the referential-attributive distinction, even though the classes of statements Russell thought his distinction determined are not the same as the classes suggested by the referential-attributive theory. Both these distinctions are threatened by metaphysical arguments which tend to deprive the distinctions of the natural, ordinary-language examples which first suggest them.

Thus consider the possibility that when I say 'That is a lucky man' my hearers and I are suffering from a group hallucination (if that is the right word). We think there is a man standing there in the direction of my nod, when in fact there isn't. This means that 'that' hasn't had a successful referential use. Many philosophers would want to say that in this case I have simply failed in an attempt to make a statement. But I was thinking something. I had a sensory impression which led me to believe there was a man there, a man who was lucky. Merely to say that I failed to make a statement is to leave unfinished the task of describing the intellectual transactions that were involved in my utterance of 'That is a lucky man'.

The claim 'but I was thinking something' is similar to the line in the argument from illusion, where it is held that in having a hallucination of a dagger before me when there is none, I am surely seeing something. This led to the idea that we only directly perceive sensory items, not external things. And one criticism of this argument is that we do not perceive our sensory experience – we have it, and on the basis of it we perceive. It might similarly be said that when I think that that is a lucky man, that is what I am thinking, and if the thought is somehow based on sensory experience it does not follow that it is those experiences I am thinking about.

These are not sound objections. Sensory experience has a certain priority which cannot be disproven merely by showing that in various other ways it does not have priority. The idea that a person reviews his sensory experience in order to determine what is going on outside lends itself to caricature and ridicule. It can also lead to a regressive picture of perception such as that of a man 'watching' his visual experience as he would a film. Perception certainly is not like this. But in perception there are always background assumptions about the relation of the things perceived to the perceiver, including their relation to his sensory experience.

When I believe that that is a lucky man, in the case described I believe that there is something before me which is a lucky man. In another case, I may remember the man I saw and think that is a lucky man, without believing anyone is before me, but then there will be other beliefs about my experience involved. It is conceivable that I should find that I perceive scenes that are thousands of miles away with accuracy. I might see a young man standing at the altar with a lovely bride and think 'That is a lucky man', knowing this scene to be occurring somewhere without having any idea of its location. Perhaps I might even have grounds for thinking some of these scenes take place in a world not spatially related to the one in which I live. For all that, there will be some assumption of causality between the thing I perceive and my experience, and this represents an ingredient in my belief which is essential to its being belief rather than imagining or something else.

If a belief that a certain object has a certain property is purely concerned with the object and the attribute, then if there were no object, there would be no belief. There would be nothing to be either true or false. It is a traditional philosophical opinion that there cannot be such a belief about an extramental object.

This opinion is not refuted by arguments to the effect that beliefs about physical objects can be certain, just as certain as beliefs about sense experiences, or by arguments to the effect that one could not even have sensory experience unless one had some perceptions of physical objects, or by arguments to the effect that singular reference to sense experiences is only possible if prior reference is made to physical objects.

Even phenomenalism, the ontological doctrine that there is nothing besides sensory experiences, is compatible with these arguments, as I believe Jonathan Bennett (1966) has shown. The phenomenalist regards perceiving a physical object as a matter of having experience of a certain kind. And he can consistently hold that one must have experience of this kind in order to have experience at all, and that having this sort of experience and learning the appropriate linguistic response to it (physical object terms) is a necessary condition of being able to make singular reference to experiences, and so on.

However, the traditional opinion is often associated with the further doctrine that one can have direct, unmediated beliefs about sense experiences. And this leads into confusion.

Russell's obscure views about logically proper names can be understood in terms of this doctrine. The idea would be that logically proper names would be names of immediately given sensory items. With respect to such items reference failure would be impossible. Attributing a predicate to a sensory item 'couldn't miss'. This is not the same as the doctrine that sincere beliefs about sense-data cannot be mistaken, but Russell seems to have held this as well.

It is not plausible that the ultimate constituents of our beliefs would be beliefs about the properties of immediate sensory items. It seems more plausible that, so far from such beliefs being involved in every belief about a physical object, such beliefs practically never occur. But the fact that it is only with the greatest difficulty on unusual occasions, if ever, that I refer to individual items of my sensory experience, does not warrant the conclusion that I am not, in perception, continuously forming beliefs about my experience taken as a relatively undifferentiated (though not undifferentiatable) manifold. I may have visual experience, auditory experience, tactile experience, etc. and have beliefs about its causes without having the capacity to precisely describe the components of the experience. And even my recognition that I do have experience may only be possible because I have first learned to respond discriminatingly to experiences which constitute my encounters with physical objects.

It is possible that corresponding to the visual field there is storage in the brain of information about the color of each section of the field. (I mean this could have been science, not that it is.) There could be stored data such that comparison would be made by the brain, and matching would determine a response, treating the section as the color determined by the matching. Such a picture might suggest a comparison theory of universals, to the effect that a person determines the color of a thing by comparing it with a mental sample of that color.

The comparison theory of universals is regressive, because it is a theory about thinking and justification, and the question how the agent knows he has got the right sample for comparison just repeats the form of the question that was to be answered. But this difficulty does not concern the scientific doctrine of brain-comparison, because it is not a theory about justification but rather a theory of brain function.

It could be true that items of the sensory field are in a way apprehended and classified. But this would be the *basis* of thinking – not *thinking*. These 'apprehensions' are ambiguously named – they would not be judgements. They would not serve as *reasons* for beliefs about physical objects.

For all that, there is still a clear lack of immediacy in judgements about physical objects. It is always perfectly possible logically not only that the judgement should be false, but that it should involve a failure to refer. However, this is much disputed, and so some persuasion is in order.

I am now looking at an apple tree. I say 'That is an apple tree'. I might as well have said 'That which is causing us to have certain experiences is an apple tree'. Of course this would confuse some hearers, but anyone who understands me in this situation is recognizing certain experiences and the fact that I am claiming their source to be an apple tree, whether or not he is able to be very explicit about it. For me to be right, something must stand in the appropriate causal relation to our experience and be an apple tree. This statement of truth conditions is not specific. I might have, say, eight hearers, five of whom were hallucinating a tree just like the one actually there. Is the reference to 'our experience' satisfied in that case? Perhaps the speaker's experience should be the basis. It would be difficult, on anyone's account, to know how to assess a claim made in such a situation. It is not a problem arising from my view.

The essential point is that there is a similarity between the case of 'That is an apple tree' and an attributive use of a referring expression. Just as the attributive 'Her husband is a lucky man' requires only that someone be married to the girl and lucky, so my statement requires just that something cause the relevant experiences in the appropriate way and be an apple tree.

We can of course stipulate that if something else had been there, looking exactly like the tree that was in fact there, and it was an apple tree, I would have made a true statement, but a different statement. But this could be said about any attributive use too, as long as we are stipulating. There is a perfectly consistent basis for it. If the girl had been married to someone else who was lucky, I would have made a true statement. But would it have been the same statement? It involved a different act of predication, since the predicate fell on a different thing. I do not object at all to saying that, nonetheless, the same statement was made. But where is the difference from my 'That is an apple tree'?

Perhaps the difference is that in this case we have an individual thing in mind? Well, this is the problematic idea. There is a natural, common sense distinction that applies here. We may say that in the case of the tree I have a definite tree in mind, I know which tree I'm talking about, and so on. In the attributive statement about the girl's husband, I may, by contrast, not know which man he is and not have a definite man in mind.

This is a perfectly legitimate distinction, but it is not a good basis for the referential-attributive distinction. The metaphysical argument to the effect that all statements expressing thoughts about physical objects must be 'attributive' does not entail the idea that no one ever has a definite physical object in mind, though Russell seems to have thought so. After all, when one says 'Her husband is a lucky man' he is (*pace* Russell) *talking about* a definite man. That he is not *thinking of* a definite man is merely because he cannot perform various identifications. But the ability to perform such identifications is not denied in the metaphysical argument, which holds merely that anything which was causing certain features of my experience in a certain way would be the thing I was thinking was an apple tree.

Furthermore, a blind person, overhearing my remark, might reply 'That's not an apple tree – it's a peach', because he is convinced that I always mistake apple trees for peach trees. But surely his public linguistic act involves just as direct a reference, just as referential a use of 'that' as my own, despite the fact that he has no definite tree in mind.

However, it could be said that this is a 'parasitic' reference. Perhaps it could be made out that all cases of referential use involve having an individual in mind at least in a parasitic way. It still remains true that attributive uses in no way preclude having the individual referred to in mind, so this is not a basis for the distinction.

If I see one of a million identical marbles and say 'That is a marble', it is a different statement from what I would have asserted if it had been a different marble, in spite of the fact that the marbles are practically indistinguishable.

On the other hand, suppose I say 'What he has in his hand is a marble'. Now we say that it doesn't matter which of the marbles he has in his hand, the statement will be the same and be true if he has some one of them in hand. So it seems we have a clear contrast here. This is an attributive use of a referring expression, while with 'That is a marble' the case is different because it wouldn't be the same statement if it were a different marble.

It is true that my statement would not be the same if the thing referred to were a different one of the million marbles. But that does not mean the statement involves a 'purely referential' use of 'that'. We could also say that 'What he has in his hand is a marble' would not make the same statement if the thing referred to were a different one of the marbles. It is just that we do not. Either sentence might be used in a situation in which someone is holding a marble in his open hand, palm up. The same knowledge would be behind each statement, but there would be different conventional devices at work, calling into play different standards of statement individuation.

Here I am using the term 'statement' very loosely. Insofar as the content of the statement is the thought, the proposition which is believed and asserted, then no statement about a physical object can be individuated by its reference, and no convention could change this. But the act of predication is individuated by its reference, and we might choose to treat the use of the word 'that' as an instruction to attend only to the act of predication and ignore the thought, the expression of which (in assertion) achieved this act.

That this is possible I do concede to the referentialists, and I believe it would provide a basis for making good sense out of the doctrine that some singular names are non-connotative. But matters have to be put in the proper order. The thought comes first, and there the distinction between referential and attributive is not found. Merely determining the reference of 'that' does not determine what thought is expressed in asserting such a sentence as 'That is a marble'.

Wittgenstein says that 'the expression "I believe that this is the case" is used like the assertion "This is the case"; and yet the *hypothesis* that I believe this is the case is not used like the hypothesis that this is the case' (1973, II.10). It might be objected that the 'I believe that' weakens the force of the assertion so that the use is significantly different. But it does not always do so. One may assert just as firmly with the belief preface as without, in many cases. Thus in a way (to use a powerful phrase) all assertions are in indirect discourse. To say that someone believes (or believed) that that is a marble does not adequately convey what he believes (or believed). If 'that' is a ring with a large marble-like stone, then I may guess that he saw the ring at an angle which led him to take it for a marble. But if 'that' is a silver dollar, then, while I can see that the speaker's act of predication was false, I will probably have no idea what he was thinking. Perhaps Bob has been given strict orders never to give Bill a marble. The speaker sees Bob hand something to Bill and says 'That is a marble – Bob, you are in serious trouble!'. But it was only a silver dollar. To show someone the dollar and tell him that the speaker predicated being a marble of it would be speaking truly, but to say that the speaker said that it was a marble would be grossly misleading. A good account of what was said should display the thought.

In the primary cases, reference to physical objects involves reference to experiences, though of course not in the sense that if someone refers to an apple tree he may be said to have also made reference to his experiences. It is, rather, that in referring to an apple tree or in thinking about one (in the primary sort of case) one will be having a belief about his own experience or that of others. In the vast majority of cases the apple tree may be of interest while the experiences will not be, and the wording used in ordinary cases reflects this fact, as does the practice of crediting someone with referring to an apple tree without regarding him to have made a comment about his experience. But when we ask the perfectly legitimate metaphysical question as to what someone who thinks that a certain plant is an apple tree is thinking, the account of that very thought will have to begin with reference to experiences, though these references need not be specific references to individual 'feelings', 'odors', etc. Such specific references might even be impossible in practice. Nor do the references to experiences made in the course of explicitly describing the thought have to be immune to error.

19 Of course it may be questioned whether our public statement or assertion is an assertion of the same thing which is thought, even when the assertion qualifies as sincere. This can even lead to questions about the 'ontological status' of these 'objects', which must in fact be taken up later. But the answer should be yes. In the standard, primary, case, an assertion is the verbal expression of a belief. Perhaps we may say, even in a case in which someone's assertion is 'sincere' that he does not 'really believe' what he says, say, if he is deceiving himself, or the like. But that one believes what he says is the standard for a good case of assertion.

This does not mean, either, that the primary function of assertions is to convey what is believed. The primary point of asserting that the cat is on the mat may be to let people know of the location of the cat. Or it may be something varying from case to case. It is true that people do lots of things besides have beliefs, but the problems here discussed call for special attention to believing.

In the predicate calculus, we are taught to 'interpret' an atomic formula 'Fa' by having 'a' stand for something and 'F' stand for a class. How we bring about this 'reference' is irrelevant. Thus we could arrive at a picture of a 'purely referential' statement, and contrast it with a case in which the form '$F-$' is filled in with a term such as a definite description which contributes to the logical powers of the statement in a way which will also be reflected in the semantic rules for the formula.

This is all right, but it is an abstraction from natural languages which ignores certain important facts. Whenever anyone uses a referring expression, he and his hearers associate with it thoughts which would still be even if the referring expression failed to refer, which is always logically possible in the case of physical objects. These are thoughts which would then be false. Without these thoughts, the fact that the omnipresent logical possibility of failure to refer does not threaten the existence of the thought could not be accounted for.

That in the primary case the object of assertion is the object of belief does not mean that in that case asserting of, or saying of, or predicating, is the same as believing of. Mill claims that 'a person who affirmed, before the Duke of Wellington was born, that all men are mortal' *asserted* that the Duke of Wellington was mortal (II.III.3. n. 2). This is incorrect, because it confuses asserting with asserting of, or predicating. But it is correct, and a good insight of Mill's, that the assertion does achieve predicating mortality of the Duke. And this is clearly not the same as believing it of him, since the speaker is in no position to think of the Duke at all.

Donnellan (1966, sec. 4) gives an example in which someone asserts 'The man who murdered Smith is insane', and believes he is referring to Jones, whom he falsely believes to have murdered Smith. The speaker may nonetheless claim his statement was true, if the killer turns out to be insane. This case shows that the belief that the murderer was insane is a belief in a statement which is not individuated by the object it is in fact about. (Russell would have held otherwise: that the case shows the statement isn't really about anyone.) This means that the beliefs that Jones is insane and that Jones committed the murder and the belief with respect to Jones, that he is insane, are not part of the belief that the murderer is insane. The latter is a separate belief.

Thus Donnellan's example is not a case in which someone has sincerely asserted something different from what he believes. (Donnellan didn't say it was such a case.) I stress this because the statement which is asserted should properly be taken to also be an object of belief. To say that a sincere assertion is believed may sound redundant. But it is not trivial that that which is sincerely asserted is also something which is believed. For that thing, the 'statement' or abstract proposition, for that very reason, cannot be adequately characterized as based on a purely referential use of a term. The means of achieving reference must always be part of the statement, because (at least with statements about physical objects) failure of reference is always logically possible without the belief also failing to exist. So not the reference, but only the means whereby it is attempted (successfully or not) belongs to the statement. The term 'statement' may of course be used in a different way. But the thing itself will still remain to be taken into account by some other name.

Strawson, in his criticism of Russell, goes even further than those who ignore the content of such bare terms as 'this' and 'that' (1950). He denies that even an utterance of such a sentence as 'The King of France is wise' can make a statement if there is a failure to refer. He denies that an assertion of existence is part of what is asserted by this sentence, holding instead that when the existence condition is not satisfied, nothing is asserted.

This is to ignore the connection between assertion and belief. Surely someone can believe that the present King of France is wise, or at least be expressing a belief in asserting 'The King of France is wise'. And this belief will always be, in part, that there is a King of France.

(I must pause, though, to grant that this last claim would not be true in some of the sorts of cases produced by Donnellan. Perhaps a janitor thinks he is King of France, and we succeed in expressing, with 'The King of France is wise', a belief which does not involve believing that there is a King of France. But for the present argument with Strawson, it would suffice to observe that still, in that case, I will have some other belief corresponding to an existential condition.)

What one believes, in sincerely saying 'The present King of France is wise', is in part that there is such a King. And this which is believed is also asserted. Strawson may have mistaken the act of predication for the statement. For it is true of this act that the existence of the King is a condition of its existence, and not merely of its truth.

Thus I think that what Donnellan was calling purely referential uses of terms to make statements would better have been put as uses to perform acts of predication. In my example, 'That syphilitic is trying to seduce Mary', the act of predication may be true (or correct, if you prefer) in spite of the fact that the man is not syphilitic. Thinking that the statement is all that is important would badly misrepresent the situation. But this should not be rectified by trying to invent a new kind of statement, the 'purely referential' one, when in fact nothing like this could be an object of belief at least in a physical object case, and it would be at best trifling to look for such statements in other kinds of cases such as allegedly 'direct' statements about sense data.

20 I do not deny that Mill may have shared the tendency to think that uses of proper names produce purely referential statements. His famous pronouncements about proper names being non-connotative certainly support this. But Mill also produced reasons for denying that proper names are non-connotative, while failing to recognize that this was what he was doing. To simply take his pronouncement at face value misrepresents his philosophy.

Mill says: 'A proper name is but an unmeaning mark which we connect in our minds with the idea of the object, in order that, whenever the mark meets our eyes or occurs to our thoughts, we may think of that individual object' (I. II. 5). This remark is in keeping with his earlier definition of a name as a mark for a 'former thought' and a sign of the thought for others. One difference is the use of the word 'idea'. However, in an important footnote to a later discussion of Locke, Mill disavows 'Locke's use of the word Idea' and says that 'Where a conceptualist says that a name or proposition expresses our idea of a thing, I should generally say (instead of our idea) our knowledge, or belief, concerning the thing itself' (I.v.2 n. 2).

At any rate, according to Mill, a name, in the first instance, serves to call up mental items by association. This is true for both connotative and non-connotative names. These mental items will in neither case be attributes. For attributes are not mental items and in fact there really aren't any such things at all. But then what is the difference between the items called up by connotative names and those called up by non-connotative names? It can't be the implication of uniqueness suggested by the fact that 'all concrete general names are connotative'; for there are connotative singular names. That there really is no difference is suggested by the following passage from Mill:

A substance ... being to us nothing but either that which causes, or that which is conscious of, phenomena; and the same being true *mutatis mutandis*, of attributes; no assertion can be made, at least with a meaning, concerning these unknown and unknowable entities, except in virtue of the phenomena by which alone they manifest themselves to our faculties. When we say Socrates was contemporary with the Peloponnesian War, the foundation of this assertion, as of all assertions concerning substances, is an assertion concerning the phenomena which they exhibit, namely, that the series of facts by which Socrates manifested himself to mankind and the series of mental states which constituted his mental existence went on simultaneously with the series of facts known by the name of the Peloponnesian War. Still, the proposition as commonly understood does not assert that alone; it asserts that the thing in itself, the *noumenon* Socrates, was existing and doing or experiencing those various facts during the same time.

(I.IV.4)

If we reflect that on Mill's account the function of the name 'Socrates' in the statement 'Socrates was contemporary with the Peloponnesian War' is to call up those thoughts by virtue of which one qualifies as thinking of Socrates, and then compare this with his account of the functioning of a connotative name in the subject position, it is hard to see how he could deny that 'Socrates' has a connotation. For example, while 'All men are mortal' is concerned with an indefinite number of individuals, with the extension or range of denotation of the name 'man' (Mill speaks this way: 'in the proposition "All men are mortal" the word "man" connotes'), this extension 'is both apprehended and indicated solely through the attributes' (I.IV.3. n. 3). And those attributes in turn are apprehended solely 'on the ground of certain phenomena which they exhibit', which is the very same phrase as is used in connection with how we apprehend Socrates.

Mill says that

When we predicate of anything its proper name, when we say pointing to a man, 'This is Brown or Smith' or pointing to a city, 'It is York' we do not, merely by so doing convey to the reader any information about them except that those are their names ... by saying 'This is York' we may tell him that it contains the Minster. But this is in virtue of what he has previously heard concerning York, not by anything implied in the name. It is otherwise when objects are spoken of by connotative names. When we say 'The town is built of marble', we give the hearer what may be entirely new information, and this merely by the signification of the many worded connotative name 'built of marble'. (I.II.5)

Mill is here forgetting about his theory as to how a name like 'built of marble' *manages* to convey information. We must recall for him that on his account it is just as much a matter of what one has previously heard concerning marble as it is with 'York' a matter of what one has 'previously heard concerning York'. In either case, these names call up previous thoughts that have become associated with the word.

This may sound like the notion of connotation from which Mill was explicitly departing, since he stressed that connotation is not merely a matter of the thoughts associated with a word, but a particular kind of association. But I am not suggesting that everything one has learned about York is connoted by 'York', certainly not that it contains the Minster. That York contains the Minster is not something one has to know to understand the term 'York'. On the other hand, it is not so clear that someone who doesn't know York is a city couldn't be correctly described as not understanding the name. Still, I do not insist on this either.

There is a common use of 'This is Brown' or 'This is York' which is equivalent to 'This is denoted by the name "Brown"'. It might be called the 'disguised-mention use'. But a similar use can be made of general names. 'This is marble' or better (to avoid worrying about mass terms for now) 'This is dirty' can be used as equivalent to 'This is denoted by the name "dirty"'. (That is, it can be so used if we follow Mill in calling 'dirty' a 'name'. Otherwise, a slight rephrasal would make the same point.) This use could be made in teaching someone English, and it would involve conveying no more information than in the case of the proper name. That such uses of proper names are vastly more common is not relevant to the question whether proper names are connotative. 'Disguised-mention' uses can be made of all names and cannot be cited to prove that proper names have no connotation, because these are merely uses in which the connotation is left out. It is much commoner to be introducing someone to a proper name that is new to him than to a general name that is, but that is no basis for calling the former non-connotative.

21　The important thing to keep track of is not so much whether a name implies attributes but why it does or doesn't. Mill says 'Logic does not undertake to analyse mental facts into their ultimate elements' (I.IV.5). Why not? It can only be because we just don't base our logical classifications on such considerations. In the statement 'John is beginning to interest Mary', does 'John' imply attributes? Well, what are we going to count as implied by this statement? In the symbolism of standard predicate logic, if 'John' were symbolized as a proper name, it certainly wouldn't imply attributes. This means that the statement is perfectly consistent with John's being, well, anything you can name. John may be a person, a dog, a city, or lattice theory. But suppose someone objects to his statement being treated this way, saying that anyone who doesn't know whether it is a concrete or abstract thing that is beginning to interest Mary simply hasn't grasped his statement? Then might not his use of 'John' begin to imply attributes, very general ones?

Here we must acknowledge the fact that what is believed, in believing that John is beginning to interest Mary, may not be precisely specifiable even with the case clear before us. Suppose it is 'obvious' to the speaker and his hearers that John is a man. But in reality John is a diabolically deceptive robot from outer space. Is the claim mistaken? Mary was getting interested, but it wasn't a man. The parties to the discussion were clearly mistakenly believing that John was a man. But was this part of their belief that John was beginning to interest Mary? My opinion is that it was not.

What is necessary is that John be made an object of thought and speech. This may be, in a simple case, a matter of his being recognized as the cause of certain experiences. With a name, it is even more complicated than with 'this' or 'that'. Still, taking the name merely to express the idea of the cause of certain experiences (and all those present at John's introduction will have an adequate idea of what those experiences are) does allow for distinguishing between the belief that this thing is a man, that it is beginning to interest Mary, and so on.

However, while we have no occasion to predicate 'this' or 'that', we do say 'This is John', and the like, without being taken to make a statement which entails that the thing referred to caused certain experiences. The case of a 'disguised-mention' use can be set aside, but not all uses are like that. If someone asks me who that is sitting in the swing with Mary, I may answer 'That is John', not by way of merely giving the name, but to identify someone with whom the questioner is already acquainted. My statement would not be taken to entail that the person I refer to caused such-and-such past experiences. What it would entail may become clearer later.

The name, unlike 'this' or 'that', may be used far beyond the situation in which the thing is initially and directly encountered. The bearer of the name, if there is one, will be made the object of talk and thought from a great variety of perspectives. There will be not only identification but re-identification, and eventually talk in which the speakers would be in no position to identify the bearer. And whether one is able to identify the bearer of a name is not a single unambiguous question independent of context. In one case, someone may qualify as being able to identify John by pointing out that John is the man talking to Mary. But, if the question is as to the identity of that fellow, named 'John', who is over there talking to Mary, the observation that John is the man talking to Mary will not qualify its maker as identifying the bearer of the name 'John'.

It is logically possible, not merely that John is a robot, but that there is a team of robots, each taking a turn at making up to Mary, playing the same role so well she can tell no difference. Does this falsify the claim that John is beginning to interest Mary? Does one who claims this mean that what is now causing certain experiences on various occasions is beginning to interest Mary? There is a clear distinction here, but it may not be easy to determine what the speaker was claiming. Even when it is clear that the speaker believed (falsely, we are supposing) that what is now causing certain features of the experience of himself and his hearers is the same thing that caused certain features on earlier occasions (or perhaps merely, was present on earlier occasions, since the experience caused on those occasions may be forgotten), it is not necessary that the speaker be meaning to *claim* this, rather than the distinct claim about what is now causing certain experiences. And even if the fantastic case here imagined actually happened, so that some departures from everyday behavior would be expected, people would still not be likely to be prepared to pursue the question as to what was claimed when it was claimed that John was beginning to interest Mary. But for all that, there is an answer to this question.

However, there is no interest in the fact that John caused those experiences, and he might not have, and still have been the same person (if we may return to a regular case in which a regular fellow named 'John' is beginning to interest Mary). It is the fact that an individual is singled out, not the variety of ways in which this is done, that is important. Ten years later I may say, 'Let me see, there was a fellow there that night, "John" I believe his name was, anyway, John was beginning to interest Mary.' We may say that my closing statement is the same statement I made ten years ago, when I said 'John is beginning to interest Mary'. It is a claim about the same person, even expressing a belief about the same person. We may say 'He still thinks Mary was getting interested in John'. But the beliefs expressed are not identical.

22 While it is not possible to say what in general must be believed in believing 'Socrates drank hemlock', what is usually believed is that there was someone who bore the name 'Socrates' (allowing for variations in spelling and pronunciation) and who drank hemlock. However, lots of people have been named 'Socrates', and it would appear that to single out one of them would call for more specifications.

Along this line there arises a theory known as the 'disguised description theory of proper names'. The idea is that a proper name is some sort of abbreviation for definite descriptions which single out the bearer of the name. Thus Frege, in his essay 'On Sense and Reference' (1952), says that for some people the sense of 'Aristotle' is 'Plato's disciple and the teacher of Alexander the Great'. For others it is 'the Stagirite teacher of Alexander the Great'. The meaning of 'Aristotle was born in Stagira' will be different between these different interpretations. (Incidentally, I doubt that Frege really thought that people do think such things as that 'Aristotle' means 'the Stagirite who taught Alexander' any more than he thought that 'the King of France in 1905' denotes the null set. He was just pre-occupied with constructing an ideal language and wanted to avoid subjective variations in meaning as much as possible. His variety of choices for 'Aristotle' are a first step in the elimination of these subjective variations, not a full recognition of them.)

The same philosophers who subscribe to the distinction between referential and attributive statements also go in for attacking this theory about the meaning of proper names. Saul Kripke (1972) acknowledges that his views on this matter are not a theory, but rather a statement of what is wrong with the disguised description theory. But others regard the sort of complaints he raises to be an alternative theory about the relation of a name to its bearer, called the 'causal theory' or 'the historical explanation theory'.

The basis of this 'alternative theory' is the recognition that Frege's suggestions for meanings of 'Aristotle' have false consequences. No one smart enough to know that Aristotle was born in Stagira and taught Alexander thinks it logically impossible that the claim that if Aristotle existed at all, he taught Alexander, should be false. But anyone who means by 'Aristotle' 'the Stagirite male who taught Alexander' should regard the aforementioned claim as necessarily true.

It might be objected that someone making this claim might mean only that Aristotle wasn't necessarily Alexander's teacher, and to say that the teacher didn't necessarily teach Alexander, since he didn't have to and might have avoided it if he had so chosen, is perfectly consistent. Even if this is true, there are other statements such as 'No one could possibly qualify as Aristotle without having taught Alexander' which Frege's account would make true, which are not true. The causal theorists would hold that *all* the popular descriptions suggested as meanings for 'Aristotle' could have been false of Aristotle – all at once. One possibility is that Aristotle was really a private in Alexander's army who gave a false story and thus got credited with the work of Baconidas.

The causal theorists are right that the average person doesn't mean by 'Socrates', 'the teacher of Plato', or anything like that. For one thing, occurrence of names like 'Plato' would make such an account of 'Socrates' question begging as far as the question of bridging the historical gap is concerned. And if we did get descriptions which did single out Socrates in a non-question-begging way, they would, *if* we followed the line suggested by 'the teacher of Plato who drank hemlock, etc.', be beyond the knowledge of many people who nonetheless are able to refer to this historial Socrates.

The truth of the matter, as presented by the causal theorists, is that the average fellow who says that Socrates drank hemlock is relying on a 'division of linguistic labors'. He is sure that other people have seen Socrates and referred to him by name, and that the information about this important person has been passed along in a historical chain, perhaps with substantial changes in the original name used (so that Socrates himself might not have answered if called by the modern name) culminating in the delivery to him of the information that Socrates drank hemlock.

The particular chain which extends from a particular average man back to Socrates may differ from that for other men. Smith may have heard all he knows about Socrates from Joe Doaks. But surely the meaning of Smith's statement that Socrates drank hemlock has nothing to do with Joe Doaks? Or are we to say that Smith's assertion includes a claim about Joe?

Smith thinks that certain uses of the name 'Socrates' are historically connected with an individual who drank hemlock, and he thinks that the most recent such uses have been made by Joe Doaks. But these are separate thoughts. So the claim about Joe need not be included in Smith's assertion that Socrates drank hemlock. However, I do maintain that Smith's assertion includes a claim about the name 'Socrates' and in fact it includes a claim about his own use of that name in the making of that very assertion. This is something the referentialists avoid by leaving the condition which they hold to connect the name to the bearer out of the thought that is expressed with an assertion made by using the name. They might charge that my account has the consequence that 'we cannot use words without mentioning them'. This complaint will be discussed at length later.

When I say that the causal theorists have helped to set matters straight as to how a name is related to its bearer, I do not mean to endorse the idea that the relation between a name and its bearer is a causal one. The valuable point is rather that in many cases a certain kind of causal connection may relate a use of a name to a bearer in spite of the speaker's inability to give any other individuating description of the bearer. The idea of a 'division of linguistic labor' is worth keeping in mind as a reminder that the primary case of naming cannot be explained in terms of the way a name is passed along from one person or group to another.

Michael Devitt (1974) holds that the 'historical explanation theory' should be extended to cover what he sees as the crucial case, the first time the name is linked to the bearer, which he calls a 'naming ceremony'. His example is an occasion when he and his wife named their cat 'Nana'. Devitt says: 'As a result of the causal interaction at that ceremony among my wife, Nana, and myself, an interaction in which Nana occupied a certain place (that of an object being named) I gained my ability ... to designate Nana by "Nana"' (p. 185). That is, he gained the ability to use 'Nana' as a name for Nana. By this sort of approach we could easily construct causal theories of lots of relations. For example, 'the causal theory of love' could explain the relation '*x* loves *y*' by saying that as a result of causal interaction between *x* and *y*, it comes about that *x* loves *y*.

Devitt does say 'Our account rests on talk of "abilities to designate objects by name".' But he continues:

> What is such an ability? . . . As materialists we expect the advance of science . . . to show us that it is a certain sort of state of the central nervous system. It is a state which is brought about in a language user by perception of a naming ceremony (and in other ways to be described) and which is apt to produce (in part) certain sorts of utterances, viz. utterances using the name in question. It is such states, whatever they are, that largely constitute the links between names and their objects.   (1974, p. 186)

Those uses of the name the 'state of the central nervous system' is 'apt to produce' are presumably uses of the name as a name for its bearer. The notion of the relation of name to bearer makes it through this 'analysis' completely untouched. In a footnote, Devitt suggests these CNS states can be 'related to pointing', but does not pursue this.

Suppose that an ignoramus comes upon a window-case display at an elementary school, the purpose of which is to give thanks for great men. There are cut-and-paste sentences reading 'We are lucky to have had so many great men in history, for example, Pericles was a statesman, Plato was a philosopher' and so on. Suppose that 'So' has dropped off from higher up in the display, and a 'crates' has fallen right beside it, and they happen to be covering the 'Plato', so that our ignoramus reads 'Socrates was a philosopher' and is convinced by it, adding it to his meager store of opinions on intellectual history. What he believes is that there is just one person of suitable historical importance connected with the name 'Socrates', and this person was a philosopher. He is right in this belief. He may also believe that this person is historically connected with the use of the name he has read, or that exactly one person is so connected. In this he is mistaken. The fact that there is no causal connection between the only use of the name he knows of, and any bearer, is not, in my opinion, as important as the fact that he thinks there is such a connection. Still more important is the fact that he thinks that this connection (there really is none) reflects a more general connection, which in fact does exist, between the name 'Socrates' as it would

most commonly be used by the majority of schoolchildren, and a
historical bearer. On the basis of this fact, the ignoramus might
well be credited with making reference to Socrates when he asserts,
at his next cocktail party, 'Socrates, you know, was a philosopher'.

My purpose is to bring out the crucial role that the thought that a
condition is uniquely satisfied plays in reference. The causal theorists
have helped to show what a variety of conditions may be involved.
But I do not accept the view that the connection between a name and
its bearer is better explained in terms of a causal connection than in
terms of the satisfaction of a condition set forth in the thinking of the
speaker.

23 The notion of connection between name and bearer is too often
confused with another sort of connection between mind and object –
that of apprehension which is not based on a condition, an unconditioned apprehension. This sort of apprehension is common in
perception. Suppose, for example, that I am looking at a very large
box of identical marbles, and I focus my attention on one of them. It
might of course be possible for me to describe a publicly available
condition which this marble uniquely satisfies, such as that of being
the seventeenth one on a straight line between two marks on opposite sides of the box. But I might not be able to provide any such
condition, and more importantly, it is not by means of any such
condition that I am able to focus my attention on an object in my
visual field.

Suppose I say 'That marble is an agate'. Here I am making a claim
about a certain one of the marbles, though no one but me may know
which, and I may know which for only a few seconds. The slightest
wavering of my focus may cause me to lose track of the marble I
referred to and never be able to know again which it was. Still I am
expressing the thought that something which uniquely satisfies a
certain condition is an agate. But what is that condition? It may be
no better described than as 'the marble which I am thinking of'. (It is
good to remember that we do not have *the* description of a thought,
but a variety of better and worse descriptions whose value is determined in part by the interests of those who seek a description.)
But of course it is not grasping this condition which enables the
thinker to apprehend the marble, to focus on it. It is rather his
capacity to grasp his focusing on it that associates this condition with
the singular term 'that marble' in this case. A cat has much better

powers of resolution than a human, it can focus its eyes much better. But it cannot grasp this power it has and we are thus disinclined to credit it with much in the way of thoughts.

I maintain that the singular term 'that marble' in my example is associated with the thought that the condition of being the cause of certain features of my experience and a marble is uniquely satisfied. The assertion 'That marble is an agate' adds to this thought the further thought that this thing is also an agate. The referentialists are committed to denying this. But they are also inclined to support their denial by holding that the features of my experience caused by the marble are not adequately identified. I might as well say that the condition associated with 'that marble' is 'the marble I have in mind'. And it is like the referentialists to say that such a description 'begs the question'. But this would be to run questions together. If the condition associated with the term is saddled with the job of establishing the connection between the user of the term and the thing he refers to with it, then such a condition as 'the marble I have in mind' will not do. But the referentialists are supposed to be defending their claim that only the referent of 'that marble', and not any condition associated with it, is involved in determining the truth conditions of what is said in saying 'That marble is an agate'. And the fact that the condition of being the marble I have in mind does not enable me to have that marble in mind is no support at all for that claim. I might have an optical illusion which made me think that I was focusing on a marble when in fact I was not. In that case, it is relevant to assessing the truth of what I said that I claimed in part that something qualified as the marble I had in mind when in fact nothing so qualified. Thus what I said would be false in that version of the case. This is something the referentialist denies. But to bring up the uselessness of descriptions such as 'the one I had in mind' for establishing my apprehension of an object does not explain away the fact that even such descriptions may play a substantial role in the description of what is said as a guide to determining its truth value.

Suppose that, on the basis of my knowledge of the political structure of Baritraria, I know that that country has exactly one president, though I have no idea who he is. Since the people of that country speak Frisian, I may qualify as knowing that the president of Baritraria speaks Frisian. Here it might be said that I apprehend this person, the president of Baritraria, only by virtue of grasping the condition, being president of Baritraria, and knowing it to be uniquely satisfied. And this conditioned apprehension of the president might naturally be contrasted with the unconditioned apprehension of him which I might make in perceiving him. Such a distinction is all right, until it is mixed up with the topic of naming and reference. If I learn further that the president is named 'Jones' this does not change the quality of my apprehension of him. Perhaps my perceiving the president would make my name for him more 'vivid' in some sense, but it does not make it any more of a name. Nor does the alleged distinction between referential and attributive uses correspond to these two sorts of apprehension. It might be thought that since the apprehension of the president in this case is only achieved by grasping a condition and knowing it to be uniquely satisfied, and the condition is also part of the assertion when I assert 'The president of Baritraria speaks Frisian', that when the case is changed to one where I perceive the president, and the apprehension of him is then not achieved by grasping a condition, that similarly the assertion no longer involves the condition. But this is fallacious.

The referentialists would have it that if I nod in the direction of someone at a conference and say 'The president of Baritraria speaks Frisian', I have made a referential use of the description, as opposed to the attributive use made only on the basis of knowledge of Baritrarian government. But both assertions express the thought that what uniquely satisfies a certain condition speaks Frisian. It is just that the conditions are different. At the conference I am claiming that the person causing certain features of my experience is president of Baritraria and speaks Frisian. That is, I am claiming more in that case than in the case not involving perception, rather than less.

24 Mill says:

> A town may have been named Dartmouth, because it is situated at the mouth of the Dart. But ... If sand should choke up the mouth of the river, or an earthquake change its course, and remove it to a distance from the town, the name of the town would not necessarily be changed. That fact, therefore, can form no part of the signification of the word; for otherwise, when the fact confessedly ceased to be true, no one would any longer think of applying the name. Proper names are attached to the objects themselves, and are not dependent on the continuance of any attribute of the object. (I.II.5)

Mill's example is a very good one for illustrating an important feature of proper names. But Mill thinks the example shows that proper names are not connected with conditions at all, and that is the wrong conclusion to draw from the case. It is rather a matter of the kind of conditions that are associated with proper names and the way they are associated.

Consider, for example, a case in which we are detectives discussing a robbery, and I say, 'Okay, let's call the one who held the clerks at gunpoint while the others were in the safe "Nixon".' It seems that if I subsequently say 'Nixon drove the getaway car', I will express the thought that the one who held the clerks at gunpoint while the others were in the safe drove the getaway car. And there is no doubt that in some cases this would be a correct account of my thought. But the 'meaning' of 'Nixon' can change drastically. One way is if we capture the gang and perceive some member of it as the one who held the clerks at gunpoint. Now, when we agree to use the name 'Nixon' for this person whom we see, rather than using it as a title we are determined to assign to whoever qualifies as the one person who held the clerks at gunpoint while the others were in the safe, then asserting 'Nixon drove the getaway car' would be a different assertion than the one made when 'Nixon' really was just an abbreviation for 'the one who held the clerks etc.'. We would be claiming that the person who caused certain features of our experience drove the getaway car. The name is still associated with a condition.

Mill says, 'A man may have been named John, because that was the name of his father; a town may have been named Dartmouth because it is situated at the mouth of the Dart.' But of course 'John is sick' will not mean 'The father's son is sick' and 'Dartmouth is populous' need not mean 'The city at the mouth of the Dart is populous'. (And here again it is worth warning that this is even in my own 'sense' of 'mean'. It is obvious that the sentences are not synonymous – I am making a different point.) This is because our thought of John or of Dartmouth need not be associated with these conditions. Those who decided to name Dartmouth 'Dartmouth' because it was at the mouth of the Dart probably had a very considerable experience of the town. Someone who asserts that Dartmouth is populous may be thinking that there is a city at the mouth of the Dart called 'Dartmouth', but that thought is probably not expressed in his assertion. This is because other conditions are at the basis of his thought about Dartmouth, conditions such that if they were not satisfied he would not be making any reference at all. This could even be such a condition as 'being the town I am thinking of'. For he may have an unconditioned apprehension of Dartmouth or at least think that he has. That is, he thinks that he is apprehending a town. This is a genuine condition, which should not be overlooked just because it is not a reason for the particular word chosen as name having been chosen.

Suppose that all I know about Tegucigalpa is that it is the capital of Honduras. I know that Tegucigalpa is in Honduras. But this is more than knowing merely that the capital of Honduras is in Honduras. How can that be? If I had merely made up the name 'Tegucigalpa' as my own personal name for the capital which I know only through that description, those who understood my 'Tegucigalpa is in Honduras' would be correct in crediting me with expressing only the thought that the capital of Honduras is in Honduras. But I know that 'Tegucigalpa' is a public name for this capital. And this knowledge is expressed in part in my assertion of 'Tegucigalpa is in Honduras'. The thought that it is the capital is left out, perhaps even the thought that it is a city, rather than a river or mountain or other thing. But the thought that 'Tegucigalpa' names something is included. There could also be assertions of 'Tegucigalpa is in Honduras' that did not include this thought.

There is nothing wrong with discarding some of the logical consequences of a statement. Perhaps with proper names, it is a good policy to attend only to the act of predication and its logical consequences, ignoring those features of the statement that make the predication possible. If this is common in ordinary speech, then a good sense can be given to the idea that proper names are non-connotative – this could be a way of indicating that their connotation is generally ignored.

The truth is that when a typical American asserts that Socrates drank hemlock he is asserting what he believes (or takes for granted or presumes) – that there is a unique individual historically connected with certain uses of the name 'Socrates', and that individual drank hemlock. We have the causal theorists to thank for this insight, except that they have refused to recognize that the means of reference belong to the statement.

It might be objected that (a) 'If Socrates existed at all, then he is historically connected with the term "Socrates" as it is used in this statement' would provide a 'last ditch' example for the referentialist of something which would come out as necessarily true on my account when in fact it is contingent. The idea would be that Socrates could have existed even if there had been no term historically connected with him beyond a certain period short of the time of statement (a).

The sentence (a) could convey the thought that Socrates did exist and that a necessary condition of his existing is being historically connected with the use of 'Socrates' in (a). So interpreted, (a) is false, and my account does not change that. On the other hand, 'No one could qualify as Socrates without being historically connected with the term "Socrates" as used in this statement' is necessarily true relative to the assumption that there is such a statement. It is natural to think of a thing, and to think that it does not depend for its existence on your thinking of it. And this may be true, but you are nonetheless thinking that that thing exists. (a) is potentially misleading in that it might lead us to ignore this assumption of existence. It is good to recognize that thinking about a thing does not make its existence dependent on our thought. But it would be unfortunate if this led us to deny that every thought about the object will include a thought that singles it out.

The objection that the theory which holds that primary cases of singular terms are associated with the thought that a condition is uniquely satisfied has the consequence that certain statements using the singular term will be counted necessarily true when they should not be, can actually be turned to the advantage of the theory in connection with a related objection. It is said that someone who asserts 'Socrates drank hemlock' may indeed have many opinions concerning Socrates which take the form of thinking that a condition is uniquely satisfied. But how is some one of these conditions to be selected as the one to use in describing the thought he expresses in saying 'Socrates drank hemlock'?

This objection would be especially embarrassing in the case of someone who has only knowledge of some very esoteric individuating condition for Socrates. For how could his assertion of 'Socrates drank hemlock' *express* the thought that that esoteric condition is uniquely satisfied, when none of his hearers would ever know it? It would be fallacious to think that whenever someone thinks *that* a condition is uniquely satisfied, he is thinking *of* that condition, or is even able to formulate that condition himself. Whenever anyone says 'Socrates drank hemlock' and semantic theorists gather to give an account of what was said, the individuating condition theorist will of course want to do the talking for the speaker. For all that, he must justify his choice of a condition if there are many conditions available.

This is where the complaint about the wrong statements being necessary is helpful. For if someone associates a singular term S with the thought that a condition C is uniquely satisfied, then for the association to be semantically suitable he should regard the proposition that S does not satisfy C as necessarily false or absurd. (I say 'should' because so many people would be quite inadequate in a situation in which, having been found to use some singular term, they were asked to pass on the modal status of a proposition linking that term with the denial of some condition. They might be inadequate either out of intellectual deficiency or perversity. But the theory, though of course applicable to everyone, should not be dependent in this way on the practice of simpletons or skeptics.) It is absurd to say 'Socrates is in no way historically connected with the name "Socrates" as used in this statement'. It is, on the other hand, perfectly consistent to say 'Socrates was not the only teacher of Plato who drank hemlock'. Such considerations will disqualify most conditions that are thought to be uniquely satisfied from being semantically suitable. I am not offering an algorithm; but in general, it is far easier to select from the various conditions that a speaker takes to be uniquely satisfied the one that is expressed in his assertion, than either the referentialists or the disguised description theorists recognize.

Donnellan (1974) goes so far as to say, 'If a child says "Santa Claus will come tonight" he cannot have spoken the truth, although for various reasons, I think it better to say that he has not even expressed a proposition' (p. 21). And he gives what is probably the most prominent of these 'various reasons' (or perhaps just the upshot of them) in a footnote to this remark: 'Given that this is a statement about reality and that proper names have no descriptive content, then how are we to represent the proposition expressed?' How, indeed, if we choose to ignore the fact that in saying what he did the child gave voice to his belief that there is an individual connected with the name 'Santa Claus', as used by his parents and others, who will come tonight? Overemphasis on the act of predication has led to the idea that where there is no such act, there is nothing left.

The same overemphasis is displayed in the following passage.

> If you say 'Henry is bald' and I say 'George is bald' we express the
> same proposition if the person you referred to by using the name
> 'Henry' and I by using the name 'George' are the same person.
> But what you say is true if and only if the person you referred to –
> that is, the person historically connected – when you use the name
> 'Henry' has the property of being bald; whereas what I say is true
> if and only if what I referred to by using the name 'George' has
> the property of being bald. The truth conditions are different
> because they must be stated in terms of what is referred to by
> different expressions, in the one case my use of the name 'George'
> and in the other your use of the name 'Henry'. Yet we may
> express the same proposition.   (Donnellan 1974, pp. 28–9)

There is nothing wrong with appropriating the term 'proposition'
for application to acts of predication, except that it is also used to
apply to what is believed. But what is believed is ignored in the
above, however it may be called. Anyway, the act of predication
achieved with 'Henry is bald' does not have as a truth condition that
someone is named 'Henry'. So Donnellan cannot mean that by
'proposition'. On the other hand the Russellian proposition, that is,
the sentence understood in a certain way, does indeed have among
its truth conditions that someone is named 'Henry'. But then it is not
the same 'proposition', in that sense, as the Russellian proposition
'George is bald', so that could not be Donnellan's meaning either.
His meaning is not clear. What the proposition is, that is expressed by
two utterances with different truth conditions, is left unexplained.

This same difficulty arises for one of the philosophers who is
among Donnellan's targets – Frege. The attack on the disguised
description theory has tended to obscure the real issue, which is over
the question as to what is thought in an assertion involving a singular term, either a name or a description, given the omnipresent
logical possibility of failure of reference. Russell held that what is
thought in these cases is that a certain condition is uniquely satisfied.
Frege did not think this. This is the fundamental point at issue.
Both Frege and Russell are characterized by the referentialists as
'disguised description' theorists. This is correct, but it only shows
that the issue is mislocated if the disguised description theory is
then taken to be the main opponent for the causal or referential
theory.

Donnellan gives the following 'rule for negative existence statements':

> (R) If N is a proper name that has been used in predicative statements with the intention to refer to some individual, then ⌜N does not exist⌝ is true if and only if the history of those uses ends in a block.   (1974, p. 25)

Donnellan says that 'This rule . . . does not provide an *analysis* . . . it does not tell us what such statements mean or what proposition they express.' And he says 'Rule R may look unexciting, but its consequences are interesting . . . its form is completely antithetical to the principle of identifying descriptions, for it has nothing to do with whether an individual of a certain description existed or not.'

This is not correct. Rule R has everything to do with whether an individual of the following description existed: 'The individual at the end of the historical chain associated with name N as it is used in such-and-such predicative statements.' It is just if there is no individual of this description that 'the history of those uses ends in a block'. That description would be irrelevant to the truth of 'N does not exist' if Donnellan were right in his claim that R 'does not tell us what such statements mean or what proposition they express'. I hold that, on the contrary, a rule like R is an excellent basis for finding what proposition is expressed in a negative existence statement.

25   In 'On Sense and Reference' (1952) Frege says that the sense of the sentence 'Kepler died in misery' does not 'contain the thought that the name "Kepler" designates something'. His only argument is that otherwise

> the negation would have to run not
>   Kepler did not die in misery
> but
>   Kepler did not die in misery, or the name 'Kepler' has no reference.   (p. 69)

This same argument would apply not only to the thought that the name 'Kepler' had a reference but to the thought that Kepler existed. This thought, that Kepler existed, would, for a modern American, include a thought about the name 'Kepler', so we might as well follow Frege's example. In either case, the argument has no force.

The fact that the thought that Kepler died in misery contains or entails the thought that Kepler existed and (for us) the thought that the name, in certain uses, is connected with a historical chain leading to a bearer, does not show that the negation of the sentence 'Kepler died in misery' would need rewording. It only shows that 'Kepler did not die in misery' does not make explicit the thought it expresses in certain contexts. And by 'not explicit', I mean just that its structure is very condensed for the complexity of the thought it expresses. And by 'condensed for the complexity' I mean that in our language we have means for expressing a number of thoughts that are included in the thought that Kepler died in misery or the thought that he did not. Thus I do not regard the complexity of a thought as language independent even though the thought itself is.

Frege himself observes, a little later on, that some sentences have subordinate clauses which 'have no simple sense'. With such sentences 'we may well have more simple thoughts than clauses'. However, he was plainly reluctant to acknowledge this to be true also of such a 'simple' sentence as 'Kepler died in misery'. Frege regarded the sense of such a sentence as a thought composed of two parts: the sense of 'Kepler' and the sense of the blank form '—— died in misery'. He held that this latter sense was a concept and not an object and that 'it' could not be denoted by a substantive. Otherwise 'the parts of a thought could not hold together'.

This is my interpretation of Frege's remarks in his essay 'On Concept and Object' (1952), and it is not an uncommon one. On the other hand, it is not universally accepted. In other writings, such as *Grundgesetze der Arithmetik* (1893, 1903), the concept is not presented as the sense of an incomplete name. In my opinion, it cannot be determined whether the relation between the concept and the incomplete name is one of denotation or sense or neither, without a better account of both these relations than Frege gives. At any rate, I shall proceed on the assumption that in those of his writings with which I am concerned, Frege held the doctrine that the thought expressed by a simple sentence such as 'Kepler died in misery' is composed of the senses of the parts of the sentence.

This doctrine is in clear conflict with the facts about grammatically complex sentences which Frege recognized. It reflects Frege's uneasiness about the nature of abstract entities. He wanted the form of the concrete thing, the sentence, to be a guide to the form of the abstract thing, the thought or proposition. For otherwise what guide could we have in that realm except perhaps

Plato's 'inner eye'? But this was a pointless worry, as will be argued later.

It is this doctrine of the similarity of form between sentence and thought in the 'simple' case which is behind Frege's refusal to grant that the thought that Kepler died in misery includes the thought that Kepler existed. For if so, then 'Kepler existed, and he died in misery' would appear to be just a more tedious spelling out of the same thought as 'Kepler died in misery'. And then where is one to look, among sentences, for a guide as to the form of the thought?

Neither Frege nor Russell could grant that 'The King of France is wise' and 'There is one and only one person who is King of France and that person is wise' or 'At least one person is King of France, at most one person is a King of France, and anyone who is a King of France is wise', all express the same proposition. Their responses are different, but the underlying reason is the same. Once one recognizes the equivalence, one must grant that there is no sense in applying any notion of form derived from sentences to propositions.

If 'The King of France is wise' expresses a proposition that is composed of the sense of 'the King of France' and the sense of the blank form '—— is wise', then it would seem that 'There is exactly one King of France and he is wise' would express the same proposition only if 'There is exactly one King of France and he' had the same sense as 'the King of France'. Under this pressure, Russell gave up his platonism, and held that these sentences represent the same Russellian proposition, in the sense that one is an abbreviation (in natural language, an extremely misleading one) for the other, or both for some even purer formulation. Thus Russell clings to the idea that there is at least some language whose form is a perfect guide to the form of the thought.

Frege kept to platonism, but even this virtue does not compensate for the effect of his clinging also to the doctrine that the abstract structure must be revealed by the concrete one. Russell was at least roughly right about what someone who thinks that the King of France is wise is thinking. But Frege had to deny that the thought that the King of France is wise contains the thought that there is a King of France. And if we consider a real life example of thinking, and don't try to make up perverse examples (which might be worth saving for other discussions), it is perfectly clear that this misrepresents what is involved in thinking that the King of France is wise.

As for asserting, one can always appropriate the term for one's own technical purposes, and even perhaps find some basis in social practice, for denying that the assertion that the King of France is wise entails there is a King, rather than 'presupposing' it. But there is a good concept of assertion on which it is ideally the verbal expression of thought.

3
Platonism

26 Lockwood complains that Mill never got over his mistaken 'belief that to state the semantic conditions under which an utterance is true is to give an account of what is actually being asserted by means of that utterance' (1975, p. 409). An example is Mill's remark that 'If it be true that all oxen ruminate, it must be true that all the individuals denoted by the name ox are among those denoted by the name ruminating; and whoever asserts that all oxen ruminate, undoubtedly does assert that this relation subsists between the two names' (I.v.2).

Lockwood replies: 'That what is denoted by "S" is also denoted by "P" is no part of what is being asserted or even implied by the statement that a speaker makes in uttering a sentence of the form "S is P". Rather, it is something which is pragmatically implied by the speaker's *utterance* of this sentence' (1975, p. 490). He also charges that 'it seems not to have occurred to Mill that a Japanese might assert that all oxen ruminate without making a claim about the English word "ox"'.

Mill was a nominalist, at least in a half-hearted way. He was probably well aware that a Japanese could attribute to the same class of animals the same attribute, in the sense that similar 'phenomena' might have similarly grounded the same bogus entity, the existence of which Mill denied on occasions when the strict truth was to be told. And it is not fair to accuse Mill of confusing the truth conditions of a sentence with the proposition expressed by the sentence when this latter entity is one which Mill, in keeping with a substantial (though mistaken, but that is another matter) doctrine, would not admit exists.

However, the issue over whether the object of belief is a Russellian proposition, as Mill holds, or a non-linguistic proposition, as Lockwood implies, is not the main issue here. My own view of propositions is thoroughly platonistic. But that by itself is no guarantee that the extra-linguistic entity asserted by asserting 'Oxen ruminate' does not make reference to the English words 'oxen' and 'ruminate'. The proposition that 'oxen' is an English word is an extra-linguistic entity. But it is nonetheless about a word.

Here again, identifying the proposition with acts of predication would facilitate Lockwood's move to the conclusion that what is asserted in uttering 'Oxen ruminate' has nothing to do with those words. For in making this assertion one performs many acts of predication. One attributes to each ox the property of ruminating. And these acts of predication, though they were made by using the word 'oxen', are in no way *about* the word 'oxen'. (The position with the word 'ruminate' is not so clear, of course, because it does involve the traditional question between nominalists and platonists. Lockwood says, by way of correcting Mill, that 'The linguistic items . . . called predicates are . . . the means by which attributes are predicated . . . They are not themselves predicated of things' (1975, p. 489). As a platonist, I agree with most of that claim, but it should not be directed to Mill as a mere correction, as if the matter were now settled.) But the object of the belief that oxen ruminate is not the same as these acts of predication. One who believes that oxen ruminate need not believe that my ox ruminates. He may not know my ox. To describe what someone believes in believing that oxen ruminate requires something other than an indication of what acts of predication are performed in asserting what is believed. For that matter, indicating all the acts of predication involved in asserting that oxen ruminate is not practically possible.

Whenever anyone believes that oxen ruminate, there will be words corresponding to 'ox' and 'ruminates' such that that person believes those words are related in the way Mill says they are asserted to be related by anyone who asserts that all oxen ruminate. The question is whether this belief which must be had by anyone who believes that oxen ruminate is a separate belief or just a part of the belief that oxen ruminate, in which case a more accurate description would bring out that the belief that oxen ruminate is not the very same belief from one language speaker to another. The acts of predication performed in the assertion would be the same, and Mill was a great one for stressing that. But the beliefs would be different because they would include beliefs about different words.

Someone seeking to preserve, in the face of this, the idea that there is a common assertion to the effect that oxen ruminate, performable in different languages, might focus on an especially important act of predication that is performed in asserting 'Oxen ruminate'. This is the act of predicating of the property of being an ox and the property of ruminating, the relation of subsumption, the first property to the second. This act of predication is about properties, not about words. Furthermore, performing this act of predication is entailed by asserting that oxen ruminate. When someone asserts that oxen ruminate, he makes the concrete predication (probably without knowing it) of ruminating of my ox. But though this is done in fact, it is not necessarily done by every possible assertion that oxen ruminate, because it is possible that my ox should not have existed. But it is impossible to assert that oxen ruminate without performing the act of predicating the subsumption of the property of being an ox under the property of ruminating.

When he was a platonist, Russell was a much more straight-forward one than Frege. He held that while one could not be directly acquainted with physical objects or the mental states of others, one could be directly acquainted with one's own mental states and with such things as *properties*. This is sometimes ridiculed as the idea that one has an 'inner eye' that somehow 'sees' these eternal entities or properties. But the doctrine of direct acquaintance may have been merely a reflection of the conviction that it is possible for people to hold in common various objective beliefs. Thus the thought that oxen ruminate would be seen as a thought relating two properties, that of being an ox and that of being a ruminant. The Japanese might associate with these properties other words than ours, and the words might be an aid in thinking, but the thought would concern only the properties, not the words. If someone assumed that anything not directly apprehended must be apprehended by means of thoughts which will then be incorporated into any thought about that thing, then if he thinks that the thought that oxen ruminate only involves the properties of being an ox and being a ruminant, he will naturally conclude that the apprehension of these properties must be direct.

This could be accepted even by a non-platonist. It might be said that apprehending a property, say, that of being an ox, is a matter of having a complex range of dispositions to produce words in response to stimulation, and so on, rather than a matter of entering into a relation to an abstract entity (not that these are incompatible). The idea that the apprehension of properties is direct, as opposed to the indirectness of apprehension of physical objects, is perfectly consistent with a reductionist analysis of the notion of apprehending a property. For the idea attributes directness to the apprehension of properties, not to the properties themselves.

With respect to any thought about a physical object, it is logically possible that the object should not have existed, and the thought be exactly the same thought. But with respect to a thought about a property, this is usually not so. Someone might say that if Bill thinks that the property Bob is thinking of is a color property, then whether Bob is thinking of a property or not, the thought is the same. Without trying to say precisely how such a case differs from the usual ones, we may simply turn our attention to the usual ones, such as someone's thinking that the property of being an ox is such that everything possessing it has the further property of being a ruminant. It is not possible that this thought should be the same even if there were no property of being an ox.

This could be trivially true to a platonist (such as myself) because the property of being an ox exists necessarily. But this is not important here. The dependence of the thought on the property is not merely a matter of the necessary existence of the property, which makes a kind of trivial dependence of everything there is on the property, since each thing there is could not exist without the property existing. This trivial consequence of the doctrine that properties exist necessarily is not needed to see that the thought would not be the same if the property it concerned did not exist. This should be granted even by those who give a reductionist analysis of the apprehension of properties.

This shows that the identification of the belief that oxen ruminate with the act of predication which holds the property of being an ox to be subsumed under that of being a ruminant (or of ruminating – I have been ignoring this ambiguity) is not open to the kind of objection I raised previously. My objection to the identification of the act of predicating having drunk hemlock of Socrates with the belief that Socrates drank hemlock was that the belief could still exist even if the logical possibility that Socrates did not were realized, while in such a case the act of predication could not exist. When the objects of the assertion are properties rather than physical objects, no such thing can happen. There would of course be a corresponding failure of existence for the acts of predication involving individual oxen if the logical possibility that there are no oxen were realized. Furthermore, it could be said that the assertion that Socrates drank hemlock achieves the act of predication, with respect to the property of being Socrates and the property of having drunk hemlock, of the property of being instantiated together. So this type of act of predication (not to be confused with 'action type'), which may be called the act of abstract predication, as opposed to the act of concrete predication such as predicating wisdom of Socrates, is not excluded from candidacy for being the thought, even in cases where the grammatical subject is a proper name. At the least, it is a great improvement over the act of concrete predication as a candidate.

For all that, it is still not correct to identify the thought with the act of abstract predication, even in the case of 'oxen ruminate'.

27 In his platonistic days, Russell was better than Frege not merely on the question of the nature of properties, but also on the question as to the nature of our 'apprehension' of them. Russell said it was direct. Perhaps it would have been better not to be so concerned about 'apprehension', as will be brought out later. But Frege treated the 'apprehension' as not direct, which is the worst account of all. He says:

> The apprehension of a thought presupposes someone who apprehends it, who thinks. He is the bearer of the thinking but not of the thought. Although the thought does not belong to the contents of the thinker's consciousness yet something in his consciousness must be aimed at the thought. But this should not be confused with the thought itself. Similarly Algol itself is different from the idea someone has of Algol.   (1956, p. 308)

What is my idea of Algol? I think, among other things, that it is a fixed star of the constellation Perseus. (Someone else might say that it is a computer language, but let us leave that out for now.) My 'apprehension' of Algol is based on this thought, which, in my opinion, includes a thought about the name 'Algol' in order to determine which star in Perseus it is (not to mention the mention of 'Perseus'). I have no image of Algol.

For Locke, someone's idea of a thing might in some cases be his visual image of it. This is not a senseless theory if the visual image is accompanied by thoughts. But Berkeley was surely right to reject the suggestion that a visual experience would qualify merely by its own structural arrangement of color and shape and the like, as resembling some physical object. Whether or not it is fair to Locke to attribute to him the view that seeing a physical object is a matter of seeing a 'sense datum' that resembles the object, in some absolute sense of resemblance, it is certainly an absurd doctrine.

I cannot offer as an alternative the idea that my idea of Algol is nothing more than certain thoughts, as opposed to images. I do not aim at anything like 'a complete theory of apprehension', only at establishing an important truth about one kind of apprehension – that it is always accompanied by the thought that such-and-such condition is uniquely satisfied. 'Accompanied by' rather than 'based on' is worth stressing for the reason pointed out earlier. The condition is not the means of access to the object that satisfies it in every case.

To return to an earlier example, I may assert 'What he has in his hand is a marble' without qualifying as 'apprehending' the marble which satisfies the condition implied in my assertion. Why I wouldn't qualify could be for a variety of reasons. Anyway, my assertion is about that marble, in the sense that the marble is the unique thing satisfying the condition implied in the assertion. (Actually the foregoing would be an even broader notion of 'about', since it leaves out the idea that the condition included a *requirement* of uniqueness and focused on the weaker point that the condition is uniquely satisfied.) To say that my *thought* that what he has in his hand is a marble is about that marble would be grossly misleading because it can be said truly that I was not, in making my assertion, thinking about or of that particular marble. But this is only an ambiguity. My claim is that the weak sort of aboutness based on the thought of a condition which the thing uniquely satisfies must be present in every case of 'apprehension', including those that require much more for 'apprehension'.

Frege does not accept this. His view is that in natural language, when the truth is told, my assertion 'What he has in his hand is a marble' would be without truth value (perhaps no assertion even – that is not important here) if his hand is in fact empty. Thus it would not, on his account, be logically equivalent to 'He has exactly one marble in his hand, and nothing else'. The same would apply with 'That is a marble', where a full-fledged apprehension of a marble is expressed. Frege's doctrine would not allow the recognition that the apprehension expressed in the assertion is based on a condition expressed in the assertion.

It is thus not possible to explain how Frege's 'thoughts' could be thought, at least not in my terms – and there are no others. It is notable that while Frege says that 'something in consciousness must be aimed at the thought' he makes no effort to describe this something. If I am right that apprehending an object requires thinking a condition to be satisfied, then the idea that all thoughts require apprehension, as Frege implies, leads to absurdity (granting that thoughts are objects, and so on). To think a thought would require thinking first some other thought, in an infinitely regressive way.

Frege's weakness on this point is not so very unlike the difficulties of the master himself. Plato worried over the connection between abstract properties and concrete things. The question how the mind 'apprehends' abstract things is just one form of this question, which can also be raised, in simplest form, as the question how a concrete thing ever manages to get related to an abstract thing as its instance.

This confusion about abstract things must be natural, since it is so common, even among thinkers of the greatest acuteness. Socrates confessed that he had not made progress at mathematics because he tended to linger over such questions as how the number one could add to itself to make two. The tendency is to think of abstract things by analogy with concrete things. It is difficult to obtain information about a very remote star. So it seems it must be that much more of a problem getting in touch with thoughts, which aren't even in the universe! There is always the consolation that the mind isn't in the universe either, but this is dissipated by Frege's warnings against psychologism, his emphasis on the fact that thoughts and properties are independent of the mind.

28   This physicalization of the abstract creates a constant pressure against the very recognition of it. Philosophers forget the reasons for holding that a property – say, that of being a rock – exists independently of the mind, independently of language, and independently of its instances. This is the doctrine of universals in its pure form. It is mixed up then with ridiculous pseudo-explanations of how the mind manages to apprehend universals and how universals manage to mingle with their instances.

These absurdities are then triumphantly exposed. It is shown that the human capacity to use language is not explained by the postulation of universals as the 'meanings' of general terms. It is shown that one does not explain how a thing qualifies as a rock by saying it is an instance of the property of being a rock.

The doctrine of universals in its pure form has no concern whatever with explaining how one apprehends properties or thoughts. The doctrine is, rather, simply a consequence of the objectivity of truth. However one recognizes rocks and learns to use the term 'rock', the important fact is that there were rocks before there were people, and there are rocks that have never been so classified by anyone. There is such a thing as being a rock, and it does not depend on people for its existence. To be a rock and to be an instance of the property of being a rock are one and the same thing.

It may be true that it is one and the same to be a rock and to be a thing, such that a properly trained and situated speaker would call it a rock, using some language or other. The fact remains that such properly trained and situated speakers are not needed at all, for being a rock.

Similarly some phenomenalists hold that 'There are unperceived objects' is equivalent to something to the effect that suitably placed perceivers would have had appropriate experiences. Critics tend to focus on denying there is such an equivalence. But even if there is, this does nothing to count against the truth of 'There are unperceived objects'. To the extent that phenomenalism denies this truth, it is false. To the extent that it does not deny it, it is obscure.

Michael Dummett says:

The picture of reality as an amorphous lump, not yet articulated into discrete objects, thus proves to be a correct one, so long as we make the right use of it. It serves to emphasize that, in learning the use both of countable general terms and of proper names, we have to learn the criterion of identity associated with them, where this means primarily learning the sense of statements of identification of the form, 'That is a' – thus of sentences involving demonstratives. Such a picture corrects the naïve conception, found for example in Mill, that the meaning of a general term consists just in its connotation (the principle whereby we determine what objects it is true of), and that of a proper name just in its denotation (i.e. which object it is the name of): for this conception presupposes that the world presents itself to us as already dissected into discrete objects, which we know how to recognize when we encounter them again, in advance of our acquiring any grasp of language at all. (1974, p. 577)

To make the right use of a 'picture of reality as an amorphous lump, not yet articulated into discrete objects', one would need to use it for a picture of a piece of melted fudge, or perhaps as a napkin. I suppose it could do as a picture of reality as well as a Rorschach ink blot might, but not from the same perspective that made it out as a picture of an amorphous lump. To use such a picture as a means of emphasizing points about what we must do in order to learn the use of 'countable general terms and proper names' is of course possible, just as one can use a string tied about a finger to remind one to mail a letter. 'What's that awful picture doing there? Oh yes, that's right, I'm supposed to remember that learning the use of countable general terms involves learning criteria of identity!'

This is, no doubt, a good thing to remember. But it is unfair to suggest that Mill forgot it. He did say that the meaning of a general term is its connotation. But then we have to ask what that meant. Dummett may think that identity criteria for, say, dogs, are part of the meaning of the term 'dog'. I do not pretend to know what that means, but Dummett's words do make such a construction derivable from them. Even if it does mean something, there is no reason to suppose that Mill must have meant the same thing by 'meaning'.

This is not to claim that Mill is clear about his notion of connotation. But I do maintain that there is no basis whatever in his writings for the charge that he did not realize that we could not learn to use a count noun without learning identity criteria.

In his discussion of connotation Mill says, 'The word *white* denotes all white things, as snow, paper, the foam of the sea, etc. and implies, or in the language of the schoolmen, *connotes* the attribute *whiteness*' (1.11.5). This is a good statement, which I take as my guide to the best interpretation of his theory. For any general term, I take the connotation to be the attribute or property for which a name can be constructed from the original term in a trivial way. Mill himself complicates the task of setting out his theory. One complication is his denial that there really are such things as attributes. But I will ignore this.

Dummett ascribes to Mill the doctrine that the connotation of a name is 'the principle whereby we determine which objects it is true of'. If we apply this to the case of the connotation of the word 'white' it would have the consequence that the attribute whiteness is the principle whereby we determine which things the term 'white' is true of. I do not believe that Mill thought that attributes or properties are really principles, but he does seem to regard the existence of borderline cases for the application of a term as an indication of some sort of deficiency in the connotation of the term, as if the connotation were supposed to help settle such cases. This is, to me, quite deplorable (as I mean to illustrate soon by deploring it), but perhaps it provides some basis for Dummett's attribution to Mill of the idea that the connotation of a general term is the principle whereby we determine what objects it is true of. To me, this is a very bad idea, which does not fit at all with the good idea which simply makes the connotation of, say, 'dog' the property of being a dog.

Even if Mill did have that bad idea, that is still no basis for holding that he thought that we can learn to recognize discrete objects 'in advance of our acquiring any grasp of language at all'. The picture of a world dissected into discrete objects is the picture opposed by the 'amorphous lump' picture, and the former is the right picture, the one supported by geology and other sciences of prehistory. The differences between Brontosaurs and Tyrannosaurs obtained without benefit of language. Whether creatures can learn to recognize discrete objects before they have language may not be so obvious. Perhaps my dogs cannot recognize cats or rabbits and are only misleading machines. Whatever the truth of this matter may be, taking the meaning of a word to be as Dummett says Mill took it does not entail a commitment on the question, unless one so uses 'meaning' that a position on the question follows automatically. But then there is no basis for holding that Mill was calling the connotation the meaning in that sense, still less for holding that he took the meaning to be a principle for determining the application of a term.

Nor did Mill hold that the meaning of a proper name is its denotation. He said that proper names do not have meaning. In saying this he misrepresents his theory badly, but attributing to him the opposite of what he said is not the required corrective. When the matter is put to rights for him it will turn out that the connotation of a proper name comes out to be its meaning.

Now it is time to deplore Mill's estimation of the role played by connotation in our determining the application of a term. He says, for example,

> In some cases it is not easy to decide precisely how much a particular word does or does not connote ... it is clear that the word man, besides animal life and rationality, connotes also a

certain external form, but it would be impossible to say precisely what form . . . In all such cases, the meaning of the general
name is so far unsettled and vague.   (1.11.5)

I would say, on the contrary, that we know exactly what the word
'man' connotes – it connotes the property of being a man. Being
able to tell whether something is a man in at least some kinds of
cases is no doubt a requirement for qualifying as grasping the
property of being a man. But the possibility of borderline cases does
not signal any gap in the connotation of 'man'. I do not object to
Mill's saying that the connotation or meaning of 'man' is *vague*.
But this is not an 'uncertainty in the connotation' of 'man', it is
rather a matter of possible uncertainty in us, as to whether something is a man.

It is common for philosophers to warn that not every general term
is such that there are necessary and sufficient conditions for its
application. There is a reasonable idea behind this warning, but this
style of presenting it is a rich source of confusion. There are, logically, necessary and sufficient conditions for the application of each
general term. One logically necessary and sufficient condition for
being a man is being a man. This is, of course, a trivial condition.
But triviality is not a logical matter. It is easy to move away from
obvious triviality, as with the move from 'brother' to 'male sibling',
but my purpose is not to argue that even non-trivial or not obviously
trivial necessary conditions can be produced for every general term.
It is rather to show that such facts as that necessary and sufficient
conditions in the logical sense may not be any help in resolving
borderline cases should not be run together with such logical
mistakes as that some general terms have no necessary and sufficient
conditions.

There may be a distinction between natural kinds and unnatural
kinds, but they are all kinds. Things that are horses or algorithms
are a kind just as much as any more natural kind. Perhaps the kinds
we choose to give non-compound names are important to some
enquiry, and the distinction between simple and compound is even
important in logic. But properties are properties, natural or not.

From the standpoint of logic, we need to know in a systematic
way what is asserted, what is claimed, what is thought. How a person acquires the capacity to assert, to think, is another matter.
Ontology will, in a way, involve both these questions, but differ-

ently. Anyway, it is a mistake to run them together. To know the connotation and the denotation of a term is not to know how a language user manages to learn the connotation and the denotation. Those terms are not introduced in order to facilitate the performance of that task of explanation.

29 I am not here arguing for the truth of the pure doctrine of universals, that properties exist apart from their instances and apart from the mind. I do regard it as merely the expression of the plainest common sense, also supported by science. The doctrine, in the case of the property of being a rock, is merely a way of expressing the fact that there were rocks before there were people, and that even if there were no rocks, it would be possible that there should be.

Unfortunately, this doctrine has gotten mixed with such notions as that the apprehension of a property requires an 'inner eye', and the like. Then there is the argument that the soul is immortal because it apprehends eternal things. One might as well argue that a fried egg is immortal since it is an instance of an eternal thing – the property of being a fried egg. There is no need to turn against properties to deal with such arguments.

The idea that things can have properties perfectly well without there being any people around to help them is a good basis for the pure doctrine of universals. However, it has been popular for platonistically inclined philosophers, especially around the turn of the century, to rather overwork the idea. They would say that properties clearly have instances without people around, but then they would say that surely this is not possible unless there is a God to oversee the transaction! This was especially popular with the application of the doctrine to the objectivity of morality. It would be held that what is right would be right regardless of people, and then it would be said that it is not possible for there to be rightness where personality does not exist! And this was presented as an argument for the existence of a personal God. In these arguments, the mind-independence of properties is first held to be indisputable and then held to be impossible.

Rationalistic metaphysics, of which platonism is a prime example, has a profoundly religious aspect. And its critics very commonly mistake objections to this religious aspect for objections to ontological doctrines, such as the pure doctrine of universals, or the substantiality of the soul, which are not based on religious considerations.

In his autobiography Russell says that his rejection of the platonistic conception of mathematics was a deep disappointment to him. It is as if he were reporting the loss of a religious belief. The eternal numbers and properties, 'above' language and mind and the concrete instances, are spoken of as of a god no longer believed in.

Quine, in his essay 'Identity, Ostension, and Hypostasis', says, 'It would be agreeable to be driven, by these or other considerations, to belief in a changeless and therefore immortal soul as the vehicle of my persisting self-identity' (1953, p. 65). Thus is the rationalistic doctrine that 'I' in 'I am a teacher' denotes a thing, substance or entity, which is not the same as a physical body, taken to be inseparable from the doctrine that this thing is immortal. Kant's largely incomprehensible attack (1972, 'The Paralogisms of Pure Reason') on the rationalistic doctrine that the soul or self is a substance has what value it has as an attack on the idea that this doctrine is a good basis for belief in personal immortality. But, like Quine, Kant does not separate the religious aspect of the doctrine of the soul from the ontological aspect. That there is such a thing as me, and that I am not my body, are at least highly plausible. That I am immortal is not so obvious. But surely these claims aren't one and the same.

I do not mean to suggest that the religious aspect of the eternal should be rejected out of hand. One reason some people despise atheism is not that it is a fearsome doctrine, depriving them of a needed illusion, but because they think it a doctrine which renders a man incapable of reverence. If it were, then atheism would truly be a misfortune. A capacity for reverence is essential to nobility of character, and a contemplation of the truths of ontology can be a source of awe and reverence. But a religion based solely on the objectivity of truth will be at best a very austere one. The bland optimism of popular religiosity, which will soon be giving us such books as 'How to Have a Better Sex Life after Death', can find no basis here.

The dispute between realists and nominalists is certainly not simply a conflict between a religious attitude and an anti-religious one. In fact it was conducted most extensively among medieval logicians, who, on both sides, used 'God exists' as an example of a tautology. But in those days it took very little to keep an argument going. At any rate, I do think the historical controversy has been magnified by the tendency for both sides to run together the religious with the purely ontological aspect of realism.

30 One reason why philosophers have been interested in the topic (or subject) of subject-predicate form is that some of them think that lots of philosophical confusion arises from the tendency to follow the cues of grammar and assume, every time one meets a grammatical substantive, that it must stand for something.

There is something plainly true about this, namely that it would be a bad mistake to think that every substantive stands for something. But the idea that lots of serious philosophical confusion has arisen from this error is not so plausible. Following the cues of ordinary language about substantives need not involve anything so crude as this.

In this connection it is crucial to distinguish between Meinongianism and platonism. Meinongianism is close to the crude doctrine that every grammatical substantive denotes. Meinong did not apply this doctrine to such grammatical substantives as 'everything' or 'nothing', and I think he also refrained from applying it in the case of abstract singular terms. But I am no scholar. 'Nothing' could be said not to be a true substantive but rather a running together of the quantifier 'no' and the substantive 'thing'. With such roughly drawn exceptions as this, I will assume that Meinongianism is the doctrine that all substantives denote, and ignore the scholarly question whether Meinong might not have thought that, say, 'The average Englishman is a beer drinker' does not fall under this doctrine. (I do think Meinong would not have thought it did, but that is a scholarly question I am not qualified to answer.)

At any rate, Meinongianism, even as much of it as Meinong clearly did hold, is an absurd doctrine, which will be criticized more extensively later. It is grossly unjust to Plato that platonism is commonly treated as similar to this absurd doctrine. For example, in his famous essay 'On What There Is' (1953, pp. 1–19), Quine has the intellectually repellent character, 'McX', represent both the Meinongian view that 'Pegasus' must stand for something and the platonic view that there are universals such as redness. This would be fair if both these doctrines simply resulted from the tendency to assume, upon encountering a substantive in a statement, that it stands for something. But in fact the ordinary language cues behind these two doctrines are not the same.

This is to grant that there are ordinary language cues such that relaxing and following their lead will lead to Meinongianism. And I do hold that such cues should not be rejected without strong reasons. There are such reasons in the case of Meinongianism. Following the cues leads to an incoherent doctrine. There are no such reasons in the case of platonism, which offends only against such things as 'tastes for desert landscapes' and the like.

It is more than enough, for platonism, to assume that when a substantive occurs in a true atomic statement that term denotes something. This is a cue of ordinary language which does not, in my opinion, need resisting. It is obviously not enough for Meinongianism. A Meinongian holds that when someone says that the King of France in 1905 is wise, he is talking about something. If he weren't talking about anything, he wouldn't have said anything, which he clearly did. Whether saying the King of France in 1905 was wise is true or not will depend, according to this view, on whether the subsistent entity referred to is wise. How this ridiculous doctrine settles the question whether the entity in question is wise is no matter. The main point is that the Meinongian must reject the idea that it is precisely because 'the King of France in 1905' does not denote anything that the statement is not true. But this is an idea that Plato would have accepted.

The Meinongian idea that whenever one is talking sense, one is talking about something, and the correlative idea that every substantive denotes, must be rejected, for reasons that will be given later. But the doctrine that every substantive in a true atomic statement denotes is a respectable support for platonism that involves no absurdities. It does call for explanation, particularly of the terms 'substantive', 'atomic', and 'denotes'. It is perfectly natural to think that 'Pegasus is a flying horse' or 'The solution to the general quintic was once widely expected' are true atomic statements, and this would not fit well with the present view. This must be taken up later.

My view leads to what Quine would call a very 'lush' ontology. Personally, I find the application of such terms to ontology thoroughly misleading, as if someone who liked a 'spartan' or 'austere' ontology might be expected to be physically lean and rugged. It is easy to see how someone inclined to associations of this sort might be nervous about 'ontological proliferation'. But I do not object to the idea that there exist minds, mental states, properties, numbers, facial expressions, rates, prices, appearances, sakes, and so on. The perils of such an admission are grossly over-rated. Ryle says it is a muddle to say that there exist minds and there exist bodies 'in the same logical tone of voice' (1962, p. 23). He also says 'exist' has a different sense in the two statements 'somewhat as "rising" has different senses in "the tide is rising", "hopes are rising" and "the average age of death is rising"'. Since I do not know what it means to say that the word 'rising' has different senses in these cases, I cannot find anything to object to in saying that 'exists' has different 'senses', perhaps dozens. As for the tone of voice, my views do not depend on how they are read aloud.

On the other hand I reject such things as Pegasus, the solution to the general quintic, and the average Englishman, though I do not reject the somewhat misleading style of speech which makes it sound as if there are such things to be rejecting. But it does call for the sort of reconstrual which is so often and needlessly and inaccurately undertaken with respect to properties. These rejections also call for later discussion. Even 'There is no such thing as the average Englishman' might be taken to mean, in everyday speech, merely that Englishmen are too multifarious a lot for there to be any good generalizations about them. These rejections can be a very untidy matter, a source of frustration and disappointment for those who aspire to formal criteria for 'ontological commitment'.

Entities cannot be eliminated in ontology, and they should not be ignored. When a substantive term does not denote, that is interesting to know. The ways of finding this out differ for different kinds of substantives, but these are all the protection that should ever be invoked against the danger of being misled by substantives.

31 It is impossible to place restrictions on what can be said in a natural language. A nominalist understands as well as anyone such a remark as 'This is an instance of the property of being a rock'. He can't prevent this from being a way of saying this is a rock which brings out an ontological feature.

It is sometimes suggested that very foreign languages may be so different from English that our ontological classifications could not be translated into their language or theirs into ours (if we can even speak meaningfully of their having 'ontological classifications').

Of course, examples are unlikely to be convincing, because they will of necessity end up expressing in English things that, the idea was, should be inexpressible. The unsatisfactoriness of some examples can be interesting.

For example, I've read that Basque and classical Tibetan are 'ergative' languages lacking our subject-predicate style. Where we would say 'Buddha has taught the doctrine', they would have a construction corresponding more closely to 'There has been teaching with respect to the doctrine by Buddha'. Somewhere else it is reported that the Nootka Indians have a language in which their way of saying 'A stone is falling' would be more literally put in English as something like 'It is stoning down hereabouts'. We could say that this is a language in which the 'feature-placing' style of 'It is raining' is used on a grand scale.

Now 'It is stoning down hereabouts' is not good English grammar, but it could be understood perfectly well by an intelligent person without his having to merely learn it as an abbreviation for the regular way of speaking. I believe something similar would be possible in Basque or Tibetan as well as Nootka. An illusion to the contrary might be generated, especially with Nootka, by the mere lack of speakers of that language with sufficient talent in the subject of metaphysics. Any language on the face of the earth is up to talking about the creatures of the earth and their properties. In some there may be no recognized device for making explicit, direct reference to properties. But that will be because the speakers have neglected metaphysics. When the time for that comes, they can break the 'rules' and be understood. When the thought is there, the means of expression will be also.

There was a time when speakers of Greek were not ready to attend to properties as things. But when more intellectual progress was made, helpful substantives were added for referring directly to properties themselves. Nominalists might bemoan this development, but there is no stopping progress.

In 'Logic and the Reification of Universals' Quine says:

Relative to a really alien language L it may happen, despite the most sympathetic effort, that we cannot make even the roughest and remotest sense of ontological commitment. There may well be no objective way of so correlating L with our familiar type of language as to determine in L any firm analogue of quantification, or 'there is'. Such a correlation might be out of the question even for a man who has a native fluency in both languages and can interpret back and forth in paragraph units at a business level. In this event, to seek the ontological commitments of L is simply to project a provincial trait of the conceptual scheme of our culture circle beyond its range of significance. Entity, objectuality, is foreign to the L-speaker's conceptual scheme.   (1953, p. 107)

There are plenty of English speakers who might naturally be described as having no notion of entity or objectuality. At least, if asked about entity, objectuality, or thinghood, they would be utterly uncomprehending. Quine claims that we can do business all right with the L-ians, it's just ontology that's out of the question. This makes the L-ians sound just like the average American. Presumably, the L-ians could be good workers. At the harbor, our translator would have no trouble explaining to them that there is a load of bananas on the dock, which they are to muscle on board the ship. But the English order expresses an ontological commitment to bananas, while the translation does not.

I was once inclined to deny that when a dock worker comes home with a friend after a hard day's work and says 'There's a beer in the refrigerator', he is expressing an ontological commitment. Similarly I was inclined to deny that those who say there is a monster in Loch Ness or an Abominable Snowman are engaged in ontology. It is claims about universals, sense data, minds, processes, events, and such like that go on in ontology, not arguments over whether there is any lunch meat left.

Now I give up, and agree with Quine that these are all ontological claims, and I applaud his wisdom in setting the standards for being in an ontological discussion so very low. But then how can it be that an American dock worker's statement that there are bananas on the dock expresses an ontological claim, while its perfectly adequate translation into L does not? After all, it isn't how the dock worker understands his claim that matters. It's how we ontologists understand it.

Quine has observed elsewhere that in empirically studying the speech of other people in order to correlate features of their utterances with features of the physical situations that appear to provide occasion for them, there will always be more than one logically consistent correlation. Thus it might be logically possible that the

L-ian term 'bananavagai' is being applied to undetached banana peels and not to bananas.

This does not seem to me a very good example. But the same point could be made with the possibility that the L-ians really apply 'bananavagai' to a thing only if it is such that it is a banana, and the sun has been visible at some time during the past twenty-four hours. We would be unable to spot this divergence by empirical tests in the land of L, where it is always sunny. And who would dream that the L-ians worked like this? They might not notice the difference themselves, even if they became bilingual. Their response would be completely a matter of unarticulated habit. But when we took some L-ians along on an Arctic cruise, they would start reporting, after the first day in the polar darkness, that we were out of bananavagai, even though we had plenty of bananas left.

If this is a genuine logical possibility (and the failure of the particular example would not refute the possibility) it is like Descartes' logical possibility that despite all the appearances of mentality in others, I alone am the only person with consciousness, the rest being like robots. Quinean philosophers appear ready to consider this a scientific hypothesis, to be weighed against 'the other minds' hypothesis, just as they sometimes speak of 'ordinary physical object theory' as if it were merely a rather elementary, pre-scientific hypothesis (about, I suppose, the causes of our experience?)

The logical possibility of 'translational indeterminacy' is no more an obstacle to our knowing the exactness of translation than the logical possibility of Descartes' evil genius is an obstacle to our knowledge about physical objects. But even when the possibility is granted it does not provide an example of people who lack the concept of objectuality. What it means to call an interest of our culture 'provincial' I do not know – perhaps Quine has some vision of the ultimate 'Big City' – but at any rate, when anyone develops an interest in ontology, language will not stop him.

While I cannot imagine people who are not up to talking about bananas (I mean regular unhandicapped people, of course), it is all too easy to give examples of people who can't handle talk about properties. And nominalists, though able to do so, pretend not to understand it. But this is a limitation of the people, not something in the nature of their language.

Of course one could insist that whenever the speakers of a language develop new forms of speech, it is no longer the same language.

With formal languages this insistence is correct. That is why a formal language may have definite limits on what it can express. But a natural language can naturally be extended to express anything that can be expressed in language without losing its identity.

32   Quine speaks of 'one important aspect of philosophical analysis – the creative aspect, which is involved in the progressive refinement of scientific language'. He continues:

> In this aspect of philosophical analysis any revision of notational forms and usages which will simplify theory, any which will facilitate computations, any which will eliminate a philosophical perplexity, is freely adopted as long as all statements of science can be translated into the revised idiom without loss of content germane to the scientific enterprise. Ordinary language remains indeed fundamental, not only genetically but also as a medium for the ultimate clarification, by however elaborate paraphrase, of such more artificial usages. But it is not with ordinary language, it is rather with one or another present or proposed refinement of scientific language, that we are concerned when we expound the laws of logical inference or such analyses as Frege's of the integer, Dedekind's of the real number, Weierstrass's of the limit, or Russell's of the singular description.   (1953, p. 106)

This is a very tendentious description of philosophical analysis. The theories of Frege, Dedekind and Weierstrass did not even require the development of a formal language, though Frege did happen to develop one in connection with his theory. Russell's theory of singular descriptions is an altogether different matter. Russell presents a formal language in which formulae containing singular descriptions are merely abbreviations for formulae that do not. The status of the abbreviating formulae as abbreviations is made clear by the rules of the formal language. But Russell also held that this formal language showed what any possible language would really be like, though its grammar might not be as reliable a guide to the real form – that is, to the real substantives – as the grammar of Russell's formal language. It is not true that 'it is not with ordinary language' that Russell was concerned. He was concerned with *all* language.

Ruling out certain forms of speech is never the 'creative aspect' of 'refinement of language'. It may be creative to show how much can be expressed under the restrictive conditions. But the possibility of having restrictions in a formal language can at best support the claim that it is only an illusion that natural languages go beyond the restrictions, by showing that everything that can be expressed without the restrictions can be adequately expressed with them. It cannot justify rejecting what is untranslatable. Some philosophers favored making rules for a language in which things like 'The Nothing nothings itself' would be mechanically branded as 'not well-formed'. But this has not the slightest tendency to show that Heidegger's effort to express a thought was a failure. When someone uses the tools of language in a strange way, he may or may not succeed in expressing a thought. That a system exists for which such a use is not counted as well-formed is always irrelevant.

To say that a thing is an instance of the property of being a rock is to express exactly the same thought as saying that it is a rock. The former way of speaking only brings out more explicitly an onto-logical feature. But no new problem of explanation is introduced. To explain how that manages to be an instance of the timeless, mind-independent property of being a rock is no more difficult than explaining how it manages to be a rock. Not that this is easy to explain. It may be neither easy nor difficult to explain. In any case it is not a problem for the doctrine of universals, whether or not it is a problem at all.

Similarly, explaining how someone apprehends an eternal, mind-independent thought, say, that all men are mortal, comes to nothing more than explaining how someone manages to think that all men are mortal. And noting that such an explanation will not benefit at all from explicit mention of the thought as an entity only shows that the explanation is a matter of psychology and not ontology.

In order to think that all men are mortal, one may have to have a variety of other thoughts. It is impossible that someone should have just one thought! But even if the 'apprehension' of some thought involves other thoughts in a non-trivial way, we are obviously not going to give any general account of the apprehension of a thought in terms of *thinking*, as Frege implies we might have to do; because thinking is thinking thoughts, so that an account of apprehending a thought in terms of thinking will be either regressive or circular. The psychological or neuro-physiological explanation would not presuppose thinking.

33 As I have described the pure doctrine of universals, it is a doctrine about properties, that they exist independently of the mind and of their instances. This doctrine is just one of many that have been called 'platonism' or 'platonistic'. The term 'platonism' is used by contemporary philosophers in a very loose way, which in itself, of course, is not objectionable. Far be it from me to condemn a casual use of terms! But there is also a deplorable tendency to proceed as if all the various doctrines rounded up under the name 'platonistic' are as bad as the worst of the doctrines so called.

Paul Bernays (1967) says, 'The tendency of which we are speaking consists of viewing the objects as cut off from all links with the reflecting subject. Since this tendency asserted itself especially in the philosophy of Plato, allow me to call it "platonism"' (p. 275). Later on he says 'Several mathematicians and philosophers interpret the methods of platonism in the sense of conceptual realism, postulating the existence of a world of ideal objects containing all the objects and relations of mathematics. It is this absolute platonism which has been shown untenable by the antinomies, particularly by those surrounding the Russell-Zermelo paradox' (p. 277).

Now how could it be inconsistent to postulate the existence of all the objects and relations of mathematics? Perhaps Bernays only means all the *alleged* objects and relations, or some such. But even so, what does the additional feature of supposing these objects and relations to be contained in 'a world of ideal objects' contribute to the inconsistencies? To say these objects are 'cut off from all links with the reflecting subject' is certainly not in the spirit of the philosophy of Plato. To say that mathematical objects are independent of the reflecting subject in that they exist whether or not there are people is platonistic. But if being thought about is a link to a reflective subject, then Plato certainly did not regard mathematical objects as cut off from all links. Anyway, there is no basis for Bernay's implication that the platonistic attitude towards mathematical objects as having an objective existence independent of the mind contributes to the derivation of Russell's paradox.

Some philosophers write as if platonism is just a general eagerness to make existence assumptions. In 'Logic and the Reification of Universals' Quine says, 'The platonist can stomach anything short of contradiction; and when contradiction does appear, he is content to remove it with an *ad hoc* restriction' (1953, p. 127). If that is platonism, it doesn't take anything as subtle as Russell's paradox to make it look bad. Suppose the 'platonist' postulates the existence of a set containing the Washington Monument which is larger than every other set, and also postulates the existence of a set not containing the Washington Monument which is larger than every other set. This 'platonist' is obviously in trouble about consistency. Why would he make such idiotic assumptions? Well, he just can't help himself. Existence assumptions are almost impossible for him to resist. There is the contradiction, which means something will have to be done – maybe if he leaves out the Washington Monument . . . And then from the sad tale of this poor fellow we are to draw the moral that existence assumptions should be avoided wherever possible!

It is fair to say that a platonist, in accepting the existence of properties, is granting the existence of things that could be called 'universals' or 'abstract entities'. But one must be wary of thinking that just any assumption of the existence of abstract entities will be platonism, unless this term is really meant only to apply to a certain kind of admission, which can be made in a great variety of ways, rather than to a view. Or if the view is just that 'There are universals or abstract entities', this is all right, but it must be remembered that, so characterized, platonism is not a doctrine that could be refuted by showing the falsity of one or another specific claim about universals.

My own 'platonism' is the pure doctrine of universals (that is, properties), combined with the assumption of the unrestricted applicability of the laws of classical logic in all their various formulations, semantic and otherwise, and with the added assumption that there are propositions, which also exist independently of the mind and of language.

34   The proposition is certainly separable from the pure doctrine of universals. Ontological reductionism does not begin with the blanket rejection of universals. Some might hope to analyze away the notion of propositions in terms of the notion of properties. The reasons for supposing there are propositions are not the same as for properties. Here are some of the reasons that have traditionally been given for holding there are propositions.

Reason 1. The argument 'John is a bachelor; therefore, John is unmarried' is logically valid (or an instance of it with a reference for 'John' is). This is partly explained by saying it is logically impossible for the premise to be true and the conclusion false. But for any pair of sentences, it is logically possible for one to be true and the other false (since their meanings may change). So this partial account of validity must relate, not to the sentences which are the premise and the conclusion, but to the propositions they express. Of course the form of the sentences which are premise and conclusion may be the basis for a judgement of validity. But the necessary connection between premise and conclusion really holds between the propositions they express and not the premise and conclusion taken as sentences.

Reason 2. Different people may say or believe the same thing, and that thing which both say or believe is not a sentence. A German schoolboy knows that the square of the hypotenuse of a right triangle is equal to the sum of the squares of the adjacent sides. And this which he knows is the same thing that an American schoolboy knows. And it cannot be a sentence.

Reason 3. Before there were any languages or sentences or words or letters it was true that two plus two equals four. Since this truth existed before there were sentences, it could not be a sentence. That two plus two equals four is a proposition, and all the linguistic changes in history will not affect it.

To these reasons, nominalists will reply that they are ready to give up talking about necessity, or saying such things as 'John believes something Bill doesn't believe'. Or they will give preposterous 'analyses' of such ways of speaking. Why do they so trouble themselves? Here is where we must turn to the idea that there are pressing reasons for avoiding talk of propositions, which override the reasons in their favor.

One common criticism of propositions turns on setting forth a confused reason for introducing them, exposing the confusion, and assuming there are no good reasons. Specifically, it is suggested that propositions are introduced to *explain* what it is for two persons to believe the same thing, or to *explain* what it is to understand a sentence. It is suggested that the proposition theorist *explains* understanding a sentence as 'grasping the proposition it expresses', and then it is pointed out that this is a ridiculous explanation, and that, in reality, we account for someone's understanding a sentence in terms of his being able to use it correctly, to answer questions about it, and such like. And of course this is true. To say that propositions existed before language is not to say that our understanding of propositions is not entirely dependent on language. Anyone who undertakes to explain what it is to grasp a proposition or a concept or property is bound to be struck by the fact that ontological assumptions about the existence of these entities will not be helpful in his task. But these assumptions are not based on their being useful in this way. To see whether someone grasps the proposition that all men are mortal, one operates with sentences. It is being impressed by the fact that it can be sentences of different languages that is a consideration in favor of propositions.

We say that two people believe or assert the same proposition though they speak different languages. But the explanatory value of this remark does not depend on ontology. We may explain that these people behaved in such-and-such a way because they both believe that *p*. The ontological significance of this remark is irrelevant to the explanation. If one expects the ontological doctrine to contribute to the explanation, it is no wonder the doctrine may come to seem absurd!

Some philosophers say that the claim 'There are propositions' is a mere form of speech (or 'language game' or some such). But everything we say is some form of speech. If we ask for an explanation of what makes 'There are tables' more than a mere form of speech and 'There are propositions' only a mere form of speech, the best we are likely to get is an account of the difference between tables and propositions, plus the gratuitous assumption that things of the latter sort aren't real.

35   Perhaps the principal complaint about properties or propositions is that they do not have satisfactory criteria of individuation, or identity. This is an obscure but very influential view. A problem of individuation arises, for example, when we ask whether the heavenly body known as 'Hesperus' is the same one as the one known as 'Phosphorus'. In natural language such a question can be awkwardly put as the question whether 'these two things' are identical. (Such an example should serve on the side as a lesson against making too much ontologically out of a distinction between singular and plural forms of speech.) At any rate, a criterion of identity or individuation would presumably help with such a question as this one about Hesperus and Phosphorus.

Besides such questions of identity, there are questions of individuation raised in counting instances of general terms or properties. For example, the question may be raised, how many tadpoles there are in a certain aquarium. Counting may be hampered by the presence of individuals that are not easily classifiable between tadpole or not. Here again, it would seem that identity criteria would be helpful.

Or rather, I should say 'should be helpful', for I am not prepared to give examples of their *being* helpful, any more than the proponents of the need for identity criteria do. My being unprepared is a matter of not knowing what criteria of identity are, in the sense in which not having them for certain alleged things or kinds of things is a reason for saying there really are no such things or kinds of things.

Consider the question whether Hesperus is Phosphorus. Someone tackling this question might really wonder how he could possibly hope to settle it. He might be helped by being told to calculate orbits and times and see if 'both' planets had the same orbit and schedule. You might say that satisfying the condition of having the same orbit and schedule was a criterion of identity for non-terrestrial planets in our solar system. But then suppose, as is logically possible, that while earthly physics is the same, bodies at a great distance from the earth are managed by an evil genius, and don't have orbits. Suppose that we named a planet seen one evening 'Hesperus' and one seen the next morning 'Phosphorus'. We would be in no position to answer the question whether Hesperus is Phosphorus, and we shouldn't assert they are the same or that they are not. But should it follow from this that there are no such things? Lest this example seem too far fetched, I wager that in the business of particle physics, the policy that if we are in principle unable to answer whether two identifiable things are identical, we must conclude there are no such things, would lead to denying the existence of things usually accepted in that subject.

Again, should we conclude, from our inability to decide whether there are more than five tadpoles in a certain aquarium, that there are no such things as tadpoles? If such steps as these were the consequence of the slogan 'No entity without identity', then it would be clear – clearly false. However, advocates of this slogan no doubt mean something else, in which case we are back to a matter of obscurity.

Quine holds that it is hard to avoid postulating the existence of abstract entities (and he explains what he means by saying this). But he prefers to meet this need by postulating the existence of classes, rather than properties or attributes. His reason is the one under discussion, that properties do not have good identity criteria, while classes do. My principal reply is that on a clear account of identity criteria, neither classes nor properties, nor any other kind of thing, is such that situations cannot arise in which such criteria as we have for things of that type will be insufficient to allow us to determine whether we are dealing with two things of that type or one.

In his essay 'On the Individuation of Attributes,' Quine (1975) argues that there is a significant difference between the kind of difficulties that arise for individuating attributes and the apparently similar cases involving physical objects. He grants that we may be unable to know whether the physical object that satisfies condition *C* is or is not identical with the physical object that satisfies condition *D*, just as we may be unable to know whether property *P* is or is not identical with property *Q*. However, Quine says of physical objects, 'Nevertheless they *all* have their impeccable principle of individuation; physical objects are identical if and only if coextensive' (p. 3).

If such slogans as that are all that is needed, then we can reply that 'Properties are identical if and only if cointensive'. Quine says, 'Where coextensiveness is not quite fully *verifiable*, neither is identity, but the identity is still well *defined*' (p. 3). Well, so is identity for properties. They have their own equally neat formula.

Moore (1944) wondered whether the proposition that the sun is larger than the moon is the same proposition as the proposition that the moon is smaller than the sun, and said that in one sense they are identical and in one sense not. I think it is wrong to ask such a question without references to a subject. For people who fully grasp the fact that being larger is just the converse of being smaller, the sentences express the same proposition. Someone with less grasp may not get the same proposition from both sentences. But the predicate 'expresses to Jones the proposition that the sun is larger than the moon' is vague, because for some values of 'Jones' we may be unable to tell whether, say, 'The moon is smaller than the sun' satisfies this predicate. In this the predicate is no worse off than 'mountain', 'tadpole', 'city' or a host of other predicates no one wishes to give up using.

36 As I argued (or claimed) in my paper 'The Sorites Paradox' (1969), vagueness is not a logical matter, but an epistemological one.

The laws of classical logic guarantee that vagueness is not in things themselves. For every thing and every predicate, the thing either has the predicate or not, and not both. But when it comes to our knowing which is the case, it is another matter. The laws of classical logic guarantee that if a thing ceases to be a tadpole, then there is a last second when it is a tadpole, such that the very next second, it is not. That the laws of classical logic have this consequence is a mildly surprising result which deserves its ancient title of the 'Sorites paradox'.

Some philosophers will go to considerable trouble to reject this result. In my paper I pointed out that rejecting the classical law of excluded middle as the Intuitionists do is not sufficient to avoid essentially the same paradoxical conclusion. This is not much of a point, even though it is true, for some philosophers will go to any lengths, even the necessary ones, to avoid the conclusion. Their results speak for themselves. However, there is a common way in which they are misleading. They may develop a way of formulating the Sorites argument so that the conclusion does not follow, and on that basis claim to avoid it, when in fact essentially the same argument can be expressed in other terms in their systems, so that conclusion does follow. This is true, for example, of Bas van Fraassen's ingenious semantics of 'supervaluations'. His logic makes it possible to say, for example, that 'That is a tadpole' is neither true nor false. And yet 'Either that is a tadpole or that is not a tadpole' is still derivable! In these latter, 'non-semantic' terms, the 'paradoxical' reasoning is still possible. I do not presume to criticize this system of logic – only to stress that it provides no reason for rejecting my view that vagueness is only a matter of human knowledge and its limitations.

This insistence on definiteness in reality, as opposed to the indefiniteness of our knowledge, is a perennial source of dissatisfaction with platonism. Bergson (1944) charged that it was a doctrine that does not square with the facts of human experience. But reasoning is a thoroughly human experience. That there is a first millionth of a second when a certain creature ceases to be a tadpole sounds absurd only because, in everyday practice, when someone says there is something of a certain kind we tend to expect that he might at least be able to discover such a thing if he were willing to take the trouble. But these instants of change are obviously not discoverable and it would be silly to try. All that is needed is a reminder that to be is one thing, and to be known another.

It is ironic that platonism is criticized severely both for lack of ontological economy, and for failing to do justice to the plurality of things. Perhaps the thinking is as follows: besides being excess baggage ontologically, the mind-independent property, seen as grasped by many, even by speakers of different languages, gives a false impression of the great variation between people as to what considerations determine their use of a given word.

Suppose, for example, that we go to a strange planet, and find there a species of man-like creatures who appear to speak English just as we do. A difference comes out only when we remark among ourselves on the quantity of rocks strewn about and they, overhearing, break into derisive laughter, popping some of the rocks into their mouths and crunching them up with incredibly strong jaws and hard teeth. They explain that these are various kinds of food, and they cite as rock what we would count as extraordinarily hard rock. Now it might be said that what is rock to us is not to them, and that my view that rocks would still be rocks even if no beings ever had any dealings with them conflicts with this fact about the relativity of rockhood.

This is not true. However, it is true that the property we express by 'rock' is not the same property as they express. And when one person counts something as no longer a tadpole on the basis of some feature which another person regards as irrelevant, we may well wonder if they express the same property 'tadpole'. Then it may seem more efficient to describe this sort of case in terms of a common word and different applications rather than worrying over whether a common property is involved.

This may be right, but even a question that is not worth raising may have an answer. If 'being a tadpole to Jones' is objective, then there were tadpoles-by-Jones' standard before there was Jones and being such a tadpole is quite independent of Jones, even if it is logically equivalent to 'being such that Jones would call it a tadpole if he were following these standards'. On the other hand, if being a tadpole to Jones is just like tasting good to Jones, a mere matter of actual subjective response, then there is nothing to being such a tadpole, no property to enquire after even if one were willing to take the time to do so. There is merely a rather interesting relation between Jones and some things. That relation might be merely a

matter of his calling something by the sound 'tadpole', or it could
be a matter of his treating it like a tadpole, where the property
involved was the quality of his treatment of the thing.

The distinction between subjective and objective is often not well
understood. There is actually no dichotomy between these two
notions, except according to extreme relativist or subjectivist views
that are incoherent anyway. When a property is said to be subjective,
it is really just a relation rather than a property, with a place for a
subject. Thus the subjectivist objection to the doctrine that good-
ness is a property should be put as the claim that there is no being
good *simpliciter*, only being good to this or that person. Then, even
if this complaint were true, someone who asserts 'X is good' could
be making a perfectly objective relational claim, say, to the effect that
he approves of X. Or it might be held that he is not asserting this but
only exhibiting behavior which is a standard sign that he approves.
And there could of course be other doctrines on this topic. The point
here is that being subjective only involves relations with a subject as
one of the terms of the relation. And the relation is objective.

However, there is an important division of subjective properties,
into those that depend on the subject, and those that do not. Being a
tadpole by Jones' standards may involve a merely external relation
to Jones if it is a matter of Jones' being impressed by considerations
that exist independently of him. Then Jones is only needed in our
articulation of the relation because we may be unable to describe
Jones' considerations in a way independent of him.

This is not a matter of Jones having an ability to recognize tadpoles which we cannot explain, in the way that a chicken sexer may
be able to tell the sex of a chicken without explaining how. For there
is no disagreement about the ultimate criteria for chickens' sex (that
is, borderline cases of that sort are not at issue in chicken sexing).
However, there may be an analogy in the notion of being a male-
looking chick, as long as this is recognized as a property that could
be possessed by a female chick. Then we might say a chicken sexer
grasps this property, which he cannot articulate in words, in the
same way that Jones may grasp a property which he associates with
'tadpole' which we can only describe as being a tadpole to Jones.
(When I speak, as I just did, of *Jones* associating a property with
'tadpole', I must immediately stress that this is not the sort of
association I consider in the account of connoting to be given later.
The idea that someone who thinks 'That is a tadpole' is, in that act

of thinking, associating a property with the term 'tadpole', is dangerously misleading, though it can be explained away as a harmless figure of speech.)

Even 'tasting good to Jones' can be independent of Jones, if it refers to a feature which generally or in certain situations affects Jones in a certain way. But when the sole consideration is Jones' actual response, then we should say 'tastes good to Jones as of this occasion of sampling', and we then have a radically subjective property, which is a relation depending on Jones, from which no Jones-independent property can be extracted.

Even a radically subjective property is a perfectly objective relation, and the denial of this does not even make sense. That is, those who deny this, as the Protagoreans did, do not even give a good meaning to 'subjective'. If they say there is no objective being a tadpole, only being regarded as a tadpole by some person, they have to explain what it would be to be regarded as a tadpole by some person. And to keep up their doctrine they should say there is no objective being regarded as a tadpole by some person but only being regarded as a case of being regarded as a tadpole by some person by some person. That is, they ought to get into an infinite regress. But of course Protagoreans are not likely to be constrained by such logical considerations. And incoherent doctrines are very far from all alike. Some are obviously trifling, while others are enormously persuasive and forceful, and for many purposes may actually be preferable to the truth. But not for present purposes.

At any rate, every assertion predicates or attempts to predicate some property or relation which is objective. The pure doctrine of universals is required to justify regarding our assertions as worth making. This ontological doctrine has its basis in the objectivity of truth, not in any evidence to be gained by ignoring the enormous subjective variation in standards for the use of words. A good explanation of grasping a property will analyze away 'grasping a property'. But it will not analyze away properties, because the value of the notion of a property does not lie in any role in the explanation of how we come to know or understand.

It is sometimes said that if we think of properties as independent of the mind and of language, we will be led to a false theory of meaning by thinking that someone can assign a term to a property simply by 'apprehending' or 'grasping' the property and arbitrarily making a word stand for it. Now this is actually something that one can do, as if I were to let the word 'roob' stand for the property of being a rock. But the idea that this is how words in natural language which express properties came to express properties is so false and trifling that it is even rather trifling to spend much time saying so. It is a complete mistake to think that such an absurd theory is a consequence of the altogether independent view, based on quite separate considerations, which is the pure doctrine of universals.

37 Some philosophers might be tempted to reduce the notion of a proposition to that of properties. In my opinion, this is a mistake which naturally contributes to worries about how the parts of a proposition or thought 'hold together'. For if the proposition is just properties, it will be some number of them and there will inevitably be a question about what brings them together. But a proposition, say, that the property of being a man is subsumed under the property of being a mortal, isn't made by bringing these properties together in a certain way. Rather the proposition is to the effect that they go together in a certain way.

The most interesting question of ontological economy is between properties and classes or sets. One of the most misleading things about the use of the term 'platonism' by contemporary philosophers of mathematics is the tendency to associate this term with generous existence postulates for sets or classes. Plato himself had nothing to say about classes in the modern sense (if there is one). Russell, even when he was a platonist, was inclined towards a 'no-class' theory, according to which language using terms for classes is merely something like an abbreviation for language without class terms but only terms for properties instead. When this doctrine of Russell's received its fullest expression, he was no longer a platonist, at least by intention. However, Quine argues that even the no-class theory presented in *Principia Mathematica*, where the intention was to avoid abstract entities altogether, involved using propositional functions as attributes or properties. So Quine holds that Russell's 'no-class' theory was a failure and, as a mere 'reduction of certain universals to others, classes to attributes', is 'pretty idle' (1953, p. 123).

This might be true if Quine were right in his view that classes are preferable to properties if one has to admit abstract entities at all. But the reverse is the case. The notion of a property is much more important than that of a class or set, and much clearer. Modern set theory is no doubt a great intellectual achievement, and I unhesitatingly accept those who understand it well as my intellectual superiors. But it is nonetheless an ad hoc and epicyclic business,[1] and people who take the notion of set or class as their paradigm of a notion or concept will naturally be seduced into very relativistic views.

Quine holds that classes have excellent principles of individuation and are, in general, relatively unproblematic entities. He says classes 'are as satisfactorily individuated as their members'. But for the alleged 'very large' classes, such as the universal class and other candidates difficult to distinguish from it, this does not seem to be true. And Quine never discusses such a question as whether the class of apples existing in 1970 still exists even though most of its members do not.

As a basis for answering questions about sets or classes, such as are raised by paradoxes involving them, I favor a no-class theory. However, it is difficult to develop such a theory for natural language. In a formal language, formulae containing class terms can be introduced as abbreviations for formulae not containing such terms. But in English, even if one can find an equivalent statement without class terms, the equivalence alone by no means justifies talk of abbreviation or calling the class statement a 'mere form of speech'.

For all that, I believe that modern theories of sets should be justified, if at all, by showing how their claims can be expressed without using any references to classes or sets, and it is only in that way that I aim to answer paradoxes involving sets.

One thing is plain: there is no such thing as an empty set or class. In fact, giving a sense to use of such a term as 'the empty class' (which Russell's 'no-class' theory does) is a good paradigm of how legitimate use of a substantive does not imply that it really denotes. It is perfectly (well, nothing is perfect) all right to say that X belongs to the null set as a mere form of speech for saying that X satisfies a contradictory condition. And to say that the null set is a subset of every set is all right as a way of saying that anything that satisfies a contradictory condition satisfies every other condition. But we all know that if there really are classes, they have members.

At least they do if classes are treated extensionally. The class of

---

[1] From this generalization I except various 'constructive' theories of sets. They are a different matter and are taken up in section 94.

men is spoken of in ordinary life as something whose membership varies with births and deaths, and perhaps from that perspective someone might meaningfully worry that a nuclear holocaust would render it an empty class. This is another difficulty for a no-class theory for natural language. Perhaps such a theory should not be expected to eliminate classes that are not individuated by their membership, but only the purely extensional ones.

A no-class theory could reinstate the slogan that every property determines a class, but with a different meaning. Since a class term would merely be a style of speech to be replaced by talk of a property, the class term could not bring any logical trouble not already involved in the property term, so there might be no basis for distinguishing between properties that determine classes and those that do not. Rather, the system of definitions that explained and justified the introduction of class terms would apply equally to all properties.

While it is obvious that there is no null class, it is not at all obvious that there are no classes at all. Our language is full of terms most naturally interpreted as class terms. The whole grammatical classification of plural as opposed to singular is traditionally explained in terms of classes (though this may not be significant in favor of classes, since the explanations are so bad).

I have seen able philosophers ask whether the following rule is true: 'Given any well-determined objects, they can be collected together into a set by an application of the *set of* operation.' But on the usual account of 'they' this rule is a tautology. It might as well have read, 'Given any collection of well-determined objects ...' The collecting comes automatically with the form of reference. But a no-class theory would assign a tautological character to this rule without assigning it any ontological consequences.

Quine suggests that attributes might be identified with what he calls 'ultimate classes' – classes that do not belong to any classes. This is like offering the position of court buffoon to the rightful heir to the throne. Postulating ultimate classes may be truly wonderful mathematics, but it is also a strong indication of something philosophically wrong with a theory that leads to such uninterpretable formal gimmicks.

The 'iterative' notion of set is introduced in modern set theory for the sake of avoiding inconsistency and perhaps because it is intrinsically interesting mathematically. It may constitute a marvelous subject of mathematical enquiry and a great help in the foundations of mathematics. But philosophically it is aptly evaluated by Quine in 'Logic and the Reification of Universals': 'for the conceptualist, classes exist only in so far as they admit of ordered generation. This way of keynoting the conceptualist position is indeed vague and metaphorical, and in seeming to infuse logical laws with temporal process it is puzzling and misleading' (1953, p. 126). However, Quine follows this superbly accurate characterization with, 'For a strict formulation of the position, however, free of metaphor, we can point to the above system itself.' That is unfortunate. For philosophy, it isn't a question of how a formal system manages to avoid inconsistency, but of what the results mean for ontology. It is bad of Quine to hint at the idea that a formal set theory of his displays sets as creations of the human mind when no justification for that claim can be given. The restrictions on intuitive doctrines about sets imposed to avoid contradictions do not have a rationale. This does not prevent their being important in many ways. But if the paradoxes involving properties and propositions can be dealt with on a firm metaphysical basis, this is a good reason for wanting talk of sets to be reduced to talk of properties, even if this is not made into an ontological reduction. For it should point the way to the right treatment of set theoretic paradoxes and to the proper interpretation of the technical devices introduced to avoid them.

38   The idea that all thoughts need thinking to apprehend them has been criticized. We must now consider whether some thoughts *include* thoughts about words. Is it true that, as Lockwood says, the thought that oxen ruminate does not include, as part of that very thought, any thoughts about the word 'ox' or 'ruminate'? It might seem that, on the contrary, an English speaker must have beliefs about certain English words as an essential condition of his thinking that oxen ruminate, so that there would be no language-independent thought that oxen ruminate.

How can it be otherwise? Well, to believe that oxen ruminate requires beliefs about words, but no particular set of beliefs is necessary. An English speaker may have one set of beliefs about words, in believing that oxen ruminate, while a Japanese has a completely different set. On the other hand, someone who believes what an average American believes in believing that Socrates drank hemlock, must have a belief about the word 'Socrates', to the effect that it is linked by a certain historical chain to an individual who drank hemlock. We can of course say truly that a Japanese speaker who knows no English believes that Socrates drank hemlock, or for that matter, we may say that Phaedo believed, because he saw, that Socrates drank hemlock. But these beliefs are only alike in being about the same person and ascribing to him the same predicate. The Japanese belief concerns a slightly different historical chain from that of the English speaker. Phaedo's belief did not concern any historical chain and need not even have concerned the name 'Socrates'. To have the very same belief as the American who only knows of Socrates by name is to have the very same belief about the historical connection of that name to its bearer.

When someone believes that oxen ruminate, he believes that whatever has the property of being an ox has the property of being a ruminant. Similarly, one who believes that Socrates drank hemlock believes that whoever has the property of being Socrates has the property of having drunk hemlock. 'The property of being Socrates' is a phrase which often identifies different properties, with reference to the thoughts of different people. With reference to a typical American, and the thought he expresses in asserting 'Socrates drank hemlock', the phrase identifies the property of being at the end of a certain historical chain involving the name 'Socrates'. With respect to the thinking of Phaedo, the phrase may not identify a property involving the name 'Socrates'.

The case could sometimes be similar with 'the property of being an ox'. There could be someone who knows only that the word 'ox' has a plural form 'oxen' and that the word 'ruminate' combines with this latter to form a true sentence. If such a person is an English speaker, we might describe him as believing that oxen ruminate. He would believe that 'Oxen ruminate' conveys a true statement. It would mean no more to him than 'Poxen buminate', and he might think this latter expression to convey a true statement as well. But it would be confusing to say that 'he believes that poxen buminate'.

Unfortunately, there is no rule against using 'that' – clauses which do not represent a thought accurately. Perhaps this isn't so unfortunate. It may avoid what would otherwise be an impractical over-concern with an unnecessary accuracy. It is still more accurate to say that the man described above believes that 'Poxen buminate' is a true sentence than to say that he believes that poxen buminate.

Suppose I am walking with a friend when one of my dogs comes upon a foul carrion and begins to devour it enthusiastically. My friend exclaims, 'How can he stand to go near that thing?' I reply, 'He thinks that it is delicious.' I have not reported a thought to which my dog subscribes, but have merely indicated in a potentially misleading way that my dog has a pro-attitude towards the carrion, which attitude need not involve any thoughts.

'Potentially misleading' can be a rather prissy way of speaking. Anything can mislead some people. 'He thinks that it is delicious' would be as unlikely to mislead as any form of speech, except that someone who is concerned with *that which is thought* will naturally take 'that'-clauses as his guide, and such an unusual person needs to be warned that such clauses are not always an indication that there is an object of thought.

Some philosophers hold that 'the thought that such-and-such is good' is like 'the thought that it is delicious', for in that case too there is no ascription of a property, but only the reporting of a pro-attitude. And some philosophers would say the same about every candidate for a property. 'The thought that such-and-such is a dog' might be viewed merely as a way of reporting a certain attitude someone has towards a certain thing, including perhaps the disposition to utter the term 'dog' in its presence. This might do for Protagoras, but otherwise one who grants that it is objectively true or false that the thing is a dog cannot take this line. Most will admit that it is not objectively true or false that a thing is delicious. Some will say the same about the question whether a thing is good. But only an unfortunate few will say this about every question.

Someone could be in the position of believing, even knowing, that whatever is denoted by the word 'ox' is denoted by the word 'ruminates', without having the slightest conception of what it is to be an ox or to ruminate. Surely this man's thought could not be shared by someone who knows nothing whatever of the English language? But then such a man does not, in assertively intoning 'Oxen ruminate', assert that oxen ruminate. He might be mistakenly taken to assert this, if his hearers thought he knew what he was saying. But when we know that someone does not understand certain words we do not take him to assert them.

However, there is a great variety of cases between one like this and one in which we feel the speaker understands perfectly what he is saying. And rather than recognizing a variety of assertions to go along with this we naturally tend rather to say at some point simply that *the* assertion that oxen ruminate has been made. Perhaps, for example, someone who knows what an ox is, but doesn't know at all what ruminating is, would be counted. Or perhaps knowing that rumination has something to do with digestion would be required. At any rate, here assertion is a social matter of what we hold a speaker responsible for. We may thus sometimes ignore what the speaker is thinking, since 'we can't read his mind', and say simply that he *said* that all oxen ruminate.

39   This tendency runs strongly contrary to my identification of what is asserted with what is thought. It might be objected that this identification is unrealistic (though in one sense it is all too 'Realistic'). How can an assertion be the verbal expression of a thought if the words are such a poor indication of what is thought that we have to say that 'the thought that Socrates drank hemlock' or 'the thought that oxen ruminate' represent a great variety of different thoughts with respect to different people?

This objection would be natural for those philosophers who deny that the thought is a non-linguistic entity to which a person stands in the relation of believing. They might say that on the contrary, we only attribute a predicate when we say of someone that he believes that oxen ruminate – we do not ascribe to the person a relation to some entity but rather a property for which there is a great variety of criteria. A great variety of verbal and other dispositions and capacities qualify someone as believing that oxen ruminate, and the doctrine of the extra-linguistic entity, the thought, represents a naïve ignorance of this variety due to overconcern with the idea that different people can have the same beliefs.

There is no need, though, for the doctrine that different people, even without a common language, may have exactly the same belief, to lead to an oversimplification of the variety of criteria for saying someone believes, for example, that oxen ruminate. That is granted by recognizing that a variety of thoughts may be connected with these words.

More importantly, the fact that we often, for practical reasons, do not concern ourselves with knowing exactly what thought someone is expressing when he makes an assertion, does not mean that we cannot know this, and see that different thoughts are adequately expressed by the same words. This is obvious with indexical sentences such as 'I am hungry', but it applies more generally as well.

Someone who does not know what ruminating is shouldn't say 'Oxen ruminate'. He should say, 'I've heard that oxen do something called "ruminating", though I don't know what that is.'

What if someone knows that ruminating involves chewing a cud, but doesn't know that the cud is regurgitated grass? Perhaps the poor fellow thinks an ox just keeps a wad of grass tucked in the corner of his mouth like a baseball player with tobacco. The question of what he should have said may be difficult, given the social tendency to drop the question of what he believes and 'look at what he said'. But this doesn't mean there is not a good conception of accurately saying what you think. My view is that expressing what you think is the *ideal* case of assertion, and that this is not an unrealistic ideal, even though there is considerable departure from it in practice. The question 'When you say that oxen ruminate, exactly what do you mean, what do you have in mind?' is not an impossible question, though it may be an impractical one for which people usually do not take time. When Socrates asked such questions, they did have considerable trouble, but that was largely because of the topics, and perhaps also because the concern was over *definitions*. I am not suggesting that it is definition that is needed in order to find out exactly what thought someone is expressing in an assertion.

When I say that my friend Robert is in room four, I do not express the belief that the person who caused certain features of my experience this morning at breakfast is in room four, or that the person who caused certain features of my experience yesterday afternoon is in room four, even though I had breakfast with Robert and saw him yesterday afternoon. I express the belief that the person who has caused a great variety of my experiences on a great number of occasions is in room four. This reference to the occasions, and still more, to the experiences, is extremely vague, in the sense that it is quite unclear exactly how many occasions, even which occasions, count in the great number, and even less clear which experiences count in the great variety. But this does not make the belief vague, or especially difficult for a knowledgeable hearer to gather from my words 'Robert is in room four'. It is logically possible that sometimes what I thought to be Robert was instead a diabolically disguised robot. If a team of robots were all I have ever encountered, my claim that Robert is in room four would be false. But it could be true if two percent of what I took to be encounters with Robert were really the robots. Of course there is in reality an exact cut-off in the percentages of robot substitutes compatible with the truth of my claim, but what it is we will never know, and would be foolish to try to learn.

The foregoing is one of many cases in which an assertion using a proper name need not express a belief about the name, even though of course the person making the assertion will have beliefs about that name. Sometimes the belief expressed essentially involves the name, as with modern American beliefs about Socrates. (When I say 'essentially involves', I do not mean that a related belief also about Socrates, to the effect that he drank hemlock, could not be achieved by a modern American which wouldn't involve the name 'Socrates'. Perhaps intensive historical research, or extra-sensory perception, would lead to a belief that Socrates drank hemlock which did not involve this or any proper names. I mean that the belief the American in fact has, *includes* a belief about the name.) Other times, the belief does not essentially involve the name, even though it will of course be related to distinçt beliefs which are about the name.

With general terms, there is at least this much similarity, that in many cases beliefs expressed using general terms include beliefs about the term. In some cases, as has been observed, the dependence of the belief on the term is so great that the term should have been mentioned, rather than used, in the assertion.

40 Phaedo's belief that Socrates drank hemlock did not require any beliefs about words, at least not about a word for Socrates. This is not to say that Phaedo 'directly apprehended' Socrates, or to say that he did not. Insofar as it was logically possible for Phaedo to have had the same experiences and thoughts without Socrates existing, we might call his apprehension 'indirect'. There is obviously some directness about it too. Anyway, the mediation of words was not required.

When I say the mediation of words was not required, I do not mean it would have been possible for Phaedo to have recognized that Socrates drank hemlock without having any beliefs about words. He could have known that Socrates drank hemlock without knowing any name for Socrates, but he would nonetheless have known some singular term to be applicable to him. And it is obscure to speculate whether he would have been able to know Socrates drank hemlock without knowing a name for him, or, with respect to a given singular term, whether Phaedo might not have known Socrates drank hemlock without knowing that particular singular term to apply. If Phaedo had not known a name for Socrates, he probably would not have been invited to the execution.

So what, then, do I mean? Well, I mean something which it would have been nice to be able to explain in terms of Phaedo's being able to have the same belief about Socrates while not having the belief he did have about the word. And as was just observed, this is obscure.

Phaedo's belief could have been the same belief even if Socrates hadn't existed. (It would have been the same belief, though the belief wouldn't have been the same, since it would have been false.) There are many different stories that would illustrate this possibility. Some would show Phaedo that he had been taken in by an incredibly grand-scale hoax, over a period of years. Such a revelation would no doubt be very upsetting.

On the other hand, suppose that all that happened was that due to a mix-up at the registrary of births, Socrates was legally named 'Wisdom' as a child. Just after his execution, Phaedo and others are told that in all official records it is to be written that Wisdom drank hemlock, taught Plato, argued with Protagoras, was wise, and so on. Phaedo realizes that the fame of his late friend is spreading rapidly, and soon, more people will know him as 'Wisdom' than as 'Socrates'. It will soon be a popular put-down to correct people who speak of 'Socrates' with 'You mean "Wisdom"?'

Faced with this, Phaedo and his friends might give up using the name 'Socrates' and correct themselves when they did so inadvertently. Of course they might not respond this way. The successful overthrow of a name isn't guaranteed by a formula here. But if Phaedo did give up his belief that 'Socrates' named a certain drinker of hemlock, for these reasons, as opposed to the kind of reasons provided by the hoax, then it would not change the content of his thought. That is, Phaedo might, in saying 'Wisdom drank hemlock', express the very same thought as he did with 'Socrates drank hemlock'.

This possibility would be a triviality for the referentialists. Recall Donnellan's claim that 'Henry is bald' and 'George is bald' 'express the same proposition' when the reference of 'George' and 'Henry' is the same (1974, pp. 28–9). For me, being concerned with saying what the proposition is, it is not so simple. I hold that 'Henry is bald' and 'George is bald' *could* express the same proposition in my sense of 'proposition', but only under certain conditions, which are much more restrictive than Donnellan's.

For example, it is far from obvious that if Phaedo said, thirty years after the death of Socrates, that Socrates drank hemlock, he would be expressing exactly the same thought as he would express saying this just after the death of Socrates. (Here when I speak of 'saying this', this is a mere convenience – 'that Socrates drank hemlock' does not always refer to the same thought.) Thirty years later, what he thought could be mistaken in ways his earlier thought could not be.

So it is, for me, no triviality that Phaedo could express the same thought with 'Wisdom was wise' as with 'Socrates was wise'. His thought was that a man caused a certain range of experiences, some remembered, others not, and was wise. The name, as Mill held, is but a marker for these thoughts, and a different marker can be introduced for the same thoughts, in order for Phaedo to bring his associations into line with those that will henceforth be produced in others by the newly accepted name.

Nothing like this can happen to the average American, for whom the name is not merely a marker for beliefs, but an ingredient in them. One who is told 'Jones robbed the bank' and believes only that someone related to the name Jones (in a way I have no intention of trying to specify in any detail, the way they call a 'historical' or 'causal' connection of the right sort) robbed the bank, may indeed switch from this to the belief that Smith robbed the bank if he is told they got the name wrong the first time. But this move from 'Jones' to 'Smith' is different from that which might be made by someone acquainted with Jones who merely decided, for one reason or other, to stop calling him 'Jones' and start calling him 'Smith'. Both the transitions involve beliefs about the names. But in the one, the names are markers of ingredients, in the other, they are ingredients.

41   This is not overpoweringly obvious. But I think it is the best resort against the obnoxious doctrine that most beliefs include beliefs about names. It is much better than yielding to the temptation to resort to an infinite regress argument. Such an argument might be built on the idea that if having belief 1 required having belief 2 about words then having belief 2 would require verbal belief 3 and so on. The trouble with this kind of argument is that any competent

speaker of English knows thousands of words, and if grammatically constructed terms are counted in, the number stretches to millions in a 'recursive' manner which many philosophers count as infinity. Dedekind (1901, part II, chap. 5, § 66) argued that the set of possible objects of his thought was infinite, appealing to the idea that for every s which is a possible object of his thought, there would be a distinct s', the thought that s is a possible object of his thought, and so on, ad infinitum. This resembles the infinite regress argument under discussion except that the thoughts in the regress argument are actual while Dedekind's are called possible, and Dedekind is speaking more generally of objects of thought, rather than of thoughts, which are a highly restricted kind of object of thought. This latter difference is unimportant, since Dedekind's argument obviously applies to thoughts as well as to objects of thought. And the distinction between possible and actual is not important either. If I believe that p, and it is possible for me to believe that I believe that p, that is, if this is a meaningful thought, then I should be credited with having it, whether or not I have actually considered the question, since if I were to consider the question, I would affirm that I believed.

This is not to say that believing entails believing you believe. I have elsewhere described a case of a man who believes something but does not believe he believes it (Cargile 1967). And I do not endorse the idea that iterated 'believes' are always meaningful. But in a normal, unproblematic case of belief, the fact that a man would, if asked, grant that he had the belief, is enough for crediting him with it, assuming there is such a thing to believe.

Of course someone might believe that no one could believe a tenth power iterated belief statement. So he might believe that pork comes from pigs while positively disbelieving that he believes[10] that pork comes from pigs. But such a person is a mere nuisance. We might dismiss him, like a lawyer screening candidates for a jury. And remember, the argument is not for my client anyway.

Let us pick a nice fellow who believes that pork comes from pigs. When he agrees that he believes this, we point out that it is true that he believes this. He agrees. We then get him to admit that he believes that he believes, stressing how easy it was. Soon we have him owning up to believing he believes he believes he etc. Now we can credit the poor fellow with an infinite series of beliefs. He will even have been let in on the mystery of generating this miracle.

This is a very dubious procedure. But it is enough to cast doubt on the argument that the doctrine that every thought includes a thought about words leads to an infinite regress which would make thinking impossible. For it provides a reason to think that there might be an infinite series of beliefs about words behind each belief about words, with no harmful regress. The argument would be like one to the effect that there couldn't be negative integers, since for one to exist, there must be one preceding it, and so on ad infinitum.

Still, the idea that all beliefs include beliefs about words should be rejected, and so my argument against the idea should be adopted, if only on the basis of need. It was oversimplified to make it too easy for people of different linguistic communities to have the same belief, but we do not want it to be impossible.

42   The formula distinguishing between being a mark of an ingredient in a belief and being an ingredient which has been described for names in the restricted (as opposed to Mill's) sense can also be applied to general terms. Some general terms are associated, for me, with properties in such a way that the term is unimportant to me. I know what I mean by 'dog', and I could use another term for the same property.

On the other hand, I know that my lamp is lighted by electricity. But what is electricity to me? Suppose the scientists announce that they have discovered that there are two very different currents, previously undistinguished, one called 'AC', the other 'DC'. The 'DC' current is called 'electric', the other, 'selectric'. It turns out that most current has always been electric, but recent changes in the perihelion of Mercury have caused an increase in selectricity. Why procedures that produced electricity until a year ago should now be producing selectricity due to the change in the perihelion is just one of those scientific matters we uninitiated must take on faith. So there it is. I thought my lamp was lit by electricity, but I was wrong. What I thought was that the power lighting my lamp is the one named 'electricity', when it is the different one recently named 'selectricity'.

This does not mean that a Japanese speaker might not be in a similar position to mine. And this similar position would be some basis for saying we could have the same belief about electricity. But he would probably be taking the word of Japanese scientists, so our sources would be different. He would be counting on no hoax involving Japanese scientists. But such a possibility would not be relevant to my belief.

Things are very different with other properties. Suppose that a panel of scientists come to me with the news that I am a mouse. The X-rays, EEGs, blood cell-counts, and so on, are conclusive. I represent the most freakishly developed mouse yet studied. Such news, coming from a panel of eminent scientists, would not be a matter to take lightly. It is for them to decide what happened with all those tests. Furthermore, their predictions might be of considerable concern to me. Perhaps my wife, too, is a mouse, and our children are just more fortunate freaks. But the strain is bound to breed true in the next generation, so that I might have real cause to worry lest my grandchildren end up living on stale cheese and dodging cats. For all that, there is some limit as to what I will put up with, even from scientists. I am a man, not a mouse! However others may be persuaded to use the words 'man' and 'mouse' I know what I mean by them, and my grasp of it does not depend on those words.

It is possible that a Japanese should have such a grasp of what it is to be an ox and to ruminate that he uses words only as marks for these ideas, which might be the same ideas as an English speaker has. But some speakers of Japanese, or of English, are not this well-off with respect to being an ox and ruminating. They might be said anyway to make the same assertion, if we do not regard the assertion as the assertion of what is thought, and if we tie the assertion mainly to the acts of predication that are performed. But the thought would not be the same, because their thought would be in part about words.

It was said earlier that the act of abstract predication is not a good candidate for the proposition, or thought. One reason is that predicating, say, the property of being lighted by electricity, is accomplished in asserting that the lamp is lit by electricity, even if the assertor does not grasp the property independently of the name 'electricity'. The dependence on the word is a feature of the thought and the thought is in part about the word, while the predication, though it could not have been performed by that speaker without the word, is not about the word.

It might be objected that it is obvious that the proposition that oxen ruminate could be true even if there were no languages whatsoever, and so how can I claim that many assertions of this proposition include claims about the word 'oxen'? My answer is that there is indeed a proposition which could be true in the absence of language, but many people are not able to assert this proposition without asserting something additional about words, the words playing such a role in their thinking that they can make no separation between them and the proposition. And the idea of making a separation between words and proposition must be interpreted carefully, since it is primarily a matter merely of having more verbal flexibility than those less knowledgeable. I can assert that the proposition expressed to a suitable hearer by 'Oxen ruminate' is one that is not concerned with language even if I am not such a suitable hearer. Thus even the true assertion 'that the proposition that oxen ruminate could be true even if there were no languages' is not one assertion for all who can use those words. For some it will involve a claim about the word 'oxen' while for others it will not.

4

Denotation and connotation

43 With respect to physical objects, failure of reference is always logically possible. Reference to properties is different, since they exist necessarily. And yet someone may think that a word expresses some property which he does not know, and be mistaken in thinking so. But if he is not mistaken, then it is not possible for him to be. It is rather like guessing the answer to a multiplication problem. A wrong answer can be given, but an answer which is right is right necessarily. Yet we may wish to say of someone who has guessed, that it is possible that his answer should be wrong, and that can't be a logical possibility, since the answer is logically either necessary or impossible. Of course if it is necessary, then it is possible, but we could not assert positively that it was possible without determining it to be necessary. We are dealing in some other kind of possibility. There is the possibility of that which is not known to be false, sometimes called epistemic possibility. However, someone may know perfectly well that a term expresses some property, though having no idea what property. It is then not epistemically possible for him that the term expresses no property. Furthermore, it may not be epistemically possible for him that the property should not exist, because he may know that the property exists but just not know that that particular term expresses it. So it seems that the possibility of the property not existing and the thought being the same is neither logical nor epistemic. There are cases here of the thought's being independent of a property in a way analogous to the independence of a thought about a physical object, of that object, and yet I know of no handy kind of possibility to use to express this independence.

With experiences, matters are even less clear. Some hold that it would be impossible for a thought about the experiences of the thinker to exist if the experiences did not exist. If all singular thoughts about physical objects involve thoughts about experiences, this would mean that two people could not have the same singular thought about a physical object, because each one's thought would be independent of the experiences of the other, but not of his own.

Experiences are almost always referred to in general terms, and with support from physical object terms. For example, I may speak of my visual experience on seeing a desk. The fact that reference to experience usually depends on physical object terms does not mean that it depends logically on successful reference to physical objects. Perhaps grand-scale possibility-candidates, such as that one has never encountered any physical objects, can be ruled out by Kantian arguments. But the logical possibility for each particular case is omnipresent.

The method of studying the thought by asking what could possibly not exist while the thought remained the same, is, to me, a good basis for understanding *one* sort of traditional enquiry concerning 'meaning'. But it may be said that as one progresses through these possibilities, one will be led to an absurd position – the 'solipsism of the present moment', since beliefs about physical objects, other people's experiences, and your own past experiences will progressively be shown to be logically independent of the existence of these things.

I do not believe that every judgement I make is in part about myself. Among others, mathematical judgements are not. But perhaps every singular statement about a physical object does include a claim about myself. Even if this is so, it does not follow that the statement is not also about a physical object. I believe that no singular statement about a physical object is essentially about it, but that is not an ontological doctrine.

Furthermore, there is a difference between finding that, for any item not part of my present experience (that is, experience at the time of the statement), it is logically possible for the item not to exist and the belief expressed by the statement to remain, and finding that it is logically possible for no items of those kinds to exist, and the belief remain. (Not to mention the fact that the logical possibility of something not existing does not establish that it does not!)

I am writing with a pen. It is logically possible, though, that this impression is mistaken. Item by item of my world can be similarly dismissed. But it does not follow that they can be dismissed collectively. It is a mistake to move in either direction here – from the fact that they can be dismissed individually to the conclusion that they can be dismissed collectively, or from the fact that they cannot be dismissed collectively to the conclusion that they cannot be dismissed individually.

Similar considerations apply with respect to time. I think it is logically possible that I do not now have a body, but rather, only a very extreme case of phantom limb. But the idea that I could conceivably never have had a body, even having the beliefs and experiences I now have, is dubious. I will not attempt to discuss the question of solipsism in relation to time, except to indicate that even as a view about logical possibility, rather than an ontological doctrine, it is doubtful.

Norman Malcolm (1963) holds that, with respect to a case in which he is looking at an inkwell directly in front of him, there is nothing conceivable which he would count as evidence that there is no inkwell there. That is, no conceivable subsequent happening would qualify, as estimated by him at the time of his observing the inkwell, as sufficient to show that he had been mistaken.

As it stands, this is merely an expression of an attitude, though Malcolm would no doubt hold that it is the correct attitude to take. Now if an evil genie suddenly appeared to Malcolm and told him that there never had been an inkwell there and that he had merely supplemented the regular course of Malcolm's experience with the proper experiences to make him think there was one, then Malcolm might well reply that he has no reason to trust an evil genie. Or he could hold that all there is to there being an inkwell then has been satisfied, so that nothing the evil genie could now do could change that fact. But for all this, it is possible that, while the surroundings of 'the inkwell' were causing his experiences of them in the usual way, 'the inkwell' was not. The causes of Malcolm's experience *could be* as the evil genie says, even though the evil genie's assurance that they are so might have no probative value whatever.

However, this is not the place to attempt an adequate defense of this view about the extent of the logical possibility of error about physical objects. Even if some examples are found in which beliefs about physical objects are such that they could not exist and be mistaken, it is enough for my doctrine about the nature of thought that a very great number of cases of the sort discussed by the referentialists are ones where the thought could exist in the absence of the reference. I have already had occasion to note, in connection with some thoughts about properties, that the thought could be independent of those properties even though the independence cannot be explained in terms of the possibility of the thought existing while the property does not (since the property exists necessarily). The project of determining what is thought by asking what the thought is independent of, does not depend on the possibility of non-existence. However, this possibility, in the case of physical objects, gives the project a persuasive set of examples with which to begin. It is not necessary to the project to determine exactly how far the logical possibilities of error go.

44 There is, however, a more serious threat of isolation. If a singular proposition about a physical object always involves a thought about the experiences of the thinker, then it might seem that such a proposition could only be thought by one person. Suppose for example that Jones and Smith are standing side by side before a marble, and both say 'That is a marble'. Suppose that this is a case which we would naturally regard as a paradigm of two people making the same statement. (Not that my description of the case constitutes a paradigm – that is to be provided by a charitable imagination.) Further, let us suppose that the statement of each speaker expresses his belief. As has been stressed, this requirement is not standard for the ordinary use of 'statement' and in fact this would be a natural case in which to treat the act of predication as the statement. But we want a precise description of what is thought. Suppose that each man is thinking 'What is causing these experiences is a marble'. Perhaps 'these experiences' are the experiences both are having, perhaps it is just experiences of Jones that Jones refers to with 'these experiences', and Smith's experiences for Smith's use of the phrase.

When I speak of Jones as thinking that what is causing these experiences is a marble, I do not mean that he is internally pronouncing such words as 'What is causing these features of my experience is a marble'. Far from it. In fact, it might not only be very difficult to bring out, in discussion with Jones, that this is his belief; it might be impossible – especially if Jones is a philosopher opposed to my view. Jones might quite sincerely maintain that he has no belief about causes of his experience.

This is an unavoidable source of complexity in the description of beliefs, reflecting the fact that the evidence for someone's holding a certain belief can be complex and conflicting. It especially complicates questions about whether believing or knowing entails believing or knowing that you believe or know. A skeptic who says he knows nothing may know a great deal. And he may know that he knows a lot about one thing, and not about another, even though he sincerely denies that he knows anything. His sincerity reflects a belief that he doesn't know. But this will be a (mistaken) verbal belief. His belief that he knows, on the other hand, may be expressed in other terms, or may not be articulated in words at all, but indicated by verbal and other behavior. And some iterations (belief that he believes, etc.) may be indicated in a similar way.

Whether we start with the supposition that Jones is thinking in terms of the causes of features of the experiences of both him and Smith, or not, we will come back to the situation of reference based strictly on reference to his own experiences. For Jones' reference to the experiences of Smith is based on his belief that there is a person causing certain of his (Jones') experiences. (If the person is treated in a Cartesian way, this causation will be peculiarly indirect, but that is no matter for now.)

It would be possible for Jones and Smith to be thinking about only the causes of their own experience. It would seem likely that even if they held the belief concerning their common experience, which would come to a complicated belief concerning their own experience, they would also subscribe to the simpler belief concerned with their own experience. But this simpler belief could not be all they thought, if we are to have any hope of taking the case as one involving a common thought, rather than merely a common act of predication. Thus if Jones and Smith were separated by a partition, and each did not know of the existence of the other, we would get a clear case of what would popularly be called their making the same statement. And probably it would popularly be said that each believed exactly what he said, 'namely', that 'That is a marble'. It is a sad duty to have to insist that while 'statement' may be used in such a way that this part of the popular claim is all right, it can't be used that way with belief.

This makes the prospects for sharing a thought about a physical object much less straightforward than Frege makes it out to be. But he makes the apprehension of a thought thoroughly mysterious, as the price of oversimplifying the nature of the thought. At any rate, it does not follow from what has been said that Jones and Smith cannot think the same thought about the marble.

Suppose that Jones, standing with Smith, hears him say 'That is a marble' and knows exactly what thought Smith is expressing – the thought that what is causing certain features of his (Smith's) experiences is a marble. To simplify, we may suppose that neither Smith nor Jones knows who they are or where they are. They may be two amnesiacs who have just met before a marble. (Those who wonder why this makes things simpler must not confuse the bizarre with the complex.) Smith is thinking, 'What is causing certain features of my (whoever that is) experience is a marble.' (Actually he needn't be thinking these words at all, but the first person needs to be presented in quotes here, and it makes no difference if we suppose that Smith was explicit to himself.) And Jones knows that this is what Smith is thinking, 'in a way'; that is, he knows this is what Smith is thinking even though he does not know it is Smith who is thinking it. He knows, with reference to Smith, that he thinks that what is causing certain features of his experience is a marble. Furthermore, there is no reason why he should not know just as well as Smith what Smith's experience in this case is like. The fact that it is logically possible that Smith's experience is qualitatively different from Jones' does not mean that, in fact, Jones may not know perfectly well that Smith's experience is qualitatively the same as his own.

'Asserting that what Smith asserted is true' can be ambiguous. It can mean simply predicating truth of what Smith asserted, or it can mean doing something more. If I assert that what Smith said at noon is true, without even knowing what he said, and he said that that is a marble, then I predicated truth of the proposition that that is a marble, and in that sense I might be said to have asserted that the proposition that that is a marble is true. But it is natural to infer from the premise that someone asserted that the proposition that that is a marble is true, that he asserted that that is a marble. And it is natural to infer from the premise that someone asserted that that is a marble, that when he did this, he knew that he was doing so. But in the present case, this chain of natural inferences leads from the true premise that I asserted that what Smith asserted at noon is true, to the false conclusion that, in doing this, I knew that I was asserting that that is a marble.

My view is that what is generally counted as assertion is an idealized case, and that predicating truth of a proposition is asserting it, even when you do not know what you have asserted. This will be important later.

In our case, though, Jones knows perfectly well what Smith asserted. He may describe it just as precisely as Smith could, saying that what that person has asserted is that what is causing certain features of his experience is a marble. ('Certain features' of course is an abbreviation which has been saving us *some* tedium, but it should be clear how to make good on its promisory feature, recognizing that terms invoking physical object properties such as 'marble-appearance' are all right.) If Jones then went on 'and this assertion is true', would he then have asserted what Smith asserted? If so, he could have done so more simply, by asserting 'What is causing certain features of his experiences is a marble'.

It might be thought to follow from what has been said that the assertions of Jones and Smith must differ because what Jones asserts could exist even if Smith did not exist, while what Smith asserts could not exist in such a case. But this does not follow, though it is another matter to determine whether it is true. What I have said is that the proposition believed and asserted by Jones could exist without Smith and his experiences. Whether the proposition believed and asserted by Smith could also exist without Smith and his experiences, I do not know.

It could reasonably be maintained that any person that exists at all exists at all times, both before his bodily birth and after his bodily death. For a person does not have to have experiences in order to exist. It is only necessary that it be possible that he should have experiences, and it is a plausible doctrine, true or not, that it is always possible, at any time, that a person should have experience at that time.

If this is right, it is of course no proof at all of anything like the immortality of the soul in the popular sense, which latter is not a question to be settled by *a priori* reflection. I mention it here only because it raises a difficulty in describing the independence between the existence of Jones' belief about Smith and the existence of Smith which is analogous to the one previously discussed in connection with a belief about a word expressing a property when the believer does not know what property it is. It is just the general difficulty of explaining independence between a thing and a necessarily existent thing. As before, I can only warn that there is such an independence, even if it cannot be explicated in terms of any familiar sort of possibility.

In 'The Thought', Frege says:

Now everyone is presented to himself in a particular and primitive way, in which he is presented to no-one else. So, when Dr. Lauben thinks that he has been wounded, he will probably take as a basis this primitive way in which he is presented to himself. And only Dr. Lauben himself can grasp thoughts determined in this way. But now he may want to communicate with others. He cannot communicate a thought which he alone can grasp. Therefore, if he now says 'I have been wounded', he must use the 'I' in a sense which can be grasped by others, perhaps in the sense of 'he who is speaking to you at this moment', by doing which he makes the associated conditions of his utterance serve for the expression of his thought.

Yet there is a doubt. Is it at all the same thought which first that man expresses and now this one? (1956, p. 298)

In this quotation, I have omitted a footnote in which Frege observes that it is hard to present the thought. This is a true observation, and Frege's doubt is also a reasonable one. In speaking of Dr Lauben's thought that he is wounded, Frege uses the words, 'this primitive way in which he is presented to himself', such that 'only Dr. Lauben himself can grasp thoughts determined in this way'.

What is this 'primitive way'? It must be a way of being presented *in thought*, as the thing determined by the sense of the word 'I', where this sense is one which no one other than the thinker is capable of grasping. Presumably, we can talk about it, as Frege would have to do to fully explain his doctrine, but we cannot grasp it. What we can grasp is some other sense of 'I' which is employed in public assertions, and which we may equally well express using 'he'. That is, we express, using 'he', the public sense he expresses using 'I'.

Even if this were true, it would not establish that people have thoughts in common. For it does not establish that when Smith says 'I see a marble' and Jones says 'He sees a marble', the abstract predication of the subsumption of the property of being him (which is my version of Frege's common sense of 'I' and 'he') under the property of seeing a marble is the same as the thought of both Jones and Smith. In other words, even if there is a property, with respect to Smith, of being him, which is expressed by Smith with 'I' and by Jones with 'he', it does not follow that the abstract predication involving this property which would be performed both by the assertion of Jones and the assertion of Smith would be the thought, the proposition, believed by both, rather than merely being a common part of distinct thoughts.

Frege worries that 'If every thought requires a bearer, to the contents of whose consciousness it belongs, then it would be a thought of this bearer only and there could be no science common to many, on which many could work' (1956, p. 301). But this worry is mistaken. Even if singular thoughts about physical objects did turn out to be private, acts of predication would still be public and would provide an adequate basis for a common science. Frege's worry led him to take as the thought something that would require thinking to apprehend. And since that thinking would have to be thinking thoughts, this was a mistake. He had hold of some public things – various kinds of predication. He should not have let his worry lead him to call such things the thought.

There is no similar problem with general or mathematical thoughts. Both Jones and Smith can straightforwardly have the common belief that all men are mortal, because this belief does not involve indicating which man. Nor does 'Exactly one man is mortal' or 'The tallest man is mortal'. This latter example shows that a singular judgement about a physical object need not bring in a judgement about the person making the judgement. 'I think' accompanies all my judgements in the trivial sense that they are all things I think. But 'I think' is an ingredient of all singular judgements about things that do not have individuating properties that can be grasped by a person (except for the property of being related to a certain person in perception, if that is an individuating property).

It is not the notion of the self or person that is responsible for this isolation. A similar problem arises even for a theory that ignores the person and focuses merely on the experiences.

Suppose that Smith thinks just 'These experiences are caused by a marble', and Jones, with reference to those same experiences, thinks 'Those experiences are caused by a marble'. The question remains as to which experiences. If it is the ones caused in a certain body (Smith's) by the marble, then the body and marble, since they could fail to exist while the belief still existed, would be thought of in the belief as the cause of certain other experiences, and their identification leads back to 'I' and 'he'.

Or consider one of Frege's public senses of 'I'. Jones says 'He sees a marble', meaning by 'he' the cause of certain of his experiences. Then Smith must be using 'I' for 'I – the cause of certain of *his* experiences'. And this must be a public 'his', for Smith, 'the cause of certain of *my* experiences', and this public 'my' will be 'the cause of certain of *his* experiences'. It is a vicious circle.

Whether or not Frege is right in his claim that there is both a public and a private sense which can be connected with my use of 'I', I hope it has been made clear that this has no connection with the obstacle to two people expressing exactly the same thought with 'That is a marble'. The problem is that my saying it brings in a reference to me, while your saying it brings in a reference to you, and my saying it does not bring in a reference to you and your saying it does not bring in a reference to me. Even those (such as referentialists) who reject this should recognize that this being so does not entail there being any mysterious 'private sense' of 'I'. However, I do not claim to have shown there is no such sense, but only to have shown its irrelevance to the question of making assertions in common.

Thus while it is not a part of my view about meaning that no two people can have the same singular thought about a physical object (except for those involving properties which individuate without including reference to the thinker, such as the property of being the tallest man), it is probably true. But it does not have the dark consequences Frege thought it did.

The impossibility of two people having the same thought about a physical object does not entail that one person cannot know perfectly well what some other person is thinking about a physical object – know it just as well as the thinker. It is just that, in order to think that thought himself, the observer must inevitably add something to it. Thus even if some propositions are only thinkable or assertible by one person, for each such proposition it is always possible for anyone to assert something that entails it. Furthermore, the fact (if it is) that some propositions can only be asserted by one person does not entail that those propositions depend for their existence on the existence of the related person. But that particular metaphysical topic need not be discussed here.

45   It has been said that such a question as whether Betty is the girl of John's dreams is a matter for John to decide, not in the sense that only John can discover whether Betty is the girl of his dreams but

rather, because it is his deciding that she is the girl of his dreams that makes it so. Similarly, it might be said that in some cases the question whether John, in asserting certain words, was expressing such-and-such belief, can only be answered by John's deciding whether that is what he thought. And this might seem to imply that in many cases, if John will not or cannot decide, there will be no truth of the matter. By contrast, the question whether John uttered such-and-such words will never be so indefinite.

Along this same line, it might be held that the doctrine that the meaning of a name is a matter of the thought, or part of a thought, which the name expresses or is correlated with would be circular if the thought itself were a linguistic item, as it is in Mill's account. For the meaning of a word would merely be other words, and their meaning more words, and so on. And a platonistic version of Mill's theory might seem to be only an arbitrary attempt to dodge the difficulty by introducing a special class of obscure entities whose only function is to create an illusion of freedom from circularity. If the project is one of explaining what makes the difference between words having no meaning for someone and their having meaning, then the notion of sense or connotation, and of the thought or pro-position, will contribute nothing.

My project here arises from the question as to the significance of failure of reference for the truth of what is said. This is a question of 'truth conditions', but of course what is said is a statement of truth conditions – it is just that what is said can be put in a variety of ways. To understand well enough what is said is to know the truth conditions. To say that someone has said that that is a marble may not be enough to give a good understanding, especially if we consider the possibility that 'that' has no reference. Here I say that even if the logical possibility is realized, and there is nothing there, the speaker is thinking something. But of course he may not be thinking anything, just reciting the words. I am not asking what it is that distinguishes 'meaning' something from meaning nothing, but rather, what the speaker thinks in those cases where he does think something.

Failure to distinguish these questions is one of the prime sources of confusion in discussions of meaning. Mill is not the only philosopher who fell into the error of thinking that a theory of connotation and denotation would provide an explanation of what it is for a word, such as 'dog', to have a meaning for someone. Any such explanation derived from the theory of connotation will be circular. The words that either are the connotation of 'dog', or express the connotation of 'dog', are just fellow words with 'dog', no more exalted for having been used in giving the connotation of 'dog'. If one wonders what it is for 'dog' to be meaningful to Jones, one can equally well wonder what it is for the words that give its connotation to be meaningful to Jones.

My question is as to what is said. Unlike the question what it is for a word to be meaningful to someone, this question tends to sound so easy that it is possible it is overlooked for that reason. If someone says 'Nixon was threatened with impeachment', then most of us know perfectly well what he said – namely, that Nixon was threatened with impeachment. But if he had said 'The present King of France is wise', or 'What I am now saying is false', the problem of adequately reporting what, if anything, he has said, is more difficult. It is in fact a formidable philosophical problem which has not been properly answered, partly because of failure to keep it distinct from other questions about meaning. In this study, the connotation of a word is not something that endows the word with meaning. Rather, when we regard the word as part of a sentence which expresses a thought, the connotation of the word is that part of the thought expressed by that sentence with which we correlate the word. 'Meaning' can mean many other things, some of them even worthy of interest, but here it is limited to the project of studying what is said.

This brings us back to the idea that what is said may be a question which in some cases depends on a mere decision by the speaker, a question which it is naive to assume must have an answer.

I will not attempt to defend the law of excluded middle here. I simply assume that a speaker always is expressing some definite belief, or is not. Perhaps uttering words without thereby expressing any definite belief is common and perhaps this is an important fact about language use or thinking. Still, in a typical case of saying 'That is a marble', the speaker is thinking some definite thing such that he would still be thinking that very same thing if certain logical possibilities were realized, which would make it the case that there was nothing there even though everything seemed the same to him. We need a description of the belief which is appropriate for this possibility. This description will provide us with a guide to the truth conditions of the statement that that is a marble in the case where there is failure of reference. In general, the adequate description of the belief in the face of all the logical possibilities can be a difficult enquiry for which the average speaker is not suited. This description can perfectly well be called the meaning of the sentence that was asserted, as long as we realize that 'meaning' is also used in connection with very different projects. And we should remember that this project does not require the assumption that every declarative utterance made in earnest expresses a definite belief. It is only assumed that it either does or does not. The difficulty of determining an answer does not prove there is none.

46 We are now in a position to further explain the notion of a singular term, though only from a certain perspective, one which ties the theory of meaning to the theory of the nature of the thought. I will define an *ontological singular term* as one for which there exists a condition such that the term is associated with the thought that that condition is uniquely satisfied.

This association is provided by a thinker, and in that sense a term is an ontological singular term only relative to a thinker. On the other hand, this does not license the conclusion that a thinker is free to choose what he likes as the thought to associate with a term. It does not depict him as the creator of his language.

The association is not necessarily one of the thinker's *thinking* the thought, only of grasping it and associating it with the term. Someone who believes that it is not true that Socrates drank hemlock on the grounds that the story of this allegedly historical character is a hoax, does not think that someone satisfies the condition of being related to the name 'Socrates' in such-and-such way. Rather, he thinks this condition is not satisfied. But he could not think this without making the association of the thought that the condition is satisfied with the name, or rather, without being of a state of mind which provides the basis for naturally and properly making this association, for someone analyzing his thought (which the thinker himself may not be doing).

Suppose that Bill hears Bob say 'Condition C is uniquely satisfied' and believes him without knowing what condition C is. Does he believe this condition to be uniquely satisfied? There is no rule of common speech against saying so, but it is better to say that he does not and say instead that he believes a condition is associated with the term 'condition C' and is uniquely satisfied.

The actual variation, among speakers who communicate with each other, of conditions associated with terms is probably not great. However, the possible variation is considerable. When it comes to determining truth, this can raise problems.

One rule previously suggested is that of focusing on the predication. If one speaker associates condition C with term t and asserts that t is Φ' while another associates D with t, and asserts 't is Φ', we may say they are both right if the common thing determined by C and D is Φ, ignoring their different thoughts. We may so use 'statement' that they both made the same statement.

This variation among speakers is not the most serious problem. Variation with one speaker on one occasion is more troublesome. Suppose, for example, someone has said 'That table is covered with books', where in fact, it is a television set with a cloth over it. The speaker was thinking there is a table before him, which is covered with books, which is false. He was also thinking that there is something causing certain features of his experience, which is a table and covered with books, which is also false. But he was thinking that there is something causing certain features of his experience, which is covered with books. And this (let us suppose) is true. Now we can credit the speaker with a true predication easily enough. But which of those distinct beliefs is to be identified as his assertion?

I will say that it is the second of those beliefs, so that the assertion is false. But insofar as one doubts that this is the belief he expresses by assertively uttering 'That table is covered with books', this determination of falsity is doubtful. What is important here is the basis for determining what is to be assessed for truth or falsity.

Here is the basis for my contention that when a singular term in an atomic statement fails to refer, the statement is false. Such a term, of course, cannot be a logical singular term, since that requires reference. But it will be an ontological singular term, or otherwise the statement will not qualify as atomic. An atomic statement represents the thought that something uniquely satisfies a certain condition and also has some further property. And this thought will be false, since the failure to refer will be due to the falsity of the thought that the condition is uniquely satisfied. This provides a proper metaphysical foundation for a fundamental semantic rule.

It is important to emphasize that my notion of an atomic statement is a functional, not a formal, classification. 'At least one person is a King of France, at most one person is a King of France, and any

King of France is wise' qualifies on my account as atomic, because it achieves the function of expressing the thought that something uniquely satisfies a condition and has a further property. However, this function is not achieved by the use of a single ontologically singular term, and thus there is not a single logically singular term as subject, so the statement would not be of logically subject-predicate form even if there were a unique King of France. If there were such a King, I would say the statement is *functionally* of subject-predicate form.

It is customary usage to use 'atomic' for a formal, syntactic feature. But my departure from this usage should be amply compensated by my recognition of the distinction between the function of singling out, or of attempting to single out, a thing (which will be associated with a condition) and attribute to it a further property, and one particular form of language among the many forms which may accomplish this function. Furthermore, the rules of standard symbolic logic which make it possible to say 'Fa is 'atomic' and see to it that the function fits the form, are not enforceable with respect to a natural language.

'Atomic' could be restricted to a formal classification if we define an 'ontologically subject-predicate statement' after the fashion of our earlier definition of a logically subject-predicate statement, merely replacing 'logically singular term' in that definition by 'ontologically singular term'. Then the rule is simpler, that when the subject of an ontologically subject-predicate statement (or ontologically atomic statement) fails to denote, the statement is false. The broader rule, with the broader conception of 'atomic', is also true, and both rules have a firm metaphysical foundation.

47 On a natural occasion of use, 'There is exactly one King of France' would be (very) naturally correlated with the thought that a certain condition is uniquely satisfied, and would thus seem to qualify, on my account, as an ontologically singular term. Frege's account, which would have this sentence denoting the truth value 'False', would also, in a different way, depict the sentence as a singular term. In 'Bill asserted all men are mortal', the sentence 'all men are mortal' can be treated as a singular term for the proposition that all men are mortal, just as if the phrase 'The proposition that all men are mortal' had been used instead of it. With 'There is exactly one King of France' there would be no denotation, or in the days of

Louis XVI, Louis would be the denotation, if my account were applied in this way.

There is no harm in this, but it does blur the distinction between a sentence and a singular term, which is a genuine one. Yet although, as observed above, a sentence may function as a singular term, even 'There is exactly one King of France' does not usually so function.

The primary function of a singular term is to serve, in the atomic case of a logically singular statement, to introduce the subject of the predication. This formal role is not usually assigned to a sentence. When someone says 'There is exactly one King of France. He is wise', the singular term 'He' introduces the subject of predication (if there is one) even though it depends for its success, even in the attempt, on the preceding sentence.

Generally, in the basic case, a singular term introduces a thing into discourse in which a predicate is attributed to it in an act of predication distinct from any used in the introduction of the thing. When I say 'There is exactly one King of France . . .' I can go on with 'who is wise' or 'and he is wise', where 'who' and 'he' are both grammatical and ontological singular terms. On the other hand, if I say 'There is exactly one wise King of France' the statement is not logically equivalent to the former two, and, even where it accomplishes the same predication, it does not formally represent its purpose as that of singling out a thing for attribution of a predicate, but merely as that of singling out a thing. This is not to say that a speaker's intentions must correspond to this formal representation of purpose. But 'There is exactly one wise King of France' provides a basis for the impression that the speaker is not sure but that there may be other kings of France who are not wise. This impression need not be true, but it has a formal basis. It is this fact, that a singular term serves to single out a thing for the purpose of a further predication, that distinguishes a sentence which has the formal purpose of merely singling out a thing from an ontological singular term.

When I say 'further predication' I refer to a distinct act of predication (or attempt) separate from the singling out (or attempt), not to a distinct predicate. I regard 'The King of France exists' as an ontologically singular subject-predicate statement. What is attributed (or attempted) with 'exists' is profoundly redundant, but is nonetheless a distinct attribution (or attempt). On a natural occasion, this sentence expresses the same proposition as 'There is exactly one King of France'. But it does not follow from this that this latter sentence is also an ontologically singular subject-predicate statement. What it is must be discussed later.

48 The distinction between sense and reference, or connotation and denotation, has been employed in explaining and defending my claim that when the subject of an ontologically singular subject-predicate statement fails to refer, the statement is false. This distinction has had other uses, some of which may have created more puzzlement than they dispelled.

Frege (1952, 'On Sense and Reference') answered his question as to why a statement of identity such as 'The morning star is the evening star' is more informative than 'The morning star is the morning star', by saying that it was due to the fact that the referring expressions in the first statement differed in sense while in the second the senses are the same.

This seems correct to me. I would say that the first statement expresses the thought that the same thing satisfies two distinct conditions while the second introduces only one of those conditions.

Identity statements are a particularly simple case in which the sense-reference distinction is useful. On the other side, they are an embarrassment to the referentialists, who are apt to be unable to distinguish trivial from non-trivial identities or even end up holding that identity statements are necessarily true if they are true at all. Their tendency to focus on acts of predication to the exclusion of all else leads them to think that a true statement of identity merely attributes self-identity.

Unfortunately, even at this point where his distinction between sense and reference is so well employed, Frege was incorporating a mistaken emphasis which leads to later deep confusions. This emphasis is not made very explicit. But he seems to divide his options three ways: $a=b$ either states a relation between that which the names 'a' and 'b' designate ('if we were to regard equality as a relation between that which the names "a" and "b" designate'), or a relation between the names 'a' and 'b' ('those signs themselves would be under discussion; a relation between them would be asserted'), or a relation between the senses of the names 'a' and 'b'. For this third alternative, which I present as Frege's alternative to the other two, I do not have a quotation. Frege might well have denied meaning to say that a statement of identity states a relation between senses and might even more likely have rejected the idea that equality is such a relation. So I do not assert that this threefold division is Frege's. He is not clear about whether it is or not.

At any rate, it is wrong to suggest that these three alternatives are incompatible. And I do believe that Frege assumed that the sense of a term, though it somehow connects the term with its reference, does not ever itself refer to the term and is never about the term. I hope that enough has been said earlier to bring out that these are questionable assumptions.

Frege also used his distinction between sense and reference to justify his claim that, if two singular terms have the same reference, they can be substituted one for the other without changing the truth value of the statements in which they thus occur. This rule, though all right in certain restricted contexts, such as the usual mathematical arguments represent, seems plainly false in natural language. 'Bill believes Tegucigalpa is in Honduras' may be false even when 'Bill believes the capital of Honduras is in Honduras' is true, in spite of the fact that 'Tegucigalpa' and 'the capital of Honduras' have the same reference.

Frege's answer was that, in the context 'Bill believes —— is in Honduras', the two terms do not have the same reference. He held that in such a context 'Tegucigalpa' refers to the sense of 'Tegucigalpa' as it occurs in 'Tegucigalpa is in Honduras', and 'the capital of Honduras' refers to the sense of that term as it occurs in 'The capital of Honduras is in Honduras'.

This doctrine of Frege's is extremely obscure, especially from my point of view, which explains denotation in terms of connotation. For this requires that in the so-called 'indirect' contexts, the name has a different sense than what Frege calls its 'customary' sense. And Frege does not adequately explain what this sense would be. He seems to imply that the indirect sense of a term A would be the customary sense of the expression 'the (customary) sense of A'. In 'On Sense and Reference' he says:

> In order to speak of the sense of an expression 'A' one may simply use the phrase 'The sense of the expression "A"'. In reported speech, one talks about the sense, e.g. of another person's remarks. It is quite clear that in this way of speaking words do not have their customary reference but designate what is usually their sense.   (1952, p. 59)

The sense in which it is true that in reported speech one talks about the sense of another person's remarks, is that in which, in reported speech, we refer to the proposition or thought the other person expressed in his remarks. Thus if we report 'Bill said that Caesar is dead', we report that Bill stood in the assertion relation to the proposition that Caesar is dead. 'That Caesar is dead' in that context has the reference which 'the proposition that Caesar is dead' does, namely, the proposition that Caesar is dead.

(From my point of view, 'Bill said that Caesar is dead' would not be a good report of what Bill said. It serves everyday purposes and follows the everyday rule of staying as close as possible to the actual words the speaker used, even in indirect speech. But it does not make explicit the condition associated with the term 'Caesar' in the thought Bill expressed with his assertion. This does not make it mistaken, only less adequate for indicating the thought.)

Since Frege would regard the proposition that Caesar is dead to be the sense of the words Bill uttered, he is entitled to his claim that in reporting what Bill said we are talking about the sense of Bill's words, that is, the proposition they express. But it does not follow from this that we are *not* talking about their (customary) reference. No basis has been provided for regarding talking about the sense as somehow excluding talking about the reference in the same act.

Still, I am granting Frege the assumption that, in 'Bill said that Caesar is dead', 'that Caesar is dead' refers to the sense of the words 'Caesar is dead', namely, the proposition that Caesar is dead. It does not follow from this that in that context 'Caesar' refers to its customary sense.

(A) 'Caesar is dead' is logically equivalent to (B) 'The proposition that Caesar is dead is true' (or rather, these sentences express logically equivalent propositions). Surely the reference of 'Caesar' in these two sentences (in an appropriate context of use, of course) is the same. But (C) 'The proposition that Caesar is dead is believed by Bill' is equivalent to (D) 'Bill believes that Caesar is dead', and the reference of 'The proposition that Caesar is dead' in it is the same as the reference of that phrase in (B). So how could 'Caesar' have a different reference in (A) and (D)? How could saying of the proposition that Caesar is dead that it is believed by Bill change the reference of a component term in a description denoting that proposition over the reference we would have if we had said of the proposition, not that it was believed by Bill, but that it was true? Note, at least, that there is no support whatever for this idea in the fact that 'in reported speech one talks about the sense of another person's remarks'.

49   The basic source of trouble here is that Frege did no better than Mill at distinguishing between sense and reference as relations. He says that a name 'expresses' its sense and 'stands for' or 'designates' its reference. But what distinguishes expressing from designating? Nothing is offered by Frege except remarks about what the sense is and how it functions, which does nothing to explain the relation between a name and its sense. (Frege differs from Mill over abstract singular terms such as 'the property of being a dog' by going into an incoherent theory which denies that such a term stands for the property but rather for a 'proxy' for it.)

By contrast, consider my own account of connoting. First of all, it is related to the question of what is said. The first great problem about what is said concerns reference failure. When we report that someone says that the present King of France is wise we may give the impression that we too think there is a King of France. And the question of assigning a truth value is perplexing. A proper account of what is said, relative to these concerns, describes the proposition expressed in terms that provide a clear basis for determining truth value by adequately representing the thought. We then find that there are natural correlations between parts of the sentence and 'parts' of the thought expressed. These correlations establish the relation of connotation, and also provide the basis for a distinction between general and singular terms and for an account of denoting for each of these types of term.

On this approach, there is no reason for any change of reference on moving to indirect contexts. An account of the thought Bill expresses in asserting 'Caesar is dead' already does most of the work involved in describing the thought expressed by 'Bill said that Caesar is dead'. It would be absurd to give a different account of the sense and reference of 'Caesar' merely because of the move to indirect speech.

This is not to say that there never is a need for a change in the correlation for a term when it occurs in indirect speech. There is sometimes a change because in indirect speech there is always the possibility of ambiguity between representing the thought of the user of indirect speech and the thought of the speaker or thinker whose thought it is the object of the indirect speech to describe. For example, if I say 'Bill believes Tegucigalpa is in Honduras', I might be concerned with the condition associated with 'Tegucigalpa' in an assertion of 'Tegucigalpa is in Honduras' by Bill, or I might merely be thinking of a condition of my own, with no intention of implying that the condition is believed by Bill to be uniquely satisfied. And these are only two among a variety of possibilities. I might explain one meaning by saying 'Bill believes there is a town called "Tegucigalpa" in Honduras' and another by saying 'There is a town called "Tegucigalpa" and Bill (though he does not think of the town by the name "Tegucigalpa") regards the town as being in Honduras'.

In both these descriptions, 'Tegucigalpa' would be correlated with the thought that there is exactly one town denoted by certain uses of 'Tegucigalpa'. But it is easy to see that other conditions might be appropriate, if either Bill or I associated the name with some different thought – or rather, if some different association were the correct one to make in describing the thought.

In cases of sentence ambiguity and in other cases, there may be no correlation between a part of the thought expressed and a part of the sentence. The best basis for a correlation is the fact that a certain part of the sentence is the indicator to an ideal hearer or reader of a certain part of the thought. For example, the thought that a certain condition is uniquely satisfied would be correlated with the name 'Caesar' if the (ideal) hearer (or reader) was only able to recognize the correlated feature of the thought by seeing or hearing 'Caesar' in its position in the sentence. However, this is not a guide to a general account of how correlations are drawn. It was stressed previously that in some cases 'that' contributes nothing, is only grammatical filler, and yet would be assigned a connotation. Furthermore, being the key to ability to pick out parts of a thought is not always easy to assign to a particular part of the sentence. This might trouble someone craving recursive procedures, but my project is to answer the question posed by the possibility of reference failure and other questions as to what is said that arise in problem cases, generally known as semantic paradoxes. This project calls for general applicability, but certainly not for a recursive procedure for assigning connotation to parts of sentences. Where there is a difficulty as to the reference or lack of it of a term, there we need to look for connotation and can expect to find it if there is reference or an attempt at it.

Like Mill, Frege warns that

when we say 'The Moon', we do not intend to speak of our idea of the Moon, nor are we satisfied with the sense alone, but we presuppose a reference. To assume that in the sentence 'The Moon is smaller than the Earth' the idea of the Moon is in question, would be flatly to misunderstand the sense. If this is what the speaker wanted, he would use the phrase 'my idea of the Moon'.

(1952, p. 61)

Mill says 'when I use a name for the purpose of expressing a belief, it is a belief concerning the thing itself, not my idea of it. When I say 'The sun is the cause of day', I do not mean that my idea of the sun causes . . .' (I.II.I).

If I say that the object of my idea of the moon is smaller than the earth, then I have certainly said of the moon that it is smaller than the earth. The idea of the moon's 'being in question' does not rule out the possibility that its object is the object of the predication, and is also 'in question'.

It may be true that 'Bill said that Caesar is dead' is equivalent to a statement in which the customary sense of 'Caesar' is denoted. Perhaps 'Bill asserted a subject-predicate proposition the subject of which had the sense S and predicate sense P' or some such would be equivalent. But so too is 'The property of being Caesar and the property of being dead have a common instance' equivalent to 'Caesar is dead'. Abstract singular terms which (*pace* Frege) have senses for their references do indeed have their own senses. But from the point of view of my project, these senses are unimportant. For they add nothing to the project of characterizing the thought in face of all possible reference failures, since their references are just as secure as their senses and one can be collected from the other in a trivial way. Anyway, even the equivalents which do make the customary sense a referent do not simply leave the customary reference 'out of the question'.

50 In his essay 'Quantifiers and Propositional Attitudes' Quine says:

> If we rule simultaneously that
> (12) Ralph believes that the man in the brown hat is a spy,
> (13) Ralph does not believe that the man seen at the beach is a spy, (here both the man in the brown hat and the man seen at the beach are Bernard J. Ortcutt) then we cease to affirm any

relationship between Ralph and any man at all. Both of the component 'that'-clauses are indeed about the man Ortcutt; but the 'that' must be viewed in (12) and (13) as sealing those clauses off, thereby rendering (12) and (13) compatible because not, as wholes, about Ortcutt at all. It then becomes improper to quantify as in (7) [(Ex) (Ralph believes that x is a spy)]; 'believes that' becomes, in a word, referentially opaque.   (1956, p.179)

According to Quine, (12) and (13) are not 'about the man Ortcutt' and Frege would no doubt have agreed that Ortcutt is not 'in question'. But what does this mean? Someone who knows that Ortcutt is the man in the brown hat can learn from (12) that Ortcutt is the object of a suspicion of spying harbored by Ralph. This is information about Ortcutt obtainable from (12). If a statement conveys precise, discriminating (and incriminating) information about Ortcutt, then why is the statement 'not about Ortcutt at all'?

The answer must depend on what is meant by 'about', which is usually not very much. Sometimes we say a statement is about x if it contains an expression which denotes x, but that couldn't be any help in this case, since that is the question at issue.

Quine gives two criteria for a term's occurring referentially. One is that it be possible to substitute a term with the same reference *salva veritate*. The other is that one be able to 'quantify into' the term's position. Presumably, an example of this latter would be inferring that someone is such that Ralph believes he is a spy from (12), or inferring that there is someone such that Ralph does not believe he is a spy from (13).

Quine apparently favors existential generalization ('quantifying in') as a good general rule of inference, applicable wherever a term is genuinely referential. If the applicability of this rule of inference is made one of the criteria for a term's being genuinely referential, then it is a safe rule. But this is a misleading way of ruling out other notions of reference and aboutness.

In my opinion, someone who says 'Socrates did not exist' has, in the use I have in mind, made reference to Socrates. The condition associated with the term is, contrary to his claim, uniquely satisfied. But it is obviously not a correct inference to existentially generalize his statement to 'someone is such that he did not exist'. The rule of existential generalization will be further discussed later, but it is worth noting here that it is not applicable with complete generality to non-atomic statements.

At any rate, Quine's claim that (12) and (13) are 'not about Ortcutt at all' is compatible with my claim that each contains a singular term which denotes Ortcutt, provided that we simply take Quine's claim, and his claim that in (12) 'The man in the brown hat' does not refer to Ortcutt, to mean that either the terms in question do not allow substitutivity *salva veritate* or they do not allow existential generalization. I agree that this disjunction is true, so I would only complain that saying they do not refer to Ortcutt, or that neither (12) nor (13) is about Ortcutt at all, is a misleading way of saying this. It is still consistent with my claim that both (12) and (13) contain terms which would be correlated with thoughts that a condition is uniquely satisfied, which condition in each case is uniquely satisfied by Ortcutt. And that is what I mean in saying that (12) and (13) contain terms which denote Ortcutt and that they are both about Ortcutt.

Quine holds that between 'There is someone whom Ralph believes to be a spy' and 'Ralph believes there are spies', 'the difference is vast indeed'. He says that if Ralph is like most of us, the former is false and the latter true. Quine says these two statements are 'unambiguously phrased'. I disagree. For one thing, the latter means (by Quine's intentions) that Ralph believes that there is at least one spy, and putting this as a belief that there are spies includes an additional implication that Ralph believes there is more than one spy.

More importantly, it is not true that, even if Ralph is like most of us, 'There is someone whom Ralph believes to be a spy' is false. To borrow a case from David Kaplan (1968), suppose that Ralph believes that there is a unique least spy, where being least is determined by first taking the class of shortest spies, then restricting that to the lightest among them, then to the youngest among them, and finally breaking any remaining ties in terms of proximity to the northeast corner of the Washington Monument. We may suppose that Ralph rightly believes that the least spy is a spy. Most of us who discuss these matters would agree with Ralph. But then is there not someone we believe to be a spy, namely the least spy?

Kaplan draws the opposite conclusion. He holds that 'There is someone Ralph believes to be a spy' (or a version of it) 'was originally intended to express a fact which would interest the FBI . . . and we would not expect the interest of that organization to be piqued by Ralph's conviction that no two spies share a size'. I think Kaplan is too sanguine about the FBI. An anonymous telephone call reporting that Professor Kaplan has established that no two spies share a size might well lead to an investigation of Kaplan. Anyway, even granting that the FBI would be unimpressed if it were able to follow the explanation of someone whose only basis for saying that there is someone whom Ralph believes to be a spy is that Ralph believes the least spy is a spy, why should FBI disinterest show that the assertion was incorrect?

The fact is that there is not in English a canonical form for reflecting the difference between what would and what would not interest the FBI. The FBI might be interested to know that Ralph has seen someone in a brown hat lurking at various important places, in a suspicious way, and not interested in Ralph's theory about spy size, but it is unlikely that they would mark this difference by any very careful attention to the order of introduction of quantifiers. On the contrary, if I inform the FBI that Ralph has some information for them, and then say 'Ralph believes that there is at least one person who is a spy' they are liable to reply 'Oh! and who is he?' or some such. Perhaps when I then explain that he is the least spy, I will be thrown out, but not for bad logic or grammar.

There is a distinction between believing there is at least one spy without being able to give a description uniquely satisfied by a spy, and, on the other hand, believing and being able to give such a description. (This latter also divides into a wide range of capacities.) And there is a difference between being able to give such a description while being dependent on a description (a conditioned apprehension) and, on the other hand, perceiving someone and thinking he is a spy (and recognizing that it is he whom you perceive that you think is a spy – an unconditioned apprehension). And this also divides into a wide range of cases.

Furthermore, these distinctions can be captured in a 'formal analysis', in my sense, by arbitrarily requiring that a statement reflect one of the distinctions in order to qualify as of such-and-such form. But this would be a pointless exercise. It would be a way of giving the impression that one is managing to formulate general rules of inference for indirect speech when in fact all the work of evaluating inferences would have to be done in order to assign the forms in the first place.

Similarly pointless is Frege's defense of the rule of substitution.

This is a fine rule for a system of mathematical logic, but it can be made generally applicable in natural language only by transferring the difficulty of identifying a context as one to which substitution can be applied, to the difficulty of identifying a context as one in which the reference is customary rather than indirect. It is the same difficulty, renamed and accompanied by a confused theory.

If it is asked under what conditions (a) 'There is something Ralph believes to be G', can be inferred from (b) 'Ralph believes that a is G' or (c) 'Ralph believes that the F is G', we can answer that to the extent that (a) expresses the thought that Ralph has a certain degree of acquaintance with something, (b) or (c) must express the thought that Ralph has that degree of acquaintance with a or the F. And these extents and degrees are not generally well marked.

The inference from (b') 'a is believed by Ralph to be G' or (c') 'The F is believed by Ralph to be G' to (a) is more straightforward, because (b') and (c') make clearer the assumption that a predicate is being attributed to a thing, and that the connotation of the subject term is not relevant to the predication.

Moving to the case of a context such as (b") 'It is necessarily true that a is G' or (c") 'It is necessarily true that the F is G', the inference to (a") 'There is something which is necessarily G' is not so much a problem as is the question what (a") means. If it says that something has a property, what is that property? This is not my problem, but insofar as it is accepted that the notion of a proposition's being necessarily true is comprehensible (and this is a matter for reasonable doubts) then one way of explaining (a") is to say that it says there is something which is the denotation of the subject of a necessarily true atomic proposition whose predicate is G.

Beside the difficulties raised by Frege's effort to preserve the rule that names with the same reference are substitutable *salva veritate*, his concern for the ideal of unified sense led him to overlook the subjective element in the sense of many terms. And this deprives his distinction between sense and reference of applicability in yet another case where it should have been helpful.

We can explain that 'The evening star is identical to the morning star' is more informative than 'The evening star is identical to the evening star' by appeal to a difference in senses, even in Fregean senses. But we cannot similarly explain why 'Cicero's only male sibling is identical with Cicero's only brother' is likely in some cases to be more informative than 'Cicero's only brother is identical to

Cicero's only brother'. This is the so-called 'paradox of analysis'. In Fregean terms, 'male sibling' and 'brother' express the same sense, because the property of being a male sibling just is the property of being a brother.

Here my distinction between a term's being a mark for part of a thought and its being itself part of the thought is needed. Someone for whom the fact that 'sibling' means 'brother or sister' is perfectly clear (and it may be perfectly clear even if it isn't true in other meanings of 'means') will get nothing from 'male sibling' he doesn't get from 'brother', unless the terms are presented to him in the course of presenting someone else's thought or assertion. But for some, 'John is a male sibling' can only mean that John is male and a 'sibling'. Others might think that 'male sibling', like 'male hater', need not even imply being male. Once it is recognized that words can be included in thoughts and that one is not forced to choose between thoughts always being about words and never being about them, it is easy to understand how different words which express the same property to the well-informed, may be connected in a non-trivial way for someone who knows them less well.

51   The notion of an ontological singular term fits well with Mill's notion of a singular name and its connotation, except for Mill's unfortunate error of denying that all singular names have connotations. We should interpret this denial as the view that the general practice with proper names is to ignore their connotations in the logical assessment of statements containing them, and credit Mill with assigning connotations to proper names, which he certainly does. The connotation of a singular name, on my account, is a thought. And Mill, in the previously mentioned footnote (i.v.2 n. 2; see section 20 above), says something like this about the connotation of all names, both general and singular.

The extension of my notion of the connotation of a singular name to general names is problematic. It would be nice to say that, on the contrary, while a singular name is associated with the thought that a given condition is uniquely satisfied, a general name is simply associated with a condition – not with the thought that the condition is uniquely satisfied, or with the thought that it is not, but just with the condition. This would make unnecessary Wolterstorff's distinction between general terms and contradictory terms, and would not require counting 'prime number between 7 and 10' a singular term merely because it expresses a condition satisfied by just one thing. The general term would be one expressing a condition, whether the condition was contradictory and unsatisfiable, or unsatisfied, or satisfied by one thing or by many. The singular term would have a completely different relation to a condition, that of being connected with the thought that the condition is uniquely satisfied.

This is, I think, the correct account. However, while a singular term is connected with the thought that a condition is uniquely satisfied, and a general term is associated with a condition, many singular terms can also be said to be associated simply with a condition, and many general terms are associated with the thought that a given condition is uniquely satisfied. As an account of connotation, 'association' is not adequate, not because it does not provide a reductive explanation (which I have no intention of giving), but because it does not even provide a clear distinction between connotation and denotation.

The singular term, 'the property of being a dog', denotes a certain condition and connotes the thought that the condition of being a property of being a dog is uniquely satisfied, if we accept the foregoing account. The general term 'dog' connotes, but does not denote, the property of being a dog. But is there really this difference in the connections between these two terms and the property?

It seems clear that as a matter of fact the term 'dog' denotes things that have the property of being a dog. It also denotes coal carts and some devices for keeping logs from rolling, and so on. But an important class of things the term denotes is characterized by consisting of instances of the property of being a dog. This by itself does not suggest that 'dog' 'connotes' this property. But then consider 'That is a dog'. It seems that this would, in a characteristic use, ascribe the property of being a dog to something. In this case, the term 'dog' would seem to serve to introduce that property. And that suggests that it 'stands for' or 'signifies' the property. On the other hand, in 'That dog has mange' the term 'dog' seems to function to 'signify' a certain dog. Even if it also 'signifies' the property, signifying the dog is the important task in 'That dog has mange' while signifying the property is the important task in 'That is a dog'.

Mill could have been thinking of this difference in introducing the distinction between connoting and denoting. The idea would be that denoting relates a term to a subject and connoting relates a term to a predicate. But even apart from the fact that 'subject' and 'predicate' still need explaining, this would not be a good distinction. All we would have is the fact that a term may signify various things. But there is no basis yet for a distinction in kinds of signifying. Nor is there a basis for a distinction in kinds of things signified. The sorts of things denoted by 'property' are the same sorts of things connoted by it.

It is a significant feature of Mill's theory that whether 'dog' occurs in subject position or predicate position or altogether outside a sentence has nothing to do with what it denotes and connotes. There will have to be some feature of how the term is being entertained to rule out coal carts and logging tools, but it will have to be something more than mere position in a sentence.

Mill says that a connotative name signifies what it denotes 'directly', and signifies what it connotes 'indirectly'', and he says the name 'implies, or involves, or indicates' what it connotes.

'Involves' is not helpful, nor is 'indicates', in distinguishing connoting from denoting. 'Implies' is not clear. It seems, though, that what is meant is that what is connoted by a term *F* will be being a *G* if and only if 'That is an *F*' entails 'That is a *G*'.

The defects of this definition arising in connection with the so-called paradoxes of logical implication have already been noted. And it has been stressed that the connotation should not be treated as a criterion for applying the term that connotes it.

This latter mistake, of treating the connotation as a criterion, may be responsible for Mill's failure to see the inadequacy of 'implies' as an explanation of the relation between a term and its connotation. To say that being unmarried is connoted by 'bachelor' because 'That is a bachelor' implies 'That is unmarried' sounds like an explanation of something. But the full connotation of 'bachelor' is being a bachelor, that is, the property of being a bachelor, and to say that this is due to the fact that 'That is a bachelor' implies 'That is a bachelor' is no explanation at all. This is not to say that the term 'bachelor' doesn't imply the property of being a bachelor. It is just that this triviality does not explain the connection between the term and the property it connotes.

It might be suggested that connoting and denoting really are trivial. 'The word "dog" denotes dogs and connotes the property of being a dog' is obviously derivable from a trivial formula which could be applied to most general nouns. It might be held that the constructibility of such substantives as 'being a dog' or 'the property of being a dog' is a trivial linguistic convenience that has gotten out of hand.

However, it is not a *linguistic* triviality that there is such a thing as being a dog, because the existence of this thing is independent of language. And even though I do regard it as trivially true that there is such a thing as being a dog, it is not trivially true that there is such a thing as being good, where this is understood as a property.

At any rate, we need a better distinction between connoting and denoting than that the latter is 'direct' and the former 'indirect', or that connoting is a matter of 'involving' or 'indicating' or 'implying'.

52 Mill is not even careful to be consistent about his use of 'denotes', sometimes saying the general term denotes a class, sometimes saying it denotes the members. He says that it is putting things in the wrong order to say that a general name names a class. He says it would be better to say 'A class is the indefinite multitude of individuals denoted by a general name'. He calls this 'a definition of the word "class"'. But it would be a circular definition, containing as it does the term 'multitude'. It is also ambiguous, between the name's denoting the multitude or denoting each of the individuals belonging to the multitude. But Mill's statement that a general name can be affirmed of each of several things suggests that the latter interpretation corresponds to his usage. So it seems that Mill has here merely confused the fact that, on his account, a general name defines a class, with the mistaken idea that 'class' can be defined in terms of the concept of a general name. In other words, on Mill's account, a given general name will determine a class – the class of things X such that X is denoted by that name. But that a name determines a class is not at all the same as providing a definition for the term 'class'.

There is, of course the dispute over the ontological status of classes, which was mentioned earlier. One might stretch Mill's inaccurate remark about the priority of names to classes into the familiar doctrine that we ought to think in terms not of 'the class of men' but the general name 'men'. The idea might be that we can say what we need to say using 'the class of men' by using instead merely the general name 'men', and never get into the question about separate entities, since 'Is men a thing separate from individual men?'

makes no sense. It is likely that Mill's intentions were for a '-no-class' theory.

At any rate, Mill should not, according to this interpretation, have allowed himself to speak of 'the denotation of the name' or 'the class of things denoted by the name', without warning that these are merely convenient figures of speech. Instead he runs them together with the proper style, as when he says, 'The word *man*, for example, denotes Peter, Jane, John, and an indefinite number of other individuals, of whom, taken as a class, it is the name.' Here we might take him to mean that the name names a class and denotes each of its members. It would be nice to avoid saying that 'man' is a *name* of Peter, since that conflicts with ordinary usage. But the important idea is that it does *denote* Peter.

Mill continues with a significant claim about the application of 'man' to individuals: 'it is applied to them, because they possess, and to signify that they possess, certain attributes'. The use of 'and' in this claim is misleading. If I say 'That is a man', I may have done so 'to signify that it possesses certain attributes'. But I need not have done so *because* it possesses those attributes. It might, after all, be a bear I was mistaking for a man. On the other hand, when I assert 'Every man is mortal', my assertion applies to men I know nothing of *because* they possess a certain attribute, namely that of being a man. I may be firmly convinced that the creature that raided our camp was not a man. But if it was a man, then my claim that every man is mortal applies as much to it as it does to my own father, who I am positive is a man.

The difference here is reminiscent of the earlier discussion of the distinction between a term's applying to a thing and a person's applying a term to a thing. But for the present, the important thing is not the disentangling of these separate matters that are entangled in Mill's claim, but rather, Mill's claim that it is *because* the things have the attributes connoted by 'man' that they are denoted by 'man'. This conflicts with his claim that a name signifies what it denotes 'directly' and what it connotes 'indirectly'. For it suggests that denoting is definable in terms of connoting and the further notion of property instantiation; a name *a* denotes a thing *x* if *a* connotes a property of *x*. So the 'signification' of denoting would be reduced to the signification of connoting. While one might attempt to define connoting in terms of denoting and other logical notions, it would not be so easy to do so. To say, for example, that a term *a* connotes a property P if it denotes all and only things having property P is open to the familiar difficulty that distinct properties may apply to exactly the same things. It seems that insofar as one accepts Mill's notions of connoting and denoting, it is connoting that is the more fundamental.

Someone desiring to avoid this conclusion might analyze denoting in terms of the actual application of a term by speakers and then try to characterize connoting in terms of what features the person applying the term is impressed by. But this would be to change the subject of enquiry and would not provide a basis for rejecting our different notions, which are based on the recognition that our words denote many things we will never perceive.

53 Wolterstorff holds that to distinguish between singular and general terms in terms of denoting 'has no chance of success', on the grounds that, in 'Socrates is wise', 'there seems to be nothing against our saying' that 'wise' stands for just one thing, wisdom, even though it is clearly not a singular term (1970, p. 46). He observes that while 'wise' may stand for wisdom it is not true of wisdom, so there is more hope for distinguishing the singular term 'Socrates' from the general term 'wise' by using this notion.

Mill uses this same idea in attempting to distinguish between denoting and connoting. In response to the hypothetical objection that 'white' stands for the color just as much as 'whiteness' does, Mill says, 'a name can only be said to stand for, or to be a name of, the things of which it can be predicated' (1.11.4). Thus Mill would say that while 'wise' connotes wisdom, it cannot be predicated truly of wisdom, which is the same fact Wolterstorff uses as a basis for explaining why 'wise' can be connected with a single thing, wisdom, without being a singular term.

I am not comfortable with the practice of saying that 'wise' connotes wisdom or that 'white' connotes whiteness. I prefer to speak in terms of the property of being wise or the property of being white. Wisdom or whiteness are things that something can have more or less of, which is not so with properties.

While he grants that there are abstract general terms, Mill refuses to say that there are abstract singular terms, even though he admits that there are abstract terms such that 'only one attribute ... is designated by the name'. He says he makes this refusal 'to avoid needless logomachies'. This is a remarkable suggestion to make in the very

thick of a discourse about words. Unless 'designating only one attribute' is something different from 'denoting only one attribute',
Mill's refusal is inconsistent with his definition of a singular term.
And if designating is different from denoting, that would be worth
following up.

Mill says that the word 'whiteness' is a name of 'the color' and
also that it is a name of an attribute. He also says that it is a name 'not
of one single and definite attribute, but of a class of attributes . . . in
respect of the different shades of whiteness to which it is applied in
common' (1.11.4). This mixture of claims could make it difficult to
confidently state Mill's views in a precise way. But I propose to
ignore the conflicting cues and treat 'white' as connoting the
property of being white, which property is possessed by anything
which is any shade of white. And I will consider the compound
abstract singular name 'the property of being white' rather than the
simple abstract singular name 'whiteness'. Then Mill's point would
be that 'the property of being white' denotes the property because
it can be predicated truly of the property, while 'white' does not
denote the property because it cannot be predicated truly of it.

However, it is not true that no general term is truly predicable of
its connotation. 'Property' is just one example. (This fact is pointed
out by Wolterstorff.) So the notion of predicability does not provide
a basis for an adequate distinction between denoting and connoting,
or for Wolterstorff's distinction between singular and general terms.

Furthermore, even if the counter-examples to the idea that a term
cannot be predicated truly of what it connotes were rounded up and
ruled out by some special clause, it would still be unsatisfactory to
distinguish denoting and connoting in terms of predication in the
above way. For predication is usually achievable only by means of
denoting of some sort. Thus to predicate being a dog of a thing, one
either singles the thing out, as with 'That is a dog', or catches the
thing with a general term, as with 'All spaniels are dogs', or in some
other way makes use of denoting.

However, one may merely point and say 'dog', or in some other way
attribute the predicate without using an expression which denotes
the thing predicated. Anyway, it might be said that Mill's use of the
notion of being truly predicable should be exchanged for Wolterstorff's simpler notion of 'being true of', which latter does not involve
any considerations about the means whereby predication is achieved.

The trouble with this is that being true of is too good an equivalent for denoting to have any explanatory value whatever. It just is denoting. There is the same problem of distinguishing between being true of and connoting as there is with distinguishing between denoting and connoting. 'Property' is true of its connotation, and its connotation is one of the things it denotes, and there are lots of other examples.

(Of course, if I indicate something with 'this' it seems odd to say that in that case the word 'this' is true of that thing, though it does denote that thing. But I would be speaking truly if I said, with reference to that thing, 'This is this'. I would be speaking truly if I uttered that sentence with reference to anything, but the 'this' would have different 'meanings' in those cases.)

54 Consider a case in which someone asserts 'That table is square'. On our account of connotation, the transaction involves an association between the thought that something uniquely satisfies the condition of being, among other things, a table and 'that table', and an association between the condition or property of being square and 'square'. We have not had much to say about verbs, but '—— is ——' in this case may be said to serve the function of indicating the thought that the thing which satisfies the subject condition satisfies, or is an instance of, the predicate condition. (This is an association between '—— is ——' and the two-place relation of instantiation. Whether this association should be called 'connotation' will be discussed later.)

On our account, the 'associations' are connotations. But we have been concerned with distinguishing these associations from other, seemingly equally natural ones. One rival is the association of 'that table' merely with the condition of being, among other things, a table, rather than our association with the thought that that condition is uniquely satisfied. Another rival is the association between 'square' and the thought that the condition of being the property of being square is uniquely satisfied.

This latter association is implausible, since we are not predicating being the property of being square of the table when we say 'That table is square'. Of course by reinterpreting the function of the blank form '—— is ——' the thought might finally be stated truly even with this connotation for the predicate. But this would be an artificial procedure that would not extend naturally to apply to other sentences.

The former association is more natural and has its defenders, notably Frege. If the earlier criticism of his views is right, then this association is unsatisfactory because the thought that something does satisfy the subject condition would be left out.

To this latter it might be replied that this thought could be assigned to '—— is ——'. But if the assignment is not to be arbitrary and worthless, there must be some evidence that this form tends to have this function in a range of cases, and there is no such evidence. In 'Every table is square', there is no implication that something uniquely satisfies the subject condition. The restriction comes from the specific subject phrase 'that table', which includes the function of a quantifier.

We can of course 'associate' anything we please with a given word. But, if we want to say what sort of association connotation is, we must be guided by the suitability of the association in a description of the thought expressed by an assertion made using the word in question. With respect to this question, my account of the connotation is the correct association to make, at least in the example considered. We can use this procedure to characterize connoting and then define denotation in terms of it in the way already indicated.

If the assertion were 'That table is an instance of the property of being square', we could proceed two ways. First, in terms of the compound general term 'an instance of the property of being square', the connotation is the property of being an instance of the property of being square, which is just the property of being square, and everything is as before, including the answer to the rival candidates for connotation.

Alternatively we could consider the copula form '—— is an instance of ——' and deal with the (on our account) abstract singular term 'the property of being square'. The thought, then, is in part that what satisfies the subject condition is an instance of what satisfies the predicate condition (rather than an instance simply of the predicate condition). The competing account here would be the same this far, and would only leave out the thought that something does satisfy the predicate condition, that is, that there is such a thing as being square.

This thought is indeed thought by anyone who thinks that some table is square, even though some, such as nominalists, would not admit to it. But not every thought that is thought in thinking a given thought is explicitly expressed by the words that express the thought. So the only advantage for our candidate for the connotation of 'the property of being square' is that it represents more explicitly what the competing account makes merely implicit.

Both these accounts treat the singular term as introducing into the assertion the thing which satisfies a condition, if there is one, while the general term simply introduces a condition. To say 'the thing is introduced' is of course figurative. A claim is made about it – it is not a constituent of the thought. The notion of a constituent in connection with something which is non-spatial is itself at best figurative. At any rate, the description of the thought expressed by 'That table has the property of being square' could use the denotation of 'the property of being square' just as well as the connotation. Instead of speaking of being an instance of what satisfies the condition of being the property of being square we would speak simply of being an instance of the property which is denoted by the phrase.

This would be natural for Mill, since he denies that terms such as 'squareness' or 'the property of being square' are connotative, saying that they merely 'signify' attributes but do not 'imply' them. With abstract singular terms, connotation does not have the importance it does with concrete singular terms, and Mill is not led into any inconsistency with this denial of connotation, as he is in the concrete case.

However, it has been shown that Mill does not give an adequate distinction between connoting and denoting, and this is because he does not give a systematic account of the role of the notion of connotation in an analysis of language. Nor have I done so. But I have indicated how one might be given, sufficiently to show that, if we take the connotation to be the element naturally assigned the term in a description of the thought expressed, my account is preferable to the alternative candidates for connotation which were discussed. For while they may do for some cases, they do not promise to extend naturally to all.

55 On this approach the confusing question 'What holds the parts of a thought together?' should not arise. It is not the function of the connotation of the copula to 'hold together' the connotations of the subject and the predicate. Rather, putting the three together in speech or writing expresses the thought that what satisfies the subject condition is an instance of the predicate condition.

On this account, the distinction between singular and general terms is real but not very important. It is primarily a matter of grammar, though there may be ontological reasons for the grammatical difference. I can say 'My dog has fleas' but not 'My the property of being a dog has fleas'. But an intelligent hearer might respond to the latter 'Don't you mean your *instance* of the property?'. The difference between 'The table is square' and 'Being square is a property of the table' is merely the difference between the relation of being an instance of, and its converse, the relation of being a property of.

Of course we may analyze 'Being square is a property of the table', so that the copula expresses instantiation rather than being a property of, and then the further property of being a property of the table is brought in. An infinite series of properties can be 'produced' in this way. This series does exist (in an actual case of talking about a table) but there is nothing problematically regressive about it. Similarly, there is an infinite series of instantiation relations, an *n*-place one for each integer *n*. There is the relation R_1 of *a*'s being an instance of *F*, the relation R_2 of *a* and *F* standing in the relation of standing in to R_1, and so on. But it is not merely using language which expresses one of these relations which brings things together in an assertion. The relations play no such role. The arrangement of the various parts of the sentence expresses the thought that the connotations of the parts are connected in a certain way (or if it is not the arrangement but some other feature of the performance, well enough).

Furthermore, the infinite series of predications that are performed in asserting that the table is square are all achieved by any of the infinite number of versions of this assertion which make one of the infinite series of predicates explicit. And there is a fairly obvious priority that 'The table is square' has over the other versions, which would make it reasonable to say that functionally the table is always the subject, even when some property is made the formal subject.

56   In his essay 'Universals' Ramsey (1931) held that 'There is no essential distinction between the subject of a proposition and its predicate.' He rejects as false the doctrine that 'if a proposition consists of two terms copulated, the two terms must be functioning in different ways, one as subject, the other as predicate'. The first view I have quoted is a bit ambiguous, between the claim that there is no

essential difference between a subject term and a predicate term, *qua* terms, and other claims such as that there is no essential difference between the position of subject and the position of predicate. I reject this latter idea, but agree with the former.

There is a difference between a subject term and a predicate term on my account, insofar as a subject term is a singular term and a predicate term is a general term. But neither of these are necessary. 'Wise is what Socrates is' can be analyzed as having a general term for subject (though it can also be differently analyzed), and whether we always insist on finding a general term for predicate term is an arbitrary matter, as when we argue over whether or not to count 'The table is an instance of the property of being square' as having 'is an instance of' for copula.

Strawson discusses 'the traditional doctrine ... that particulars, like John, and universals-cum-particulars, like being married to John, can all be referred to, by the use of referring expressions; but only universals, and universals-cum-particulars, never particulars alone, can be predicated, by means of predicative expressions' (1959, p. 136–7). This view is one rejected by Ramsey, and I agree with him on this point.

We do not have before us any account of the distinction between 'particulars', or 'individuals', and 'universals'. Everything that exists is particular, as Locke said, and is an individual. But there is a popular intuition that would say that such things as the Washington Monument, or George Washington, are not universals, while the property of being a monument is. And 'particular' or 'individual' might be used, however misleadingly, merely to mean 'non-universal'.

Strawson regards 'x is an instance of y' as a form for predicating y of x. This view should make the falsity of 'the traditional view' obvious. For the Washington Monument would be a good traditional example of a non-universal, and yet, by asserting 'Nixon is an instance of the Washington Monument', one would be, on Strawson's own (correct) account, predicating the Washington Monument of Nixon.

This might be avoided by ruling that, in 'x is an instance of y', it is the compound general term 'an instance of y' and not the singular term y which is the predicate term. Being a monument can be predicated without the 'instance of' locution as in 'That is a monument', while the Washington Monument is not so well provided for.

But this is merely a matter of grammar. As a defense of the doctrine that particulars cannot be predicated it would be just arbitrary. We could introduce a syntactic device for making a singular term into a general term suitable for use in predicating the denotation of the singular term, such as '*x* is the-Washington-Monumental'.

It might be said that the fact that our language has no such device suggests that none is needed. I agree. But does this prove that there is a fundamental difference between a property or universal and things like the Washington Monument? What are the differences?

It may be said that the Washington Monument has no instances, and could not. But neither could the property of being a rational root of two. It may be said that the property of being a rational root of two is a compound of properties that could have instances while the Washington Monument is not. But how do we know the Washington Monument is not a compound property? For that matter, it might be said to have an instance, namely, itself, as will be discussed later. Claims to the contrary, true or false, are no argument by themselves.

Again, it may be said that every property has a negation. For example, corresponding to the property of being a monument, there is the property of not being a monument, while the Washington Monument does not have a negation. But why should not the property of not being an instance of the Washington Monument, which should, if the first objection is true, be a property of everything, be the negation of the Washington Monument?

Geach argues that 'names and predicables are absolutely different' (1962, p. 31). He is not using 'name' in Mill's sense, but in the narrower ordinary sense. In his terms, with respect to 'Socrates drank hemlock', 'Socrates' is the subject and a name and '——— drank hemlock' is the predicate and a predicable.

That there is a difference between 'Socrates' and '——— drank hemlock' is plain enough, and we may as well call it absolute, since whatever is true is absolutely so. Geach says that negation is the principal difference, and this again is no doubt true. He says that predicables always occur in contradictory pairs, while names do not.

This latter claim might be taken to mean that, in English, predicables have grammatical negations while names do not. This is true, but Geach appears to have in mind an even weaker claim. He says that 'predicables always occur in contradictory pairs; and by attaching such a pair to a common subject we get a contradictory pair of propositions. But we never have a pair of names so related that by attaching the same predicates to both we always get a pair of contradictory propositions' (1962, p. 32).

On my view, predicables do not come in contradictory pairs, since a predicable and its negation, appended to a proper name successively, yield two propositions which could both be false. Geach has a different view on this question of reference failure, but that is not the main issue here.

Geach claims that 'we never have a pair of names so related that by attaching the same predicates to both we always get a pair of contradictory propositions' (1962, p. 32). I agree. But this is a trivial truth, and yet Geach concludes from this that 'We must thus make an absolute distinction between names and predicables; if a name and a predicable have the same external form, that is a defect of language' (1962, p. 34).

Of course names do not come in contradictory or even contrary pairs in the sense that attaching the same predicate to both yields a pair of contradictory or contrary propositions. But predicables do not come in contradictory or contrary pairs in this sense either. So this trivial truth does not establish any fundamental difference between names and predicables.

However, the grammatical difference remains. Geach would not accept the idea that what he calls a predicable is connected with a non-linguistic entity, a property, but what Strawson calls 'the traditional doctrine' is expressed in such terms. I only want to make clear that no support can be derived for this doctrine from Geach's argument, though he surely didn't intend to be supporting it anyway. The fact is that a phrase such as 'the property of being a monument' denotes a thing which can be predicated and there is associated with that (abstract) singular term a predicable (in Geach's sense), namely '—— is a monument'. But 'the Washington Monument' or 'Washington' do not have corresponding predicables. My contention is that this is merely a matter of grammar which could easily be arranged otherwise.

Whether the Washington Monument has a negation is far from clear. But the fact that no place is provided for it in present English grammar is not a proof that there is no such thing. Besides, 'the negation of the Washington Monument' is a perfectly proper construction which will serve for those who wish to predicate this property, if it exists.

It would seem that the negation of the Washington Monument would have everything as an instance. However, Quine (1969, pp. 31–2) defines individuals as those things which are identical with their unit sets. This is an elegant idea. If we followed an intensional analogy, each individual would be identical with the property of being it, and then, just as on Quine's account, one asks whether a thing has no members other than itself or, otherwise, either has other members or none at all, to see whether it is an individual or a proper set, so no one would ask whether a thing has any instances other than itself or, otherwise, either has other instances or none at all, to see whether it is an individual or a proper property. This is better than having individuals have no instances or members, because it distinguishes between them and the null set and contradictory properties.

I am not claiming that the Washington Monument is a property. Perhaps by 'property' we mean 'proper property' and have just collapsed this latter phrase into one word, in which case it is fairly clear that the Washington Monument is not a property. But I do claim that it can be predicated, and if it cannot be predicated by means of a certain preferred type of predicative expression, that is only a rule of grammar which could be changed, though there is no point in changing it because predicating the Washington Monument or other individuals is not such an important activity that the language needs more than the barest provisions for it – provisions which have already been made in our wonderful language, which allows the expression of every thought, however false and trifling, such as the thought that Nixon is an instance of the Washington Monument.

5

Meinongianism

57   The definitions given so far of logically subject-predicate statements, ontologically subject-predicate statements and general and
singular terms, were aimed mainly at providing a proper foundation
for the rule that reference failure never leads to lack of truth value,
but rather, in an atomic statement, to falsehood.

(A) 'The King of France is wise', on a standard occasion of use,
represents an ontologically singular subject-predicate Russellian
proposition. (B) 'At least one person is a King of France, at most
one person is a King of France, and any King of France is wise'
could be used on the same occasion to express exactly the same
thought, exactly the same Fregean proposition. Functionally, it
would be ontologically singular. But formally it is not. For it does
not have just one term which is the signal for the thought that
exactly one thing satisfies the condition of being King of France.

(A) and (B) express the same proposition but they differ in form
(though of course there are various forms they have in common).
Furthermore, (B) is a better expression of the proposition with an
eye to the problem of failure of reference. If I say 'John thinks that
——' and fill the blank with (A), I do not make clear whether I am
myself under the impression that there is a King of France. If I fill
the blank with (B), I make clear what John thought, while also
staying neutral myself about whether there is a King.

Admittedly, (B) might be misleading in the blank of 'John said
that ——', if John's words were (A). There is a bias in favor of
staying close to the speaker's wording which conflicts with more
philosophical concerns in reporting what is said. But when reference
failure and its evaluation is the concern, then the task of conveying
an approximation to the actual wording must be done separately.

From the standpoint of finding the subject term in (A), (B) is not
as good as (C) 'There is exactly one King of France, and that one is
wise', because (C) focuses attention on the thought that a certain
condition is uniquely satisfied, which thought correlates with 'the

King of France' in (A). (B) has this thought as 'At least one person is a King of France and at most one person is a King of France', which is rather less straightforward. And then it continues in a way which tends to obscure the fact that the statement's function is to attribute being wise to a thing which has (hopefully) been singled out. (B) attempts, just as (A) and (C) do, to single out a thing and say something about it. But its use of 'Any King of France is wise' obscures this fact. 'The afore-mentioned King of France is wise' would have been a less misleading ending. (B) is the favorite, in fact, of those who think that it does not involve singling a thing out at all. But it does.

(A), (B) and (C) all express the same proposition (that is they could on a natural occasion, etc.) but are different in form. I have already stressed that there is no point in asking about the 'form' of this common proposition, since it is not only not a concrete thing, but unlike types, it does not even have instances or tokens that are concrete things. However, there is some basis for the notion of a singular (Fregean) proposition. This would be similar to my notion of a Russellian proposition's being functionally singular.

The problem with this notion is that any judgement always 'singles out' several things. However, some of those things may be singled out by way of singling out something else, while one may be singled out for its own sake. Furthermore while various things may be predicated of various things, one thing may be predicated of that thing that was singled out for its own sake. And similar, though more tedious, things can be said about the case where nothing is singled out for its own sake but there is merely the attempt, as in the case of reference failure.

58   Grammatically, (C) is a conjunction. Its second conjunct has as grammatical subject 'that one'. This conjunct expresses a complete thought, part of which was already expressed by the first conjunct, so there is a certain redundancy of the sort common with pronouns. The thought is that there is just one King of France and he is wise. But in this explanation of the thought, a pronominal device is used again. Such an expansion of the second conjunct is thus unnecessary from the standpoint of bringing out the existential claim in that conjunct, since it is already preceded by such a reminder and draws part of its meaning from it.

However, the fact that 'that one' qualifies as a singular term, even though the basis for the correlation is somewhat different in such a pronominal case than in the ordinary noun case, is important because it means that the second conjunct of (C) is an ontologically subject-predicate statement. On occasions when there is no King of France, this statement is just as good an example of reference failure as (A).

It has already been observed that both Russell and Strawson held that reference failure leads to truth value gaps. This is obscured by the fact that Russell also held that there are no truth value gaps. But he held that they would occur if reference failure occurred, so he held that genuine reference failure does not occur. And Strawson, too, holds that reference failure need not concern the logician because it does not occur in statements, but only in such things as failing attempts at statement making.

Both Russell and Strawson agreed that 'There is exactly one King of France and he is wise' is false (in the appropriate context). This does not square with their views about the consequences of reference failure. For the imbedded 'he is wise' represents just as good a case of reference failure as in 'The King of France is wise'. Of the two, Strawson's position is the worse here because he would surely concede that the reference failure does occur, and yet he offers no explanation as to why this should not lead to a truth value gap. 'He is wise' is just a brief way of expressing the same thought as 'The King of France is wise', so that to say the latter fails to count as a true or false statement while the former is part of a false statement is not consistent.

It might be replied that the conjunction is false because the first conjunct is false even though the second is neither true nor false. But neither Russell nor Strawson were departing from classical two-valued logic as this step requires. Or it might be denied that 'There is exactly one King of France and he is wise' is really a conjunction. But one can perfectly correctly say 'There is exactly one King of France. He is wise.' If these are not separate statements, then the usual procedures for counting statements will need to be drastically altered. And neither Russell nor Strawson give any indications how.

Russell is not as simply inconsistent on this point as Strawson, thanks only to his being more obscure. He might just deny that reference failure occurs in 'He is wise' either. In fact, Russell did not ever present the above analysis of 'The King of France is wise' except as an 'abbreviated', less than 'strict' interpretation. The 'strict' interpretation is presented in terms of what is now called a 'substitutional' account of quantification. Nowadays, this is just a matter of reading, say, '$(Ex)\ Fx$' as 'There is a name which yields a true proposition when put in place of "x" in the form "x is F".' But Russell was not merely concerned with interpreting a formal symbolism. He was concerned with the logical analysis of language in general (a noble attitude), and he did not regard the 'substitutional' reading of '$(Ex)Fx$' as just a competitor with 'There is something such that it is F'. He regarded this latter as itself just an informal 'abbreviation' for the 'stricter' substitutional wording.

This is clearly a complete mistake. 'There is an unnamed star' is true, but comes out false on this account. There are two ways to qualify a substitutional account of quantification, but neither will preserve Russell's elimination of the 'objective' quantificational style. One way is to allow descriptions as well as names to be substitutions. This is obviously out for Russell, since it makes descriptions uneliminable. The other alternative is something along the line of a 'variable name' or phrases such as 'no matter what the name is made to stand for'. And this certainly does not restrict quantification to names.

59   Neither (B) nor (C) qualify as formally ontologically singular subject-predicate statements. One reason is that they are compound statements. Furthermore, (B) clearly does not have exactly one ontologically singular term. Whether this is because it has none, or more than one, is a more difficult question, one related to another difficulty, that of the alleged distinction between singular and general statements (not to be confused with the distinction between singular and general terms, which has been discussed already).

Both Russell and Strawson agree that 'There is exactly one King of France' is not of subject-predicate form, but is rather 'existential' or 'general'. This has already been criticized, because this sentence is grammatically of subject-predicate form, and neither Russell nor Strawson bother to explain their notion of subject-predicate form which they withhold from this sentence. I have argued that this sentence is not an ontological singular term. But whether it contains such a term remains to be discussed, as does what it is for a statement to be formally (or even functionally, for that matter) 'existential' or 'general'.

Before doing this, however, the observation that the above sentence is clearly grammatically a singular subject-predicate sentence is a reminder that we have not yet taken up the notion of grammatical subject-predicate form in detail.

The problem with grammatical subject-predicate form is that it is supposed to be possessed by such a sentence as 'The solution to the general quintic was once widely expected', and the notion is explained in naïve grammar as involving a subject term's standing for something. But the alleged subject in that sentence clearly does not stand for anything. Furthermore the notion of an ontological subject-predicate statement will not help here, because the statement is clearly not atomic. One who makes it, at least in a non-philosophical context, is not even attempting to single out something with 'the solution to the general quintic' as an ontological singular term. The thought is, rather, that it was widely thought that there was a solution to the general quintic which would be discovered. This provides the basis for classing 'the solution to the general quintic' as an ontological singular term in the problem sentence, but not for classing the problem sentence as grammatically subject-predicate, due to the compounding 'It was widely thought that'.

There is an even more fundamental reason why the notion of an ontologically singular subject-predicate statement will not do for explaining the grammatical notion. For not only does the grammatical notion run over the boundaries between the atomic and the non-atomic, it also applies to sentences whether or not they express a complete thought. 'John is sick' can express an ontologically singular atomic statement. But whether or not it does, it is grammatically subject-predicate.

Thus there are two different problems for explaining grammatical subject-predicate form; its failure to recognize atomicity, and its lack of connection with specific thoughts.

If we ignore this latter problem, then one philosophical doctrine peculiarly relevant here is Meinongianism – which I take to be the idea that every grammatical substantive (except those which are really compounds of a substantive with a quantifier, such as 'nothing', 'everything', 'someone', etc.) denotes an object, but that some substantives denote objects which do not exist, but merely subsist, and some denote objects which do not exist or subsist, but are 'beyond being'. The idea is accompanied by the slogan that existing is independent of predication and having properties, that even non-existent objects may be ascribed properties and also have them (or lack them) so that statements making such ascriptions may be true or false.

This doctrine could be pared down to nothing beyond our previous accounts of a substantive were it not for the insertion of 'grammatical'. And this is the source of considerable obscurity. From the standpoint of definition, the question whether 'the solution to the general quintic' is a logical substantive turns entirely on whether the expression stands for something. But the question whether the expression is a grammatical substantive is put in exactly the same terms. The difference lies in the tendency, from the grammatical point of view, to answer yes, and from the logical point of view, to answer no. And this is not a good basis for a formal distinction.

My view is that a sentence's being of grammatical subject-predicate form should be explained in terms of its bearing suitable syntactic resemblances to a sentence of logical subject-predicate form (or ontological subject-predicate form). And similarly being a grammatical as opposed to a logical substantive. For example, both 'the solution to the general quintic' and 'the solution to the general quartic' are of the form 'The solution to (*term designating a type of equation*)', and this fact is the sort that warrants saying the former is a grammatical substantive. To generalize and adequately characterize the sorts of resemblances involved is no project for me. But this should at least indicate how the notion of grammatical subject or substantive might be elucidated.

60 A sentence of logical subject-predicate form will be a Russellian proposition. A predicate will be attributed to something by means of the sentence. But a grammatical subject-predicate sentence need not be serving to say anything at all, in the sense in which a Russellian proposition does. However, it is natural to speak of a sentence 'saying' something in another sense. When I speak of different 'senses' of 'say', I realize that this is very imprecise. But I think that '"Nixon is hirsute" says that Nixon is hirsute' conveys (to a general audience with a certain background) with 'says' a different idea from what '"John is sick" says that John is sick' conveys with 'says'. In the former something is really said about a person. In the latter this is not the case. Perhaps this is a delicately intuitive matter. I only hope my meaning is clear. The distinction may seem rather like that between 'see' in 'John sees a tree' and 'John sees a pink elephant'. To say there are two senses of 'see' is not at all a good way to

make the distinction. And the two sentences could even be so used that there is no distinction to be drawn. But there is nonetheless a distinction suggested by the two sentences, which I think is genuine. However, it is a very precarious distinction and I hope that my distinction regarding 'say' can be put in a better state.

Corresponding to the distinction regarding 'say' is a distinction regarding 'say of', 'about' and related terms. Thus, while 'The solution to the general quintic was once widely expected' says in the full sense that the solution to the general quintic was widely expected, it may also be said to be 'about' the solution to the general quintic, or 'say of it' that it was widely expected. And this will be less than the full sense of 'about'. Similarly, 'John is sick' says John is sick only in a weak, grammatical sense and also says of John that he is sick only in a similar weak sense.

My best hope for making clear these 'weak senses' is my account of grammatical form. 'John is sick' says John is sick only in that it resembles sentences (such as tokens of it in proper contexts) that really do say something, which something would be reported by grammatically similar transformations of the original, and it says of John that he is sick only in a similar way.

It is also true that 'John is sick' can be used to say things, and to say things of someone. But this is not a good explanation for saying in the weak sense, because 'The rational square root of two was discovered by Bill' says of the rational root of two that it was discovered, in the weak sense, even though that sentence could not be used, in accordance with its present meaning, to do that in the full sense of 'say of'. It is the formal resemblance to logical substantives, not the possibility of use as a logical substantive, that qualifies an expression as a grammatical substantive. Thus it is not merely the fact that a grammatically subject-predicate sentence is not being used to say something (or otherwise 'supplemented', to borrow Russell's term) that may keep it from qualifying as logically subject-predicate.

61 When Meinongianism is applied to supplemented sentences, that is, Russellian propositions, it is an absurd doctrine. Besides the fact that 'impossible objects' such as 'the actually existent round square plane figure atop Berkeley College' are logically intolerable, Meinongianism as here applied has the consequence that someone who, laboring under the false impression that there is a King of

France, though having no one in mind, asserts sincerely 'The King of France is wise', has thereby made reference to a subsistent entity which he may have had not the slightest conception of, and with respect to which the question whether it is wise is totally and permanently unanswerable. If someone else said 'The great and wise King of France is wise' he would have referred to a wise subsistent entity. But whether it is the same entity as the one associated with 'the King of France' is unanswerable. Certainly the speaker's intentions have nothing to do with the matter.

However, the naïve grammatical definition of a 'sentence' as a group of words expressing a complete thought need not be taken as intended for Russellian propositions. The idea might be a version of saying something in the weak sense. And Meinongianism might be construed as a way of trying to express the naïve grammatical tendency to talk about 'says of' and 'about' in connection with unsupplemented sentences.

For this account of 'sentence' the Meinongian theory of meaning is at least more plausible than it was for the Russellian account. For now it does not require taking a sincere assertion of 'The King of France is wise' to be about something. Rather, the theory is available to close out dialogues such as: 'Whom does the sentence "John gave Mary a book" say John gave a book?' 'Mary.' 'Who is Mary?' Here we could give a Meinongian-sounding reply: 'Mary is a pure object.' And perhaps all this has to mean is that being able to answer 'Who is said to have been given a book?' is a common test for comprehension of English, and that the answer is not 'the word "Mary"', and that though the answer *is* 'Mary', this has nothing to do with whether there is actually someone named 'Mary', pure or not.

In this case, there is no need to enquire as to whether John did give Mary a book, or whether the King is wise. For we are not raising the question whether these sentence types are true, though we could speak of stating their 'truth conditions', for example, the 'condition' that John did give Mary a book. In speaking of 'truth conditions' here we are not doing anything like what would be appropriate in a case in which the sentence is actually used to make an assertion (or is otherwise 'supplemented'). That is, saying that the sentence 'The King of France is wise' requires for its truth that the King of France be wise is a remark reflecting an understanding of the sentence, which should not lead to pressing the question whether he *is* wise. The fact that we do press questions about the truth of assertions makes the notion of pure object much more clearly unsatisfactory when it is applied to particular assertions or otherwise 'supplemented' sentences.

There is a clear intuitive difference between those questions which are questions about the sentence by itself and those questions which are about an assertion of the sentence. However, it is difficult to state this difference precisely. If, for example, 'John gave Mary a book' says what he gave her is a book, and 'Peter gave Alice a book' says he gave her a book, we could sensibly ask if it was the same book if we were dealing with assertions. And the same question could make sense with respect to the sentences themselves if, for instance, we were studying a text with 'It was the same book' further on. But such possibilities should not obscure the fact that the questions about the sentences themselves and the questions about assertions made by them are of a quite different kind.

If this is kept in view, then the technique for teaching the grammatical classifications advocated by Miss Anscombe (1965, p. 165) may be innocent and even useful. Even saying that 'the solution to the general quintic' denotes a 'pure object' could be harmless. But too often this innocent way of speaking is extended in dubious ways.

One linguist has said: 'Anyone who doesn't think that a possible world as ordinarily conceived can contain contradictions should read *Catch-22* or the daily newspaper' (Lakoff 1968). If this sort of comment is correct, then logicians do well to try to distinguish logic from grammar. But I feel certain that the spectacular style of stating the requirements of grammar could be dispensed with, though once that is clear, there is no pressing need to give it up. For example, it is not necessary for the grammarian to say that what the sentence 'The round square plane figure atop Berkeley College is round' says is round is the round square plane figure atop Berkeley College, in order for him to identify the subject phrase in that sentence. And if it really is important to observe that that is the answer an English speaker would naturally give, it still isn't necessary for the grammarian to regard giving and defending this answer as a part of his scientific task.

Even if Meinong could be made out as a philosophical friend of grammar, it would only be by trimming his views. For he went beyond providing answers to requests for the subjects and objects of sentences to assertions as to what is true of these things. He would, I think, have to have held that 'The round square plane figure atop

Berkeley College is round' is true. And this is outside the province of grammar. This is not to say that this sentence could not be construed as usable for a true assertion. But Meinong would have called it a true predication. And this is logically intolerable.

62 It may be worth remarking that even Meinong would not have called 'The round square is round' true. I believe he said that a round square is round, or that anything which is round and square is round, and would have advanced this as a basis for saying 'The round square plane figure atop Berkeley College is round' is true. But he should not be charged with running together abstract and concrete singular terms, as some of his critics do.

Antony Kenny (1969) compares Descartes' idea of a triangle and his idea of a supremely perfect being with Meinongian 'pure objects'. He suggests that Descartes had a healthier conception of pure objects than Meinong, because he excludes from his realm of pure objects any that are 'impossible entities'.

In my opinion, if the notion of a 'pure object' is to be used in grammar, it must be so understood that there is no point whatever in ruling out pure objects that are 'impossible entities'. Descartes is concerned with things which can be conceived of, but answering 'What does the sentence say is round?' should not be saddled with such a concern. It should be irrelevant whether what the sentence says is round can be conceived of.

In his brief comments on Kenny (1969), Bernard Williams says of pure objects, 'fatal difficulties beset the account of such objects. A pure object is said to have just those properties which can be established by non-trivial argument *a priori*. This can be put by saying: a pure object of type F possesses just those properties which are possessed *necessarily* by any F' (1969, p. 55). Any object, pure or not, which is of type F had better possess all properties possessed necessarily by all F's. But trouble is supposed to arise from the idea pure objects possess only such properties. Williams advances this as leading to difficulties for the notion of a pure object even when 'impossible entities' are excluded from consideration.

Now it is true, as has been observed, that to say 'The present King of France' denotes a subsistent entity, leaves it quite undetermined whether this entity is wise or not. If this underdetermination occurs in the course of a *grammatical* observation as to the nature of the thing that is the subject of 'The present King of France is wise', it can be completely innocuous. But if the claim is made that in a present-day *assertion* the subject is an entity whose wisdom or lack of it cannot be determined, then the doctrine is absurd.

It is unlikely that Meinong would have clearly accepted this absurd doctrine. More likely, he did not clearly distinguish what might be called 'innocent grammatical Meinongianism' from other, less plausible versions. But in any case, the point to note at present is that this absurd doctrine is not open to the objection Williams raises against it.

This is because the doctrine only entails that *we cannot say* that the subsistent present King of France is wise or that he is not. We can only *say* what we can deduce from his description. But Williams attributes to Meinong a further view that entails that this subsistent entity neither is nor is not wise. And this is unfair to Meinong.

'Unfair to Meinong, indeed!', you may say, suspecting my own standards of Meinong scholarship. Well, yes, it is unfair, to Meinong the cultural object. After all, Williams does not support his attribution with any textual references either. As it stands, Williams' principle has the consequence that if a pure object X is of type (F & G) and being of type F is logically independent of being of type G, then x is neither of type F nor of type G. This follows because, according to the principle, being of type F precludes being of type G (since being of type F doesn't entail being of type G) and vice versa. But there is no reason to attribute this logical blunder to Meinong.

Williams employs this principle in deducing a conclusion which is readily obtainable without using the principle. He says, 'I shall use the expression "The polygon" to mean a certain ideal object.' He then uses the principle to prove that 'The polygon is not a polygon'. The idea is that a polygon must have either an even or an odd number of sides, but there is no reason for saying either that the polygon has an even number of sides or an odd number of sides. And, if it doesn't have either an even or an odd number of sides, then the polygon is not a polygon.

This conclusion is perfectly correct. But from it, Williams goes on to conclude:

> Results of this kind are likely to be obtainable with any 'pure object'. They seem to provide a conclusive objection to the idea that by having the additional property of existence a 'pure object' could turn into an object of the type in question.

The general shape of these results might also suggest what is wrong with the whole enterprise: that it is utterly misguided to try to represent as singular and categorical and about peculiar objects, propositions which are indeed what they seemed to be when we started: general and hypothetical, and not about peculiar objects.   (1969, p. 56)

In my opinion, Williams' suggestion that 'results of this kind are likely to be obtainable with any "pure object"' is based on ignoring the difference between abstract and concrete singular terms. He should have tried to apply his argument to the Cartesian ideal objects discussed in Kenny (1969). The triangle Descartes thought of was a triangle, and its angles summed to 180° (since it was surely a Euclidean triangle Descartes was thinking of). But there is no reason even to suppose that 'The Triangle' has angles at all. Admittedly, 'The Triangle has no angles' is an extremely misleading thing to say, but I think it is perfectly comprehensible. To give another example: *the* letter S is not *a* letter S. That is, the type is not a token of itself. Nor is there any reason to suppose the letter S is S-shaped, or has any shape at all, since tokens of it come in a vast variety of shapes, and there is no reason to assign some one of them as the shape of *the* letter S.

The idea that 'The triangle that is equilateral is also equiangular' is really not singular and categorical but is really like 'If anything is a triangle that is equilateral it is also equiangular', is at least true to the extent that these statements are equivalent. Whether this means the first statement is not really singular depends on what is meant by 'being really singular'. But setting that aside, there is not even an equivalence between 'The triangle is the principal figure in trigonometry' and 'If anything is a triangle, it is the principal figure in trigonometry'. No doubt those who resent abstract entities will find 'The triangle is the principal figure of trigonometry' very easy to replace. I have no sympathy with this attitude, but anyway, making out statements involving 'the triangle', 'the polygon', 'the letter S' as all really general and hypothetical is not as simple as Williams implies.

This is not intended as a defense of such abstract entities, which in fact deserve to be regarded with suspicion, not because they are abstract, but for other reasons that must be discussed elsewhere. My point is that such entities should not be confused with Meinong's 'pure objects'. Someone who subscribes to the letter S as an entity will be unimpressed by the observation that adding to it 'the property of existence' would not turn it into a letter S. For one thing the letter already exists; for another, it was never meant to be a token of itself.

On the other hand, with a 'pure object' such as 'the unicorn Bill is thinking of', Williams has fallen far short of establishing a 'conclusive objection to the idea that by having the additional property of existence' this imaginary creature could turn into a unicorn. Meinong would have held that it already *is* a unicorn. The existence would just make it a real one. And to make out statements about 'Bill's unicorn' as necessarily 'general and hypothetical' is quite implausible. Of course, if Williams is allowed to attribute to Meinong the principle that Bill's unicorn has only those properties deducible from its being the unicorn Bill was thinking of, he can then derive a contradiction (assuming, as everyone should, the law of excluded middle). But all the *logical* trouble is brought in by this principle, the attribution of which is unwarranted anyway.

63   However, Kenny may be quite right in thinking that if 'pure objects' are meant to include such things as 'Bill's unicorn' and are the kind of things which might come into actual existence from a previous 'pure object' existence, or the like, then the 'impossible entities' should be purged. Such entities would not be merely a matter of answering questions such as 'What does the sentence say John gave Mary?' Rather they would be subjects and objects for specific assertions. For example, St Anselm (*Proslogion*, chap. 2) claims that a painter may have a certain painting in his mind, as an object of thought, and then later, that very same painting may be ontologically upgraded by being put to canvas by the painter. The painting goes from 'merely mental' existence to existence in reality. Here the 'intentional object' is not just a matter of answering such a question as 'What does the sentence "Before it was put to canvas, Jones' painting did not exist in reality" say once did not exist in reality?' The sentence is being considered, not in itself, but as used in an assertion. Finding something for the assertion to be about is a very different enterprise from finding something for the sentence to be about in the sense in which this only amounts to a natural way of identifying its subject phrase.

'Pure objects' used in innocent ways of presenting grammatical comments on a sentence can be involved in more ways than just identifying the subject and the object. For example, consider the sentences, 'John went looking for the girl of his dreams, and he found her. She was Betty Brown.' If asked for a correct replacement for the pronoun 'she' we may cite 'the girl of John's dreams', and to the question, 'What does the second conjunct of the first sentence say John found?' we can reply 'The girl of his dreams'. Here again, the direct object (in Miss Anscombe's terms) as opposed to the direct-object phrase, is the girl of John's dreams. Miss Anscombe writes: ' "The direct object is what John sent" (= "what the sentence says John sent"). "The intentional object is what x was thinking of." These two sentences are parallel' (1965, p. 65).

In my opinion, it is quite misleading to suggest that such sentences are parallel. For one thing, it is misleading to equate 'what John sent' with 'what the sentence says John sent'. But more important is the fact that when we speak of the direct object we are talking about a sentence taken out of context without regard to whether it has been asserted. We may, of course, enquire as to the direct object of an asserted sentence, but the fact it is asserted is irrelevant to the grammatical question.

On the other hand, the intentional object, as what someone is thinking of, is not necessarily connected with what a sentence says, but if it is, it is an asserted (or otherwise supplemented) sentence that is involved. With respect to an intentional object, we can always ask whether that object really exists. But with a direct object in a grammatical analysis, such a question makes no sense. I may be said to be thinking about the solution to the general quintic. The solution to the general quintic is then an intentional object. And we may ask whether there really is, or even could be, such a thing. But when we say that a book is the direct object in the sense of being what the sentence 'John gave Mary a book' says John gave Mary, it is nonsense to ask whether any such book exists. Sometimes the question whether the direct object exists would make sense, as with 'John outlined to Mary a solution to the general quintic', but this is a mere coincidence which should not be allowed to obscure the fact that with respect to grammatical classifications the question of existence does not arise.

The standard idea is that intentional objects may not exist and yet be intentional objects, that not existing is no obstacle to being an intentional object. And Miss Anscombe may have thought that, similarly, not existing is no obstacle to being a direct object. But this is misleading, because the classification of an object as intentional always leaves a basis for raising the question whether it exists. But the grammatical classification 'direct object' provides no basis for even asking whether there really exists such an object. (Of course a basis could be provided, not altogether arbitrarily. We could ask whether the book which is the object of the assertion conveyed by the sentence exists, to which the answer is trivially 'no', because there is no such assertion.)

To distinguish between the sort of questions which are appropriate in talking about the sentence by itself from those which are appropriate when talking about an assertion of it is a subtle matter, but I think it should be intuitively clear. If I say 'John gave Mary a book' says what he gave her is a book, and 'Bill gave Betty a book' says he gave her a book, we could raise the question whether it was the same book if we were concerned with assertions. And raising this question with respect to the sentences by themselves could be given a point, say if another sentence in the list being studied is 'It was the same book'. But it should be clear that the questions raised about the sentences themselves are quite different from those raised about assertions made with them.

Suppose that someone thinks that asserting 'He did it for the sake of appearances' commits us to saying 'There are such things as sakes'. It is no use observing that 'He did it for John' has an indirect object while the other sentence does not. The grammatical classifications are of no use here. We can answer 'What (or who) does the sentence say he did it for?', with 'the sake of appearances' in the first case and 'John' in the second. An argument over 'sakes' does not come in at the level of grammatical classification, but only when we are concerned with an ontological analysis of the assertion. And to hold out for 'sakes' in the ontological analysis is very different from advocating them as helpful for grammatical classification.

Thus a philosopher may be concerned to explain that when we say 'Betty is the girl of John's dreams', we may only mean that Betty measures up to standards John set out as important, and not that she was depicted in some dream of his. Whether this is correct or important, *grammatical* questions about the sentences can yield answers which may suggest certain questionable philosophical views about mental activity, without actually expressing any such views.

64   There is considerable dispute over the acceptability of the rule of inference known as 'existential generalization'. The rule could be put as follows: if a sentence S is of singular subject-predicate form and is true, then the existential sentence derived by appropriate grammatical transformation with the predicate of S, is also true. The dispute over this rule could profit from a clear statement as to what is meant by 'subject-predicate form'.

Some logicians hold that the rule is not valid, because it is true that Pegasus is a flying horse, but false that there is a flying horse. Others, more likely philosophers, will say that there is a flying horse all right, only it exists in mythology, not in reality. (Presumably, it does in reality exist in mythology.)

Now if we are asking about the form of a specific assertion, then if that assertion is either logically or ontologically a singular subject-predicate atomic statement (this is a redundant description), then with respect to such statements existential generalization is a correct rule. On the other hand, it is not in general correct in application to negations. Here, by a 'negation', I mean the negation of a statement, such as 'It is not the case that the King of France is wise'. 'The King of France is not wise' can qualify as atomic by my standards. But forms are not fixed by the words of the sentence, only by the instructions accompanying the form. Either of those two example sentences just cited could be used to make statements which were negations. Probably, either could be used to make atomic statements. All we can be sure is that (*negation*) (*atomic statement*) gives one form of a negation. That 'It is not the case that the King of France is wise' always expresses a statement of this form cannot be guaranteed.

This fact about forms is especially important with the question as to the status of existential generalization. Consider the inference from 'The solution to the general quintic, though once widely expected, is demonstrably impossible', to 'There is a solution which, though once widely expected, is demonstrably impossible'. One might say that this is valid, but not really an existential generalization or only a grammatical, rather than a logical or ontological existential generalization. One might say that indeed, this argument is not only valid, but sound, that is, it is a valid inference to a true conclusion from a true premise, but it is not really an inference to the existence of something. We might say that if the conclusion were really existential, it would be false. But whether the conclusion is really existential cannot be discovered merely from its words. This is of course, partly because 'really existential' needs explaining.

Some logicians call 'Pegasus is a flying horse' true on the grounds that most knowledgeable people would class it as true if asked in a poll. And on this basis they reject existential generalization. They apply the usual criteria for truth to the existential conclusion of the rule, but use a poll to determine the truth of the premise.

I find this very unsatisfactory. Why ask people about 'Pegasus is a flying horse' without also asking about 'In spite of the fact that there are no flying horses, Pegasus is one', and such like? Or again, contrast 'There is no such creature as Pegasus' with 'There is no such mythological creature as Pegasus'. Perhaps it will be said that the business of setting out a formal system and then finding some way to make sense of it is much more productive than bogging down in a welter of examples.

Perhaps slightly different from the appeal to a poll is the appeal to a logical law. For example, it is said that by the law of identity, Pegasus is identical with Pegasus, but the conclusion by existential generalization, that there is something which is identical with Pegasus, is false. But do we wish to say that while nothing is identical with Pegasus, Pegasus is? It would seem that the law of identity, taken as 'Everything is identical with itself', would require that there is such a thing as Pegasus in order for us to conclude that Pegasus is identical with himself. Of course 'Pegasus is not identical with himself' is odd. But the proper denial 'It is not true that Pegasus is identical with himself (because there is no such creature)' is not so bad, and anyway, we must be guided by the interpretation, the explanation of what is said, not just by how it rings to the ear.

However, the law of identity may be put, not as 'Everything is identical with itself', but as 'For every name that is put in place of "x", "x is identical with x" is a true sentence'. But then existential generalization is being rejected on the basis of reading the quantification in the law of identity in a 'linguistic' or 'substitutional' way, while reading the quantification in the conclusion of the rule in the usual way. When the quantifiers are interpreted uniformly, the rule should be true.

My view offers the choice of classing 'Pegasus is a flying horse' as false, or finding it elliptical for something false, or finding that there is (perhaps 'in some sense') a flying horse. (Here, of course, it is assumed that we are viewing this sentence as asserted, not as part of a myth-telling.)

65 Philosophers who take the last alternative and hold that Pegasus exists (but perhaps only in mythology) can make the idea of an existential claim pretty puzzling. Zeno Vendler says 'There are things that do not really exist' (1967, p. 69). Presumably, there really are such things. There really are things which there are not, really, and so on. Meinong came straight out with: 'There are objects of which it is true that there are no such objects' (1961, p. 83).

If this deliberately paradoxical remark of Meinong's were slightly extended, to 'There are objects of a certain kind such that there are no objects of that kind', it would be clearly contradictory. But perhaps the idea is that 'There really exist things of kind k' is not equivalent to 'Things of kind k really exist'. It might be held that the 'real' in the predicate is not equivalent to the 'real' in the quantifier. This might seem to be supportable by examples. 'There really are fictional heroes' sounds true, but 'Fictional heroes really exist' sounds false. Perhaps there really exists the character, Hamlet, though the character, Hamlet, does not really exist.

In my opinion, this attempt to make plausible the view that there are things which do not really exist is unsound. The fictional character, Hamlet, does really exist. But this character is not a Danish prince (except speaking elliptically); it is *of* a Danish prince. Similarly, the mythical animal, Pegasus, really exists, but a flying horse does not really exist – the character of a flying horse exists. A purely mythical or purely fictional animal is no more an animal than a decoy duck is a duck. Names such as 'Hamlet' or 'Pegasus' are equivocal, between being names of mythical or ficticious characters, and being mythical or ficticious names. Both 'The death of Ophelia was a literary theme of Shakespeare's' and 'The death of Ophelia disturbed Hamlet' strike us as true. But Hamlet was not disturbed by any literary theme of Shakespeare's. The former statement is about the play, the latter 'goes along with the story', and is only true as part of the story. That is, it is part of the story that it is true. If this is recognized, then one cannot 'cite Hamlet as an example of there really being a man who doesn't really exist'.

To say that some things exist only in mythology is all right if it means that it is only a myth that such things exist, or that they are 'said' to exist by a myth-teller. But these sayings of the myth-teller are not assertions and are not true or false as they occur in the myth-telling.

It might be asked whether the sayings of the myth-teller *would* be true or false if asserted. This is a complex question (in the 'Have you stopped beating your wife?' sense). If a myth-teller says 'There was once a golden mountain' then he expresses a proposition, which if he asserted it, would be false. On the other hand, if he says 'There was once a man named "Bill"', there is no reason to take him even to express a proposition as he might if he asserted those words. In an assertion, there might be the implication that the name 'Bill' was historically connected with some individual, or again, the claim might be simply that some individual bore that name and did certain things, without his name being connected historically with our use of it. This would be unusual, but possible. Someone might hazard the *guess* that there was once someone named 'Socrates'. If he went on to say 'Socrates was a philosopher' we would have to take him to be making the further claim that only one person was ever so named, or we would have to interpret him as bringing in the further claim that his present use of the name will belong to a proper historical chain – without some such interpretation his utterances will not be comprehensible as assertions. They might be understood as trance remarks or in a variety of fantastic ways, but not as assertions. But this sort of particularization is not needed for names used in story-telling. So here we cannot even say that the story-telling is producing propositions at all, even unasserted.

The distinction between story-telling or play-acting on the one hand, and asserting on the other, may be exploited by an author for irony, or for other purposes. Thus a character may say 'Sometimes I feel I'm only a character in a play'. Or a pair of actors may engage in love-making before an audience while 'saying' to each other how essential they find privacy is to such relations. But these devices only exploit the distinction, rather than obliterating it.

The strict truth, then, is that nothing exists in fiction or myth-ology. Fictional or mythological characters exist in reality just as much as tables, numbers, or properties do. There is no other kind of existence besides existence in reality. Some grammatical substantives do not denote anything, and only substantives which denote something real denote anything at all.

What then, is to be made of the notion that a grammatical

substantive is a word or phrase that stands for something? Just what I made of it in my definition. A logical substantive is a term which stands for something, and a grammatical substantive is a term which bears a suitable grammatical resemblance to a logical substantive. 'The president of the US in 1956 was a Republican' is logically of subject-predicate form. 'The round square plane figure atop Berkeley College is round' is not. But it is grammatically of subject-predicate form, and this should be explained in terms of its similarity in structure to the former sentence, rather than in terms of the naïve grammatical definition, which is really a logical rather than a grammatical one. It is these intuitively felt similarities that lead us to say that what the latter sentence tells us is round is the round square plane figure atop Berkeley College.

I have already declined to attempt to describe in detail the similarities which provide a basis for classifying sentences as grammatically subject-predicate. However, one class of grammatical substantives is problematic partly because the question of corresponding logical substantives is. 'Nothing', 'something', 'everyone' and the like are not counted by Meinong as substantives. They should be treated as phrases that are run together, so that 'Something is a King of France' is like 'Some man is mortal'. But then the classification of these sentences in terms of logical subject-predicate form is problematic for reasons set forth earlier. When the logical question is taken up again, the discussion should also be helpful in connection with the grammatical classification.

At any rate, to return to 'The round square plane figure atop Berkeley College is round', it is perfectly all right to say 'What the sentence tells us is round is the round square plane figure atop Berkeley College'. But this is not logically a two-place relational sentence, though it is grammatically.

66   This is the strict truth, which requires special emphasis in this area where figurative ways of speaking are so common and so liable to mislead a logical discussion. The statement is not a logical two-place relation because the grammatical substantives in it are not ontological substantives. 'What the sentence tells us is round' is not associated with the thought that there is exactly one thing the sentence tells us is round. However, many perfectly correct things we say *sound* contrary to this. For to say 'There is just one thing the sentence tells us is round – namely, the round square plane figure

atop Berkeley College' need not be incorrect. It is only 'figurative' rather than 'strict' speech.

To distinguish between 'strict' and 'figurative' can be quite shabby philosophy. It is all too easy to palm off some paradoxical claim by admitting that it is counter to common sense but it is the 'strict' truth. It is worthwhile to justify the use of 'strict' here with some care.

It would be perfectly correct to say that some mathematical results which were once widely expected, such as the solution to the general quintic, have since been found to be impossible. To say that this isn't strictly true (though it is nonetheless true) here just means that, in spite of the grammatical similarity to an existential statement, this statement cannot be regarded both as true and as asserting the existence, in any sense, of a solution to the general quintic. There are no mathematical results which are impossible. Taken strictly, 'Everything is possible' is not an expression of boundless optimism, but an extremely cautious necessary truth. Here, in being strict, we merely apply the laws of logic.

This is not to say that those who say 'Some results are demonstrably unattainable' don't *mean* what they say. It is, rather, that the grammatical form of what they say is misleading as to the logical form.

However, this distinction between being logically existential and being grammatically existential is much more difficult than the distinction between being logically substantival and being grammatically substantival. Given a grammatical substantive, I determine whether it is a logical substantive by asking about the world, whether there is in it a thing denoted by the candidate word or phrase. But to determine whether a given grammatically existential phrase is logically existential, it is no use to enquire about the world. That enquiry only determines truth or falsity in this case, not whether the claim is existential. This latter depends on, among other things, the intentions of the one who made the claim. This is why the notion of a formal *criterion* for 'ontological commitment' is mistaken.

Thus it is possible for someone who asserts 'Some results are demonstrably unattainable' to think he is citing a counter-example to the principle that everything that exists is possible. He may thus be making a necessarily false existential assertion. But someone else may say these same words meaning no offense to logic, and then he is not making an existential claim (at least not the one most obviously suggested by the words).

What is worst of all, though, is that even what it is to mean no offense to logic is not perfectly clear, and the range of intentions with which 'Some results are demonstrably unattainable' might be said, is utterly multifarious, from logically impeccable to logically nefarious. The distinction between a logically sound person and a logically muddled one is becoming as blurred nowadays as that between a good person and a bad one. This is because the variety of ways of seeming sound (or good) are increasing. Someone who claims that there are objects, such as the round square, which do not obey the law of non-contradiction, may be a brilliant mathematical logician on the side (just as the most depraved sorts of persons may nowadays be engaged in helping the poor).

However, man does not live by bread alone, nor by brilliant technical results, either. So stands our first and perhaps foremost objection to Meinongianism. It is contrary to logic to say that a contradictory grammatical substantive denotes. But if it is said that, yes indeed, there is nothing which the contradictory substantive denotes, but that is just the sort of thing denoted by a contradictory substantive, namely, the sort of thing which there aren't any of, then the situation threatens to degenerate terribly.

It is helpful to explain being grammatically substantival in terms of being logically substantival. But the notion of being logically existential is in no condition to help with that of being grammatically existential. Comparison between existential and locative statements only brings out that both may be used with a range of intentions from logically sound to unsound, with no rule for distinguishing emerging. So it seems that we are reduced to defining grammatical existentiality by enumeration, making lists such as 'There is . . .', 'There are . . .', 'Some . . .' etc.

How then do we define a logically existential statement? I cannot. But then how can I jibe at Meinongianism for claiming there are contradictory objects, when I admit that in everyday language people may speak this way quite correctly? If the sentence 'There are contradictory objects (but not in reality, of course)' can be used to say something true, how can I show that the Meinongian use of it is to say something false? Well, I cannot give *proof*.

67 This suggests turning from our first and foremost objection

to another one, which was mentioned earlier. Suppose that someone, who sincerely but mistakenly believes there is a King of France, says 'The King of France is wise'. (Please imagine, here, a clear-cut failure to refer, which is surely a possible case, rather than some more esoteric case in which, despite the fact that there is no King of France, the speaker succeeds in referring to someone as 'the King of France'.) Meinongianism has the consequence that, in this case, the speaker's phrase 'the King of France' does denote something, regardless of the speaker's intentions. But then, whether the statement is true should depend on whether this thing is wise. And since this is quite unanswerable, we should be unable to say whether the statement is true. But even a Strawsonian would admit that in this case the speaker has not made a true statement.

There is nothing logically wrong with Meinongianism here, but it is plainly wrong. And yet the reasons for approving it in this case are the same as always. Saying what the sentence is about does not really require that the word or phrase cited denotes. The intuition behind saying 'Surely the sentence is about ——' where the grammatical subject or some other substantival component of the sentence fills the blank is a sound intuition. But the resulting 'theory of objects' must be restricted to grammar and seen as merely a style of speaking which can be accounted for in a less spectacular way. In fact, accounting for this style of speech is what it is to 'restrict it to grammar'.

It is not uncommon for philosophers to apply the Meinongian doctrine that all substantives denote in a selective way, without noting that their restrictions are quite arbitrary. Thus it may be said that dragons exist in fiction, but round squares do not, since they are logically impossible. But fiction is not concerned with logical possibility. It is true that to say that in 'Fafner was a dragon', 'Fafner' denotes a dragon, does not involve logical inconsistency or any such absurdity as that of always guaranteeing a denotation for 'the King of France'. But the reasons for saying this are essentially the same in these cases, and it is arbitrary to apply them selectively.

Even this arbitrary position requires caution against inconsistency. Thus we cannot say that a consistent substantive denotes something which exists 'at least in fiction', perhaps also requiring that fictional intent be clear, to rule out the 'King of France' case. For there could be a story about a unicorn which was the only unicorn to exist in fiction or out of it, and another story about several other unicorns. How could 'fiction' accommodate the only unicorn to exist in fiction and some other unicorns as well?

This could not be allowed unless either (a) 'exists in fiction' were given a reductionist interpretation which would make clear that it is no kind of existence at all, or (b) 'fiction' were construed as such a place that 'the only unicorn to exist in fiction' would be an inconsistent description. Alternative (b) could appeal to the idea that 'the only possible unicorn' is impossible because it is necessarily true that more than one unicorn (in fact, infinitely many) is possible.

There are two directions for a consistent Meinongianism. One is towards a grammatical version in which 'Every substantive denotes' applies without restriction to every grammatical substantive, but 'denotes' only applies to grammatical appearances as already explained. The other is towards 'possible worlds' logic, in which consistent stories determine worlds with things existing in those worlds. Then the difficulty about the King of France would be answered by distinguishing between thinking there is an actual object to which you are referring, when in fact there is not, and actually referring to a possible object, where the speaker's intentions must be consulted to see which is the case.

'Possible worlds' logic is, in my opinion, a case of a mistaken metaphysical interpretation being gratuitously attached to work in mathematical logic which is itself unassailable. But even if the notion of 'possible worlds' is not logically incoherent, it will not do as a refuge for Meinongianism, or any similar desire to make out fictional statements as referring to 'possible entities'.

This is because, even though 'There are things which are unactualized possibles' may not be logically unsound, it is nonetheless impossible to specifically *refer* to a merely possible entity. This is especially clear if merely possible entities are regarded as located in possible worlds. I can make identifying references to things in the actual world because there is only one actual world, so that adding the specification of the world, though silly, raises no conceptual problem for the actual world.

In order to make an identifying reference to a possible world, one would have to answer every factual 'yes or no' question about that world. Otherwise, if some 'yes or no' factual question were not answered, there would be at least one possible world in which the answer is 'yes' and at least one in which the answer is 'no'. To which one are you referring? This certainly can't be answered just by pointing. You must *say* which one, by description, or not be making specific reference to either. But it is impossible to answer every 'yes or no' factual question about a possible world, at least not possible if it is a 'referentially lively' world.

This qualification is added because I will not bother with such a question as whether there could be a world which contained nothing but necessary entities. Perhaps such a world would allow a blanket answer to all factual questions about it. But such a world does not provide a counter-example to my claim that it is impossible to refer to a merely possible thing, since it doesn't contain any such things.

A counter-example might be put forward of the following kind: the perfect sphere of description *D* located in the one possible world which contains that sphere as its only contingent existent. Assuming that the identity of indiscernibles applies to possible worlds (which seems gratuitous to me, but never mind), and assuming that a description *D* could be found which would answer every factual question about this sphere, then I must restrict my claim to 'referentially lively' worlds. But at the very least, I am sure that an identifying reference to a possible world has never in fact been made ('hasn't been made in this world', they might say). Certainly no novel ever written has even approached being logically complete with respect to factual questions. And since by a 'referentially lively' world I mean one for which there is no recursive procedure for answering all factual questions, my claim as qualified is fairly safe. And insofar as it is impossible to specifically refer to a possible world, still less is it possible to refer to a possible entity which inhabits one.

Of course this does not show that it is not possible to make a general reference to possible worlds and things, in the way I am doing in this very sentence *if* there are such things (which I of course do not for a minute concede). But the foregoing considerations should at least show that Meinongianism really has no comfort to find along this line, since this line does not afford even one actual example of a case of referring to something which doesn't really exist, and any possible examples are no credit to the position and are apt to be mighty thin anyway.

6

Kinds of assertion and predication

68 It is common to contrast singular statements with 'general' or 'existential' statements as if these were distinct types. Here we must be wary not to confuse distinctions of function with distinctions of form, and especially to insist on having alleged distinctions made clear.

Formally, statements called 'general' or 'existential' are apt to contain 'quantifiers', expressions such as 'all', 'every', 'some', 'most', 'at least one', 'there exists', and the like. It is not adequate to say that a quantifier functions to indicate 'number', but it is suggestive of their role.

A notable feature of quantifiers is the way they are used in connection with pronouns. We say 'Everything is such that *it* . . .', 'There is something *which* . . .', and so on. I have already argued that in 'There is exactly one King of France and he is wise', the second conjunct is a singular ontologically subject-predicate statement. Whether or not it marks an attempt to carry on a previous reference, it does mark an attempt at reference.

Though there are similarities, English pronouns have a more complex logic than the bound variables of quantification theory. One significant difference can be brought out by considering the usual English verbalization of '$(Ex)Fx$', which is 'Something is an F', or 'There is something such that it is F', or some such. To these verbalizations we can add 'and it is G', where there is a full-fledged conjunct which could have been a separate sentence. But in quantificational notation, we can only alter the sentence '$(Ex)Fx$' to '$(Ex)(Fx \ \& \ Gx)$', which does not have a conjunction for its main connective, but is, rather, governed by the existential quantifier.

Note that there is a difference here between '$(Ex)Fx$' and its logical equivalent '$\sim(x)\sim Fx$'. With the English verbalization of this latter, 'It is not the case that everything is such that it is not the case that it is F', we cannot go on to add 'and it is G' as we can with the verbalization of '$(Ex)Fx$'.

On the other hand, we can pronominalize after the English render-
ings of universally quantified formulae. For example, '$(x)(Fx{\to}Gx)$'
is 'Everything is such that if it is F, it is G'. To this we can add 'and
if it is G, it is H. So if anything is F, it is H.'

To suppose that these pronouns are carrying on a reference has
been attacked at considerable length by Geach. Consider, for
example, 'The woman every Englishman loves best is his wife. She
is the first to hear his troubles etc.' How could I say that 'she' is 'the
wife of the Englishman previously referred to'? This would indeed
be very misleading. In this example reference is not being made to
any Englishman. Rather, one is talking as if you could just pick any
Englishman and expect to find his wife in the role described. This is
not meant to be taken literally. The remark could be true if a very
impressive percentage of Englishmen were like that. This example
shows that the fact that it is perfectly correct to introduce a pronoun
does not show that there is a reference, or attempt at one, to be carried
on. There is a sort of sham reference, but that is still not reference.

However, it would be thoroughly unwarranted to move from this
to the conclusion that the apparatus of quantifiers working with
pronouns never involves reference of the same sort as in a logically
subject-predicate statement.

Geach holds that 'For the philosophical theory of reference . . . it
is all one whether we consider bound variables or pronouns of the
vernacular' (1962, p. 112). His treatment of recalcitrant cases can be
very harsh. A typical example is his treatment of '(5) Socrates
owned a dog, and it bit Socrates'. Geach says:

A medieval would treat this as a conjunctive proposition, and
enquire after the reference (suppositio) of the pronoun 'it'; I have
seen modern discussions that make the same mistake . . .

Contrary to what has been suggested (even in print) for
similar cases, it makes not a farthing's difference if in (5) . . . we
substitute 'the dog' or 'that dog' for 'it'. Any one of these three
expressions, in some contexts of utterance, could serve as subject
of the predicable 'bit Socrates', so as to yield a proposition with a
truth-value; but here, not one of them could. For no definite dog
is before the reader's eyes, or is brought by the sentence before his
mind's eye, to supply a reference for this subject-term. And the
'the' and 'that' must be parsed, like 'it', not as demonstratives but
as *relativa*, looking back to 'a dog'. (1969, p. 149)

Geach goes on to say that the right account is to treat the pronoun as a bound variable and make the main operator in (5) an existential quantifier.

Geach's appeal to a distinction between 'demonstratives' and 'relativa', as if they were mutually exclusive, is unfounded. 'Looking back to "a dog"' does not preclude the 'it' from having a reference.

The sentence (5) could be used in a variety of cases. In some, there would definitely be a referent for 'it'. A hearer might say, 'I know the dog you mean, that vicious little terrier. I wonder why Socrates never got rid of it.' There is absolutely nothing incorrect in using (5) in a discussion of a definite dog.

On the other hand, someone might assert (5) on the grounds that Socrates did own at least one dog, perhaps more, and every dog owned by Socrates bit Socrates at one time or another. Someone could know this without being able to single out any dog as belonging to Socrates. In this sort of case, the 'it' is indeed not carrying on a reference. This seems to me a less natural use for (5) than the one described in the preceding paragraph. But Geach seems to think that the words of (5) are enough to restrict the possible cases to ones like the present one. And this is not so.

69   Geach sets forth a condition which 'the dog', 'that dog' or 'it' would have to satisfy in order to 'serve as subject of the predicable "bit Socrates" so as to yield a proposition with a truth-value'. The condition is not satisfied if 'no definite dog is before the reader's eyes, or is brought by the sentence before his mind's eye, to supply a reference for this subject-term'. The phrase 'definite dog' strikes me as involving a redundancy, and the idea of a sentence bringing such a dog before the mind's eye is rather imprecise. But I am not one to press criticisms of that sort. What is important is that the implied contrast with the case of proper names is based on a very shaky theory about them, which requires genuine proper names, as the paradigms of subject terms, to serve to refer to things immediately present either to the senses or to the mind.

This theory will not be satisfied by ordinary proper names in English, even when they are serving as logical substantives in my sense. For example, suppose that, in a discussion about movies, I assert 'Lassie was a collie'. This is a true assertion, in which I refer to a 'definite dog'. I do not mean the fictional character in Eric Knight's novel. I mean one of the several dogs named 'Lassie' who starred in the movies, and I know which one I mean, and some of my hearers may be supposed to know too. For us, 'Lassie' may be supposed to serve, in my assertion, to call this dog before our minds' eyes. But suppose there is a perverse character present who sincerely believes that in movies, whenever an animal is presented as a collie (or as a wolf or coyote) it is really a disguised German shepherd dog. This man has never seen a 'Lassie' movie or even heard of Lassie, but he gathers I was talking about a canine film actor, and he says 'You're wrong! Lassie was a German shepherd!'

In this case an assertion is surely being made about Lassie. Lassie is the subject, and the referent of the term 'Lassie'. But the speaker has no idea of Lassie at all. Geach's reason for denying that referring is involved in (5) applies equally in this case, from the point of view of the speaker, but it does not fit what he elsewhere says about proper names.

To be sure, my own account is one which would allow that the perverse speaker in this example is not expressing the same thought with 'Lassie was a German shepherd' that I might have associated with this sentence, knowing Lassie as I do. That is, my account allows for subjective variations in the connotation of 'Lassie' determining the same referent. The perverse speaker might mean by 'Lassie', 'the dog you all were referring to'. But the important thing is that he can use 'Lassie' to refer to a dog which is in no way 'before' either his inner or outer eye, even allowing for the fact that the application of such notions is extremely vague.

This is not to deny the claim that pronominalization is not a sufficient indicator of reference. But Geach seems to regard quantifiers working with the pronouns as in (5) as a sufficient guarantee that there is not reference, and seems to think that such a form of speech provides a sufficient indication of its user's 'state of mind', so that we can determine from it alone that he does not have a certain degree of acquaintance with any dog belonging to Socrates.

The standard semantics for quantification theory encourages this sort of mistake. 'Fa' is interpreted by stipulating a domain, and having 'a' stand for an element in it and 'F' stand for a subclass of it. On the other hand, '$(Ex)Fx$' is interpreted by merely having 'F' stand for a subclass. It is natural to conclude from this that there is no reference to a subject in an existential statement. But this is too hasty even in the case of quantification theory and thoroughly mistaken in application to natural language.

Sometimes when someone says something of the form 'There is something such that it is F' he is making reference to something. Other times he is not. Sometimes, how he goes on to pronominalize is a good guide to which of these is the case. Other times it is not. And we cannot escape this fact, frustrating as it may be to a formalizer, by stipulating that '$(Ex)(Fx)$' is to be a 'canonical' way of representing merely the 'bare existence' claim. No such canonization in a natural language is possible. It can't stop people using an expression in any way that happens to succeed in conveying what they wish to convey. Of course 'There is something such that it is F' could be introduced to *mean* 'There is something such that it is F and I, the speaker, am not referring specifically etc.' But that isn't what the canonizer was after. The illusion of capturing the 'bare existence' statement with a non-question-begging form (as contrasted with such a form as '(bare existence statement)') is created by working in a formal system where all sorts of referential work is done which can simply be ignored in the formal calculations. For example, the fact that you and your hearers happen to know perfectly well that there is only one member of the subclass assigned to 'F' may put you in a perfectly good position to use '$(Ex)Fx$' to make an identifying reference and then go on to say something about 'the F'. But that won't be part of the formal system. However, the possibility is still a fact of language.

70 There is indeed a distinction between attributing a predicate to a thing on the one hand, and holding that the predicate is satisfied on the other. But it is a common mistake to think that these classifications are mutually exclusive. This assumption was crucial to Russell's argument that his analysis shows, for example, that 'The Queen of England is married' is not 'about' Elizabeth. Though he rejects this application, Strawson uncritically accepts this distinction between the subject-predicate and the existential. But neither attempts to clarify the distinction, or recognizes the crucial difference between the attribution of a predicate as in believing of a certain thing it has a certain predicate, and, on the other hand, as in asserting of a certain thing that it has a certain predicate.

In the case of believing a thing to have a predicate, reference failure leaves nothing. That is, if I really have a thing in mind and think it to have a certain predicate, I will be right or wrong. But if I fail to have something in mind, then I cannot attribute a predicate.

On the other hand, cases have already been described in which someone, in an assertion, attributes a predicate to a thing even though he has no idea of that thing. Thus belief-ascribing a predicate is a different matter from assertion-ascribing a predicate. With belief-ascribing, reference failure is impossible, and the mechanism, so to speak, does not allow for it. But with assertion-ascribing, the machinery is there for a meaningful act which involves failure to refer.

It seems to me that Russell might have thought as follows. When someone asserts '*a* is *F*' and is sincere, then when there is no *a*, he must nonetheless be thinking something. He cannot be thinking of a thing, that it is *F*, so he must be thinking something else, to be elucidated in terms of quantified judgements, as opposed to subject-predicate ones. A failure to assertion-ascribe a predicate cannot be matched by a failure at belief-ascription, so the words involved in such an assertion cannot be a true guide to the speaker's state of mind. Russell's hoped-for ideal language was to be one in which words picture not only reality, but thoughts. The logically proper name is conceived by Russell as nothing but a label for a thing of which you have an idea directly in mind (perhaps only an idea or mental or sensory image could qualify as such a thing).

Unfortunately for this planned ideal language, the notion of a quantified belief or judgement is not nearly so clear or forceful as that of a subject-predicate belief. The belief that a thing has a property can be clearly contrasted with an assertion that the thing has that property. But to believe, say, that every man is mortal, can only be elucidated, if at all, in terms of the public sentence 'Every man is mortal', or equivalents. If Jones asserts that every man is mortal, and Smith is a man, he has predicated mortality of Smith. But if Jones believes that every man is mortal, it by no means follows merely from Smith's being a man that Jones believes him to be mortal. For Jones may have no idea at all of Smith. Thus some philosophers will analyze such statements as 'Jones believes every man is mortal' in terms of Jones being disposed to affirm the sentence 'Every man is mortal'. Against this it might be objected that Jones could believe that every man is mortal even if he were a German unable to respond to 'Every man is mortal'. It could then be replied that he would respond affirmatively if the meaning were explained to him. (We are not trying to identify the object of Jones' belief, but to explain what it is for him to have that belief.) We could skip that issue and just say that believing that every man is mortal is being disposed to assert that every man is mortal. This isn't strictly true, since someone might believe that every man is mortal but hate having to say so and be disposed to avoid doing so. Still, it may be true that our understanding of believing that every man is mortal is based on our understanding of accepting the assertion that every man is mortal.

This must seem to be a mere triviality! But our understanding of believing that, say, that dog is vicious, is not similarly based on understanding the idea of accepting the assertion that that dog is vicious. If anything, it goes the other way, and we can explain asserting that that dog is vicious in terms of believing that the dog is vicious, which someone can do with virtually no grasp of language. Asserting every man is mortal employs a conventional device which commits the assertor to the mortality of men he may know nothing of. Believing that every man is mortal involves understanding some such device and believing that its application has yielded a truth. So the device will not be good for a reductive explanation of believing.

It may be noted that my own account of what is involved in a sincere thought that a is F is similar to the one I have suggested Russell might have had in mind. One principal difference is just that while I, like Russell, regard the existential statement as indispensable in adequately representing the thought in connection with the possibility of failure of reference, I do not regard the existential statement as automatically not a referring statement.

It is true that when we know someone has asserted that there was at least one dog such that it belonged to Socrates and it bit Socrates, we know a certain amount about what has been claimed without knowing whether there was reference. So it might be said that reference would be a matter of additional information, perhaps a matter of 'pragmatic implication' as opposed to 'semantic assertion'. Well, what is said can be divided up as much as you please, with gerrymanders to preserve the application of this or that formal scheme. There is nothing wrong with that if it is not made out to be an account of more than it is.

Even with this concession, there is nothing to salvage for those who think not only that 'There is at least one F' never involves reference, but that adding 'and there is at most one F' still does not provide a basis for a referential use of a pronoun. I do not claim that someone who asserts both of these or things that entail them, perhaps widely separated or entwined in a complex series of claims, has made a reference. That may misrepresent his state of mind. But he has certainly asserted what is the basis for one, if he were aware of it.

Though it is grammatically subject-predicate, 'There is exactly one King of France' is not ontologically subject-predicate because it is the whole sentence, not some part of it, that is correlated with the thought that a condition is uniquely satisfied. There is thus some difference, though not a profound one, between subject-predicate and existential statements at the ontological level. However, pronouns within the 'scope' of an existential quantifier in natural language are not merely devices for formulating a compound condition for the quantifier to say is satisfied, as in quantification theory. They may be indicators of reference that contribute to independent thoughts and predications.

In the case of universal quantification, it has already been observed that the bound pronoun is even less an indicator of reference than in the existential case. When I say 'Everything is such that it is F', it is as if I said 'Pick anything you please – it is F'. Here 'it' is 'the thing you just picked'. But whether the thing you picked is F is relatively unimportant, though of course it has to be F if the statement is to be true. The important thing is that it doesn't matter what you pick. And of course one usually doesn't pick anything. The style of speech is as if you could proceed in that way. That you could is the essence of the matter, whether you do is insignificant.

If I say 'Everything is such that if it's a man, then it's mortal', and someone else says 'Yes, and it's also rational', is this two separate statements? Grammatically it is. From the way Geach writes on these matters one would expect him to be warning that this is really one statement with the universal quantifier as main connective. But there is no reason to be thus guided by what holds in the nearest version of this that can be formulated in quantification theory. My claim was that every man is mortal, my hearer added the distinct claim that every man is rational, expressing this thought in a form that borrows from devices I used in making my statement. Such borrowing is not allowed in standard quantification theory. But that is no reason to pretend it doesn't exist. In natural language a pronoun can be 'governed' by a quantifier and yet belong to a separate statement.

71 The formal distinction between subject-predicate, existential and universal does not apply to the propositions expressed by sentences, only to the sentences. 'There is exactly one King of France' and 'The property of being King of France has exactly one instance' express the same proposition, yet the first is existential, while the second is both ontologically and logically subject-predicate. This is a matter of formal classification. On the other hand, the most significant functional distinction between subject-predicate and existential involves other considerations besides the sentence and the proposition. Whether someone is concerned mainly with the property of being a King of France or with the thought that there is exactly one or with something else is obviously not merely a question either of the form of words or of the thought expressed. Insofar as the subject term is characterized as the one expressing the 'main concern' of the user of the sentence, the identification of the subject will be very dependent on knowing the interests of the user. This is emphasized in my approach. The same thought, as a proposition, can be described in a variety of ways, but some are better than others for presenting the thought as the thought of some person. A peasant who has been deceived into thinking France has a King may believe the proposition that there is exactly one King of France. This is the proposition that the property of being King of France has exactly one instance, but to describe his belief in this latter way may give a misleading impression of the peasant's state of mind. In many cases, merely giving an articulate and polished presentation of someone's belief may give the false impression that the believer himself could put it that way.

Fred Dretske (1972) has pointed out that emphasis can mark a considerable difference in what is said. I would say that '*Tom* won the race', 'Tom *won* the race', and 'Tom won *the race*' could all be used on an occasion, to express the same proposition. But in the blank of 'Bill has forgotten that ——', different thoughts would be likely to be represented, as Bill would be put forward as having forgotten different features of the proposition that Tom won the race. Bill's thinking of someone else as the winner, or that Tom only finished second, or that it was the race and not the shot-put, that Tom won, would all be different thoughts suggested perhaps by different emphasis.

It might be asked how it can be that the proposition that *Tom* won the race can be the same proposition as that Tom won *the race*, while the proposition that Bill has forgotten that *Tom* won the race is not the same proposition as the proposition that Bill has forgotten that Tom won *the race.* This is just another example of the possible ambiguity of a term in indirect speech, between its representing the thought of the speaker and its representing the thought of the person whose mental attitude is being reported.

We could oppose being functionally existential to being functionally subject-predicate if we focus on the intentions and emphasis of the thinker. Alternatively, we could avoid this degree of subjective variation by recognizing that not only are the pronominal uses linked to an existential quantifier not thereby precluded from being subjects, but that even the 'bare existence' claim, as a functional notion, can be functionally merely a type of subject-predicate claim, namely one in which the subject is a property and the predicate is just that of having one or more instances. Similarly, if the subject is a property, and the predicate is that of being subsumed under another property, we can say this is a type of singular subject-predicate judgement which is universal or general. This may sound surprising to those in the habit of opposing general to singular. But no end of confusion has been generated by simply assuming that these must be exclusive categories without providing a clear basis for distinguishing them. Formally, I have distinguished between 'Socrates is wise', 'There is something which is both Socrates and wise' and 'Everything is such that Socrates exists and if it is identical with Socrates, it is wise'. But functionally, there is nothing here but difference in emphasis which is served by the formal differences. Difference in emphasis is not difference in reference.

72   This is widely overlooked. Bernard Mayo (1962) discusses what he calls the 'Ryle-Prior-Peirce thesis (hence RPP)' put by Ryle as the doctrine that 'statements in the future tense cannot convey singular, but only general propositions, where statements in the present and past tense can convey both. More strictly, a statement to the effect that something will exist or happen is, *in so far*, a general statement (Ryle 1954, p. 27).

Mayo rightly observes that this thesis calls for an explanation of what is meant by singular and general. He then cites the formula (2) 'Θc' as a symbolization of 'Socrates is wise' and the formula (7) '$(Ex)(\Theta x. x = c)$' as a symbolization of 'There is a wise man, namely

Socrates'. The formula (5) '(Ex) Θx' symbolizes 'There is a wise man'. Mayo says 'for our purposes it is enough to notice that (5), since it contains no singular terms, must be a general statement'. Already he is relying heavily on the grammar of symbolic logic. For in English grammar, 'There is a wise man' does contain a grammatically singular term. But of course neither the English grammar nor the grammar of symbolic logic is really enough for Mayo's purposes. And he himself continues to add further considerations to these grammatical ones. He cites the two-part question, 'Is there anybody who is wise, and if so, who?', the first part of which is answered by (5), and says:

> When we proceed to answer the second part of the question, 'namely who?', by saying 'namely, Socrates', we do introduce a singular term. But this singular term *is not a subject term* and the sentence remains essentially general:
>
> $$(\exists x)\,(\Theta x.\ x = c) \qquad (7)$$
>
> This is to be read, say, 'There is a wise man, namely Socrates'. In certain contexts, the sentence 'Socrates is wise' (which is normally of type Θc (2)) could be used to express what (7) expresses: namely, when it is the answer to the question 'Who, if anyone, is wise?' This ambiguity – that 'Socrates is wise' may be either of type (2) or of type (7) – will be important in the sequel.
>
> (1962, p. 10)

What sort of ambiguity is it that can be marked off by logically equivalent symbolic statements? Perhaps some syntactic ambiguities could be so distinguished, but this is not such a case. There is of course a difference between setting out to point out that there is someone who is wise, and happening on Socrates as an example, and setting out to point out that Socrates is wise. There is a great variety of possible intentions that could be served by saying 'Socrates is wise'. But no particular class of these possible intentions is signaled by the words 'There is someone who is wise, namely Socrates'.

However, if it were only a matter of such things as the impression one is likely to get as to the interests of the speaker, there is a distinction here which might be arbitrarily described as a distinction between singular and general. Unfortunately, though, the notion of singularity is tied up with that of reference. And while Mayo does not explicitly say that someone asserting 'There is someone who is wise, namely Socrates' does not refer to Socrates just as much as someone who says 'Socrates is wise', this is implied by his remarks.

Mayo says:

> We have seen how the apparently singular proposition 'Socrates is wise' can be a general proposition of type (7), if it occurs as the answer to the question 'Who, if anyone, is wise?' Similarly, we have to see that an apparently singular proposition about the future, such as 'Professor Carnap will fly to the Moon', may well be a general proposition in disguise. It could be the answer to a question 'Will anyone fly to the Moon, and if so who?' More formally, 'There is a value of x such that "x flies to the moon" and "x is Professor Carnap" are both true.'   (1962, pp. 12–13)

I have already indicated dissatisfaction with the idea that merely being an answer to such a question as 'Will anyone fly to the moon, and if so, who?' should make an apparently singular subject-predicate statement not such after all, but really 'general'. But there is worse here than an unsatisfactory new notion of generality and singularity. Mayo continues:

> What are the reasons for insisting on this move? ... The difficulty of giving a reference to singular terms occurring in future-tensed statements is not obvious in the case of the 'Professor Carnap' example, just because we have indeed got Professor Carnap ... But it remains to be pointed out that, although we have 'got' the present Professor Carnap, we have not 'got' the future Professor Carnap, which is what the sentence is supposed to be about. The difficulty of giving a reference is certainly still there, however impatient we may be at the pedantic discrimination between two Professor Carnaps ... The sentence cannot refer at all and must, therefore, if asserted at all, be asserted as a general statement, as the RPP holds.   (p. 13)

This passage involves some dubious claims which are not relevant to our current enquiry. Some would say that whenever we have got Professor Carnap (which we unfortunately no longer have) it is the same one we have at any other time; others, such as Mayo, disagree. That is a question for another work. Again, some will hold that when we say of a present individual that he will fly to the moon, it is that present individual, not the future one at the time of flight (if there is a difference) that is the subject of the claim. These are reasonable doubts which can, however, be set aside. For present purposes the important point is that Mayo mistakenly assumes that somehow disqualifying 'Socrates' as 'the subject term' automatically also disqualifies it as referring. Further, he assumes that if we can show that a sentence contains no term which qualifies as referring, the statement made by use of that sentence cannot be about anything. These are mistaken assumptions.

This is not to say that an account of reference cannot be given which rules out reference to future individuals. On my account of reference, such reference is possible. It is a matter of being the thing which uniquely satisfies the condition, such that the thought that that condition is uniquely satisfied is connoted by the referring expression. Here 'is uniquely satisfied' is tenseless in that being satisfied at any time will do. If I say 'This cow's first calf will be a heifer', the thought is that there is going to be exactly one calf first born to this cow, which calf will be a heifer. The claim is grammatically and ontologically subject-predicate, and if true, is logically subject-predicate. But if we eliminate the 'tenselessness' and define 'reference' in terms of the thought that a certain condition is presently satisfied, then 'this cow's first calf will be a heifer' does not qualify as subject-predicate on that definition. Of course this is no guarantee that there is no reference going on elsewhere in the sentence. But with a proper clarification of both one version of a singular-general distinction and one version of reference, the 'RPP' can be transformed from an obscure source of controversy to a triviality.[1]

This does not save the idea that in 1962 'Professor Carnap will fly to the moon' did not make reference to Carnap. But the future individual in that case wasn't Carnap, but his flight to the moon. More accurately, 'Professor Carnap will fly to the moon exactly one time' expresses the same proposition as 'There will occur exactly one flight to the moon by Professor Carnap'. It is a good example of how a statement can provide a basis of reference without containing anything that qualifies as an ontological singular term purporting to have that reference.

If I say 'Professor Carnap will fly to the moon exactly one time

---

[1] As was said earlier, Mayo's views are a case of a widely held doctrine. One prominent example of the same view is in Strawson (1959). Since I criticized that version in my review of *Individuals*, I have chosen a fresh example here.

and he will do it in a blue flight suit', the 'it' correlates with the thought that there is going to be exactly one flight to the moon by Professor Carnap, and can thus be regarded as referring in spite of the fact that in the preceding context there is no similar referring expression. There is merely the basis for one.[2]

73 It has been suggested that one sort of functionally existential statement could be defined as a subject-predicate statement where the subject is a property and the predicate is that of having one or more instances. Similarly we could say that a subject-predicate statement is universal if the subject is a property and the predicate is that of being subsumed under some other property.

'The property of being a man has instances' is functionally existential by this definition. What about 'The Washington Monument has instances'? Does it matter whether its subject is a property? The former proposition can also be expressed by 'There is at least one man', while the latter cannot be put in that form but only by 'There is at least one instance of the Washington Monument' (and even that doesn't express the proposition well). But that is not important. Perhaps we could say that a statement is functionally existential if there is something which it says has instances. But, on the one hand, every statement attributes having instances to something if we ignore emphasis, that is, for example, 'Every man is mortal' attributes having instances to the subsumption relation, even though this is not usually the point the user would be interested, or even able, to make; and, on the other hand, if we emphasize emphasis, 'The King of France in 1975 has instances' would fail to qualify as existential while 'The Queen of England in 1975 has instances' would qualify. This could be repaired by saying that to qualify as existential it need only be that it is represented that there is something which has instances, rather than that there must actually be a thing which is said to have instances.

These distinctions between general and singular statements are not nearly as firm as those drawn earlier between general and singular

[2] In Cargile (1970) I held (in a footnote) that it is a rule of traditional grammar that 'A pronoun requires another expression in the surrounding context which purports to have the same reference, if any, and does not purport to have no reference at all' (p. 139 n.6). On this basis I held that traditional grammar would frown on 'There are no lions – they just don't exist'. This was not an important claim in that paper but it was certainly an unwarranted one. At any rate, what traditional grammar had to say on such a topic, which I should not have presumed myself to know, is no help anyway with the question of reference.

terms. But in both cases, the important thing is to make clear the kind of basis such distinctions have, and to show that it is a mistake to think that they mark epistemological distinctions concerning such things as the degree of familiarity a speaker has with an object. The principal motive for our discussion of singular terms was to show that reference failure is no threat to the classical laws of logic and semantics. This problem is not nearly as important with general statements and does not even arise from the sort of quantification just discussed. There is a difficulty about reference in connection with the universal affirmative of traditional logic, but for general statements the principal problem as far as semantic paradoxes is concerned is to make clear what predications are performed by general statements and how such predications are related to what is said.

The modern theory of quantification takes the singular statement as basis. Generality is introduced by replacing the singular term with a variable and appending quantifiers. This makes a mathematically admirable system which should not be blamed for those adherents of it who press too far superficial formal analogies with natural language.

On the other hand, in traditional logic, the main focus was a certain kind of general statement – the 'four categorical forms' – (A) 'All A's are B's', (E) 'No A's are B's', (I) 'Some A's are B's and (O) 'Some A's are not B's'. Sometimes the singular statement would be 'represented' as being a categorical (A) statement such as 'All things that are Socrates are things that are wise' for 'Socrates is wise'. The motive, presumably, was economy in rules of inference. But it is a false economy, since it relies on the ability to make the unanalyzed inference from 'Socrates is wise' to its universal affirmative counterpart. Furthermore, there is some question about existential import for (A) statements, which does not correspond well with the question of reference for such a statement as 'Socrates is wise'.

The quantifiers so far discussed work with the general term 'thing'. In natural language this is unusual. Quantifiers are used with more restricted general terms. Rather than say 'Everything is such that if it is a man, it is a mortal', we say 'Every man is mortal'. The categorical forms further differ in that their instances use the grammatical plural form.

Consider 'All men are mortal'. Mill says that this 'asserts that the objects denoted by the subject (man) possess the attributes connoted by the predicate (mortal)'. Later on he says that what is asserted is that 'whatever has the attributes connoted by the subject, has also those connoted by the predicate; that the latter set of attributes *constantly accompany* the former set' (i.v.4). In a footnote to this claim he considers the objection that the proposition is concerned with the *extension* of the subject term and the *intension* of the predicate term, which was what was implied in Mill's own first statement of what is asserted by 'All men are mortal'. His answer is that the objection is true enough, but the extension of the subject term is 'apprehended and indicated solely through the attributes' which it connotes.

This answer may be aimed in part at maintaining the idea that a class is 'nothing beyond' the property that determines it. This idea has been discussed, and it may be set aside for now. The first problem with Mill's attempt to describe what is said in saying 'All men are mortal' is that he portrays it as making a claim about the terms 'man' and 'mortal'. I have disagreed with Lockwood's implication that this is always wrong, but I cannot accept Mill's implication that it is always right, either. For someone with the usual understanding of the terms, the terms merely introduce features of the judgement, without themselves being included.

A further problem in Mill's account is his treatment of 'man' as subject term when the grammatical fact is that the term is 'men'. Perhaps I am mistaken in speaking of the 'grammatical fact' here. 'Men' is the plural form of 'man' and it might be said that 'man' is occurring in its plural form. It does appear that Mill regards the denotation and connotation of 'men' to be the same as for 'man'. But the term 'men' is not true of the same things as the term 'man', it cannot be predicated of the same things, and that 'men' is the plural form of 'man' cannot be used to explain this difference away, without first being explained itself.

Mill's mistake of making the terms themselves subjects is easily rectified. We could simply revise his two versions of what is said by 'All men are mortal' as follows. The first would be 'The objects that are instances of the property of being a man possess the attribute mortality.' The second would be 'Whatever has the attribute of being a man has the attribute of being mortal – the latter attribute constantly *accompanies* the former.'

It is tempting to ignore the distinction between singular and plural, and I do not regard it as an important one. Still, it seems that the term 'men' is true of *classes* or groups of men. It is implausible that there is a profound difference between 'Bill and Bob are both men' and 'Bill is a man and Bob is a man'. It seems that the same property is attributed to Bill in both statements. And yet in the former, Bill and Bob are explicitly presented as a pair of men, that is, as a class or group, while in the latter, though of course this fact is expressed if there is such a fact, it is not signaled by formal devices.

It may thus be worthwhile discussing the analysis of reference in the categorical forms using the grammatical plural, in terms of classes. This is not to suggest that the classes are as described by modern set theory, or to give up my earlier announced sympathy for a 'no-class' theory.

74 For one analysis, we may start with the idea expressed by Russell (1903) that '*men* and *all men* (which I shall regard as synonyms) do denote, and I shall contend that what they denote is the class composed of all men' (p. 67; and chap. 6, sec. 67). Russell's idea here might be put by saying that the connotation of 'men' in 'All men are mortal' is 'the concept of the class' or the property of being the class, while the denotation is the class. Russell says 'men (the object denoted by the concept men) are the class'. This is confusing, and reflects Russell's worry about the distinction between 'the class as one' and 'the class as many'. The literature on this distinction could be used as inspirational matter for 'no-class' theorists. At any rate, suppose it is said that 'all men' stands for the class of men, thus making a singular reference. To complete the picture, let it be said that 'mortal' stands for the class of mortals, and that 'are' stands for being subsumed under, so that, on this analysis, the sentence would have the same form as 'The class of men is subsumed under the class of mortals'.

It is important to note that this analysis, whether or not it is plausible, is incomparably superior to the analysis of 'All men are mortal' according to which it has the form of a quantified conditional such as 'If anything is a man, then it is a mortal'. This is because the former analysis actually tells how to exhibit the sentence 'All men are mortal' (as well as the sentence 'The class of men is subsumed under the class of mortals') as a substitution instance of the restricted form '(term for a class) (term denoting the subsumption relation) (term for a class)'. In other words, this claim is supported by presenting the alleged common form, reducing the debatable part of the claim to such questions as whether 'all men' really does stand for the class of men, 'are' really does stand for subsumption, and so on. But no one who claims that 'All men are mortal' has the form of a quantified conditional has ever even *tried* to exhibit this sentence as a substitution instance of such a form. Those who make this claim have not understood what they were saying. They should have been content to claim that the function accomplished by 'All men are mortal' is equally well served by a certain quantified conditional.

If we ask whether the class subsumption analysis of 'All men are mortal' is true, we have to remember that we are dealing with a question of formal classification. Taken by itself, the exhibition of a sentence as of a certain form may be of little or no interest, unless the classifications of its parts are extendable in a natural and systematic way to other sentences, in such a way that interesting generalizations (say, about validity) can be made in terms of such formal classification.

Seen in this way, the class subsumption analysis is not very satisfactory if we consider the sentences 'Some men are mortal' and 'No men are mortal'. For what class could 'Some men' naturally be taken to denote? Still less could 'no men' be plausibly taken to denote a class. And yet it seems natural to expect a formal connection between these sentences.

75   Here is an alternative analysis: 'men' stands for the class of men, 'are' stands for being a member of (rather than for being subsumed under), 'mortal' stands for the class of mortals, and 'all', 'some' or 'no' respectively tell how many members of the class of men are being held to also be members of the class of mortals.

On this class membership analysis, a unified formal analysis is given for the traditional four categorical forms of proposition. This should incline us to rate it as better than the class subsumption analysis. But then we can say, with respect to this analysis, that 'The class of men is subsumed under the class of mortals' does not have the same form as 'All men are mortal', since it does not contain an expression which functions as 'all' does.

The class subsumption analysis makes 'All men are mortal' of logically singular subject-predicate form. With the class membership analysis, the question is not so clear. There is a term denoting exactly one thing. But is the predicate predicated of this thing? This question depends on what is identified as the predicate expression and what as the predicate. And this could be done in more than one way.

It could be said that 'are mortal' is the predicate expression and being a member of the class of mortals is the predicate. Then the sentence would not be of subject-predicate form, since the predicate is not predicated of the subject.

However, this approach has the defect that the predicate should not be viewed as predicated at all, which might make it unsatisfactory to say that it is the predicate for the sentence. For if the predicate is being a member of the class of mortals, and it is viewed as predicated, it would have to be viewed as predicated distributively of all men. But then in order to have parity of form, 'No men are mortal' would have to be viewed as predicating this same predicate, being a member of the class of mortals, distributively of no men. And this would be to say nothing of what 'No men are mortal' says, since distributing a predicate among no men amounts to nothing.

Of course it might be said that in 'No men are mortal' the property of being mortal is not predicated of no men, but withheld from all men. But this represents a change in the function of 'no' as compared with 'all'. On this account, 'all' functions to tell how many, while 'no' does something more.

Even if this is accepted, the case of 'some' would not appear to work in the same way. To say that 'some' functions to indicate that mortality is being predicated merely of some members of the class of men is usually rejected out of hand. It would usually be denied that this is even *part* of what is done in 'Some men are mortal' on the grounds that such an assertion does not predicate mortality at all. This is an issue which will be discussed later. For now, it is enough to say that even if 'Some A's are B's' does somehow in some cases achieve the function of predicating B of some A's, this cannot be generally the case because of the cases such that there are no A's. When we speak of predicating B of all the A's or denying B of all the A's, we can add 'if there are any', and claim to have covered the entire function of the categorical statement. But even if the generally rejected idea that part of the function of 'Some A is B' is to predicate B of some A's, if there are any, is let pass, there is also the function of claiming that there are some. This makes for a notorious asymmetry between the universal categoricals and the particular categoricals.

So if the predicate of the sentence is to be viewed as predicated, and a unitary formal treatment of the categorical forms is desired, it would seem that the predicate expression on the membership analysis of 'All men are mortal' would have to include the quantifier 'all' as a part. And the predicate would be having all members belonging to the class of mortals, and this would be predicated of the class of men. Then 'No men are mortal' would not have the same predicate, but would have, rather, having no members belonging to the class of mortals for the predicate. With 'Some men are mortal', having some members in the class of mortals would be the predicate. The formal unity would come from within the predicate, the difference would come from the quantifier part, and would be merely a difference in 'number'.

On this class membership analysis, it would be best to regard 'All men are mortal' as a corruption of 'All men are mortals'. In traditional logic the predicate was often revised to exhibit it as containing a term for a class. For example, 'All birds fly' might be rewritten 'All birds are flying things'. Insofar as this procedure was warranted, it must be because even in 'All birds fly', 'fly' somehow functions to denote the class of flying things. Otherwise, it must be conceded that 'All birds fly' and 'All birds are flying things' differ in form. This is probably the truth of the matter. But natural language has such a variety of forms for accomplishing the same purpose that attempts to impose an artificial economy are understandable. And of course it need not be an outright error to do such a thing as treat 'All birds fly' and 'All birds are flying things' as of the same form. It may merely involve cumbersome and implausible rulings about the function of parts of the sentences.

76 The appeal to distributive predication is more plausible for 'Every man is mortal'. Here there is some justification for the grammatical classification of singularity if we say that being mortal is being predicated of each man taken one at a time. The fact that 'man' is a general term applying to each man fits well with this. When I say 'There is a toilet for all families' I seem to describe a deplorable sanitary arrangement, while 'There is a toilet for every family' is not so outrageous. Of course this is a delicate distinction commonly obliterated in everyday speech, but then it would be too

optimistic to hope that an indisputable formal classification is forth-coming. I only hope to make clear what a formal classification should do, so that choices usually left obscure can be openly dis-cussed.

The distributive predication analysis, even if it is more plausible for the grammatical singular, still encounters essentially the same difficulty for 'some' that arose when it was applied to the gramma-tically plural case. If 'Every man is mortal' attributes mortality to each man taken singly, it seems that we should go on to say that 'Some man is mortal' predicates mortality of some man. And this is usually dismissed as absurd.

This might not seem absurd if one regarded such a technical device as Hilbert's epsilon operator to be a genuine referential device. I do not believe it was originally put forward as a genuine referring expression, but the symbol '$(\epsilon x)Fx$' is interpreted by assigning a class to 'F' and then picking a member of that class at random to be the denotation of '$(\epsilon x)Fx$'. If the class is empty (speaking in terms of modern set theory), then '$(\epsilon x)Fx$' was arbi-trarily taken to denote the null class. However, I will discuss this operator from my own perspective, and will assume that when the class assigned to F is empty, '$(\epsilon x)Fx$)' fails to denote.

In the use of the epsilon operator in mathematical logic, it was shown how to define quantifiers in terms of it. This would work well for existential quantification on my account, since $F((\epsilon x)Fx)$ is clearly equivalent to $(Ex)Fx$. But universal quantification would not be so straightforward. If it were defined from existential quantification as usual, as $\sim(Ex)\sim Fx$, then this would come to $\sim \sim F((\epsilon x) \sim Fx)$, and cancelling the double negation would give $F((\epsilon x)\sim Fx)$ which on my semantic rule about reference failure in atomic contexts could never be true.

I think this could be avoided by distinguishing between *de re* and *de dicto* negation and making the appropriate rules governing them. Without attempting to do this in detail, the idea in the above difficulty would be that '$(x)Fx$' would be defined in terms of the epsilon operator as 'It is not the case that the member hereby ran-domly selected from the non-F's is a non-F', where 'non' is *de re* negation and 'it is not the case' *de dicto*, so there is no double nega-tion to be cancelled.

The only reason for bringing up this crude sketch of a formal system is to ask if such a device would not warrant the usually rejected view that $(Ex)Fx$ involves predicating F of some F, if there are any.

A game could be arranged (I imagine) in which $(Ex)Fx$ would 'abbreviate' $F((\epsilon x)Fx)$, and asserting it would involve predicating F of some F, if there are any. There could be a referee who actually runs out and tags some F (if any) without the player who asserts '$(Ex)Fx$' getting to watch the tagging or know anything about it except that it is done. Then the player could follow '$(Ex)Fx$' with 'and furthermore, it is G' and he would be right or wrong depending whether the F assigned to his assertion by the referee was G. (To work this out, one would have to explain how the quantifier works with non-atomic formulae, and within the scope of other operators, but the simple cases are enough for present purposes.)

Would a model of this sort justify regarding 'Some man is mortal' as predicating mortality of some man, and 'Some men are mortal' likewise? I think not. For such a model only shows again how in a formal system the semantic rules can mislead by ignoring work that is done in order to apply them. One might say 'In evaluating "$(Ex)Fx$" look through the domain to see if you encounter an F. The first thing you come across that is F, mark "$(Ex)Fx$" true, and by the way, call that the *referent* of the bound variable.' This 'by the way' is a completely idle use of 'referent'. It might not be idle if the search of the domain had already been performed by the speaker and figured in the thought he expresses. But that is left out in the rule of evaluation.

To add to the semantic rules for standard predicate logic the rule that the first thing you encounter that satisfies 'Fx' is to be the 'referent' of the bound variable in '$(Ex)Fx$' makes no difference whatever to the formal valuations. And yet it involves the consequence that the thus supplemented '$(Ex)Fx$' is about the first F encountered and thus would not have been true had that thing not been F. And this does not correctly represent the natural language 'There is at least one F'.

(When I say that this extra rule makes no difference to the valuations, I mean the assignment of truth values. It would make a difference in the individuation of valuations, since two interpretations that would have been called identical on the old rules might differ because one ran through the domain looking for an F in a different order from the other, so that different 'referents' were assigned. This is not a significant difference.)

It might be said at this point that I cannot appeal to the fact that 'There is at least one *F*' is not about any *F* if there are lots of *F*'s, because I argued earlier that this is not so. That would be a misunderstanding. I argued that this is not always so, not necessarily so. But it is an essential feature of this sort of statement that it can be so in some cases. And this is eliminated in the above formal model. Some assertions of the form 'There is an *F*' are such that there is a certain individual which must be *F* in order that they be true. But the fact that other statements of this form do not have this feature must not be lost track of. A formal system based on the epsilon operator would retain certain features of pronouns that are lost in the standard theory. But it would itself eliminate other features.

77   There are two ways in which an assertion of 'Socrates owned a dog' might be true even if Phido (who in fact belongs to him) had not belonged to him. One is if Socrates actually owns a dozen dogs besides Phido. The other is if Socrates had owned some other dog, even though he in fact does not. The former sort of case is enough to establish the point of the foregoing paragraph. The latter sort of case can be a source of obscurity and puzzlement, owing to its counter-factual nature. When we say that Socrates might have owned a different dog, though he did not, this seems the sort of thing which can be true, and yet we may become confused over the basis for calling such a claim true.

I appealed to this sort of possibility in rejecting the idea that statements about physical objects are individuated by their referents. I claim that it is always logically possible that the proposition which is in fact about a certain physical object be the same proposition, and that object not exist.

However, someone might reply that, even on my own analysis, 'That is a marble' could make a statement individuated by its referent. For it could be held that the statement makes reference to the cause of certain experiences, which is my view, and could then hold that experiences are individuated by their causes. Thus if a marble is causing certain features of my experience, on this view it would not be logically possible that anything else could have caused those very same experiences.

(This radical view must be distinguished from the innocuous (though obscure, but more importantly, irrelevant) view that nothing else *could* cause those same experiences (as opposed to 'could have caused'). Suppose that Bill is Bob's brother. It might be logically impossible for Bill to cease to be Bob's brother and come to be someone else's. This could be so even if it is logically possible that Bill could have never been Bob's brother but could have been someone else's.)

The idea would be that if certain features of my experiences are caused by a marble, then in any state of affairs in which the same marble was not operating in the same way, the experiences could not be the same either, and the reference to 'these experiences' being different, the statement made with 'That is a marble' would be different. On this view, the statement made with 'That is a marble' would be, if true, necessarily true, because that very same statement could not possibly have occurred in reference to any other situation.

This view makes difficulties for my doctrine that a statement about a physical object is not individuated by its referent, and also for other common opinions about logical possibility. However, it does not affect my principal criticism of the referential-attributive distinction or of the opposition between subject-predicate and existential. If someone is holding out his hand to me, palm up, with fingers open except for the thumb, which is in the palm, and there is a marble in his palm in plain view, I may say 'That is a marble' or I may say 'There is at least one marble in his palm', allowing for the possibility that another is concealed under his thumb. No epistemological distinction is marked by these formally different statements.

However, it may be said that if a distinct but identical appearing marble had been held in the same way, the statement made with the first sentence would have been different, but not the statement made by the second.

It could be held that the first statement is concerned with causes of my experience, while the second is not, or need not be. For even if the possibility of the reference is there, I may regard 'There is at least one marble in his palm' as not concerned with this information about experiences and restricting itself to there being at least one marble there. Thus it could be held to be true even if it wasn't a marble in plain view, but a perfectly round marshmallow, if there were a marble concealed under the thumb.

As before, I stress that this is possible, but not necessary. If I add to 'There is at least one marble in his hand', 'which is an agate',

I might be merely adding a condition to being a marble. But if I add 'and it is white' one may ask what I mean by 'it', and I may mean, and in the present sort of case would quite naturally be taken to mean, '*that* marble', the one of which I said 'That is a marble'. This possibility cannot be taken away from the words 'There is at least one marble in his hand'.

When someone knows that a condition is uniquely satisfied, there is the basis for reference. When he believes that a condition is satisfied there is the basis for a sincere attempt. But there are various other cases of a borderline sort. As has been observed before, someone may have the basis of reference and not know it in various ways.

78   Suppose that Jones asserts 'There is at least one American involved in the scandal' and is, so far, quite right. However, unbeknownst to Jones, there is exactly one American involved, Aloysius P. Kirklebaum, a Boston resident. For some reason we needn't describe, Jones goes on 'and he resides in Boston'. Is this true or false? We know it is dishonest of Jones, but we know that a lie does not have to be a falsehood. However, I would say that in this case it is a falsehood, because 'he' is properly taken to mean 'the person I can single out by means of some individuating condition who was aforecited as being an American involved in the scandal'.

On the other hand, if Jones had said 'There is an American involved in the scandal and he lives in Boston', he might have spoken truly though still be lying. For then his 'he' might naturally be taken as simply cancelling any implication of indefiniteness and meaning 'the American involved in the scandal'. In this latter case, I would say that Jones has referred to Kirklebaum, in spite of the fact that Jones does not know he has referred to anyone.

When a statement expresses a condition and claims it to be uniquely satisfied, we have the basis of individuating or specific references. When it merely expresses a condition and attributes a predicate to whatever, if anything, satisfies it, we have conditional, or general, reference. Both sorts of reference are the basis for predication. 'All men are mortal' predicates mortality of Socrates just as surely as 'Socrates is mortal', though the basis of the predication is general reference in the former, and specific reference in the latter.

However, this is only equally sure because it is certain that Socrates is a man. If I say 'All males are mortal' and someone of doubtful gender is a disputed case of a male, then insofar as the issue of maleness is in doubt, it is doubtful whether being mortal has been predicated of that person. Of course this doubt is only our doubt, and in reality, it is a male or isn't and being mortal has been predicated or not, but we may not know which. I will call this sort of predication 'conditional' though with misgivings, because the term might give the impression that the predication is somehow pending, in the way a conditionally accepted student's admission is. There is no such temporal lag whatever. It is just that for us to know whether the property was predicated, we need to know if the condition is satisfied.

By contrast, a direct predication does not require the satisfaction of a condition. This is the point I argued earlier to have been misunderstood by the referentialists. Recall, for example, the case where I say 'That miserable syphilitic is trying to seduce Mary', where the man is not syphilitic but does indeed have designs on Mary. My statement is false. There is a condition the man uniquely satisfies, which I know he uniquely satisfies, which is included in the thought I express. But the condition I employ for individuating reference includes a mistake, and yet the predication is still accomplished and is true.

Perhaps this could happen even with conditional predication. If I say 'I'm afraid George's future is rather bleak, for it has now been conclusively established that all absinthe drinkers eventually go mad', I might be taken to have predicated being headed for madness of George, even if it turns out that I was mistaken in thinking him to be an absinthe drinker. There is no difference whatever between direct and conditional predication as far as predication is concerned. There is a difference in means which I name only with hesitation and with no desire for emphasis.

When someone asserts 'There is an American involved in the scandal' and he expresses the thought that a condition is uniquely satisfied, either the condition of being an American involved in the scandal or the condition of being beyond that otherwise specifiable by him, and he is right, he has the basis of specific reference. If he asserts this sentence and does not express such a thought, then even if there is only one American involved, the basis for specific reference is not in the assertion.

However, $(\text{E}x)Fx$ is logically equivalent to $(x)((y)(x \neq y \rightarrow \sim Fy)$

$\rightarrow Fx$). To assert 'There is an American involved in the scandal' is the same (in the case where there is no basis for specific reference) as asserting 'Everyone such that everyone other than him is not an American involved in the scandal is an American involved in the scandal'. And this is to predicate being an American involved in the scandal of anyone who satisfies the condition of being such that everyone other than him is not an American involved in the scandal. In the case in which Aloysius P. Kirklebaum satisfies this condition, 'There is an American involved in the scandal' predicates being an American involved in the scandal of Kirklebaum on the basis of a general reference to Kirklebaum, by virtue of his satisfying a certain condition. (That he satisfies it uniquely is incidental.)

It is the same style of predication, namely conditional, when I say 'All men are mortal', or 'If a thing is a man, it is a mortal', or 'If Socrates is a man, then Socrates is a mortal'. The latter is based on an individuating reference, even though the conditional does not claim that a condition is uniquely satisfied, but only that if a certain condition is uniquely satisfied and the thing that satisfies it is a man, then that thing is mortal.

One can also predicate mortality of Socrates by saying 'If Plato is a man, then Socrates is mortal'. This again is conditional predication, but the individual to which the predicate is attributed does not figure in the condition set out in the antecedent.

When I speak of a conditional predication, I mean a performance which is a predication if a condition is satisfied. There is also another way that an act of conditional predication can be a predication even if the condition is not satisfied. That is the case in which the performer of the conditional predication (either a person, or in the abstract case, a sentence itself) asserts that the condition is satisfied. Thus if Jones says 'If Socrates drank absinthe, Plato had mumps' and also says 'Socrates drank absinthe', then insofar as this pair of assertions are a united performance (rather than a 'flip-flop') Jones has predicated having had mumps of Plato.

Similarly, the sentence 'If Socrates drank absinthe, then Plato had mumps, and furthermore, Socrates drank absinthe' predicates having had mumps of Plato. If the assertion of the condition is conveyed by a separate sentence, then they would have to be viewed as a unit to warrant treating them as making the predication.

This sort of predication could be called 'enthymematic' to distinguish it from predications that come about not through the assertion that a condition is satisfied, but by the condition's being satisfied.

If Jones says 'If all the Straws are happy, then Socrates drank hemlock', and then says 'Furthermore, Jack Straw is happy, Mary Straw is happy, Bill Straw is happy and Betty Straw is happy', and (perhaps unbeknownst to him) that is all the Straws there are, then he has predicated having drunk hemlock of Socrates. Jones has not asserted that the condition of the predication is satisfied, but he has asserted a compound condition which satisfies that condition. He has not asserted that all the Straws are happy, but he has asserted, of every Straw, that that Straw is happy. And that is enough to make his performance include, perhaps unbeknownst to him, the predication of having drunk hemlock, of Socrates.

This theory of predication does not conflict with the traditional view of the truth conditions for any statement, except, as will be seen, for the semantic paradoxes. But it does recognize the performance of predications that are usually overlooked. I hope that I have sufficiently emphasized the need for distinguishing between the knowledge and interests of a speaker and his hearers and the logical powers of the language he employs. My theory of predication is concerned with the latter.

Stressing this point may prevent some likely, but superficial, criticisms. For example, it is a trivial consequence of my theory that whenever anyone asserts anything, he predicates something of everything. That is, to assert that p is to predicate being such that p of everything. As far as assessing truth and falsity is concerned, this is completely trivial and represents nothing new. But it might be complained that my theory thus has it that to say anything is to talk about everything. However, as long as the notion of 'talking about' is connected with such notions as 'knowing what you are talking about', it cannot be used so that 'predicating something of x' entails 'talking about x'.

While I am convinced that my theory of predication is a correct analysis of the concept of predication, a more important point is that it provides a basis for assessing truth values which corresponds exactly to the traditional assessment except for the paradoxes, which, unlike the traditional approach, it assesses correctly and consistently.

79   These facts about predication connect in an important way with assertion when we apply them to the predication of the property of

being true. When I say 'If Bill is sick then Boyd is sad' I may as well have said 'If Bill is sick then the proposition that Boyd is sad is true'. If Bill is sick, then I have predicated truth of the proposition that Boyd is sad. As was observed earlier, to predicate truth of a proposition is to assert it.

As was noted, this conflicts with our natural tendency to assume that we always know what we are asserting. I have appealed to the idea that one asserts what one believes. It seems to me a fundamental defect in Strawson's view that when someone sincerely says 'The present King of France is wise' he thereby expresses the belief that there is exactly one King of France, and yet on Strawson's account he does not assert this.

However, the fact that, when someone puts a proposition forward as an object of his belief, in the normal case he is thereby asserting that proposition, does not entail that conversely, whenever someone asserts a proposition, he puts it forward as an object of his belief. In the primary case of individuating reference, the belief is the guide to the assertion because the assertion is the expression of belief. But when the reference is general, assertion employs formal devices that apply to things that have not been made objects of thought.

What then, is asserting? What is it that all cases of asserting have in common, like the common ingredient in all alcoholic beverages, or the common property of being a game, that unites such otherwise disparate activities as chess and footsie? Well, it is attributing truth to a proposition. This is something one might well want explained further, to see how actors and parrots do not assert what they utter, and so on. But truth can be attributed to a proposition one not only does not believe (as in lying) but does not even know of. We could distinguish between knowingly asserting and asserting without knowing. But I prefer to simply modify 'assert' with 'knowingly' when that is important to convey.

If Jones says 'What Smith said at noon is true' and Smith said 'All men are mortal', then by my account, Jones has asserted that all men are mortal, whether or not he knows it. To say that Jones has asserted that all men are mortal is misleading because people naturally take 'asserted' as 'knowingly asserted'. But that can be cleared up by an explanation. A more difficult problem arises in the fact that to say that Jones, in saying that what Smith said at noon is true, asserted that all men are mortal, does not give an account of what Jones said or asserted, in full. For Jones did more than assert that all men are mortal. He also asserted that Smith said something at noon. To give a full account of what Jones said we need something like 'Jones said that what Smith said at noon (which was that all men are mortal) is true', where the parentheses help to warn that Jones may not have known that was what Smith said.

This points to a real ambiguity in the notion of asserting or saying which, though it may be aggravated by my account of asserting, does not arise from it. The ambiguity is reflected in the conflict between the following two assumptions, which are each independently plausible. First, if someone asserts '*p* and *q* and *r*' it seems that he has, in so doing, asserted *p*. Second, if someone asserts '*p* and *q* and *r*' and asserts nothing else, then he has made exactly one assertion, a compound assertion. This is an obvious conflict. By the first assumption, the number of assertions can immediately be extended to three, namely asserting *p*, asserting *q*, and asserting *r*. And then there is asserting '*p* and *q*', asserting '*p* and *r*', and so on. What I will say is that in asserting '*p* and *q* and *r*' the speaker has *non-assessably* asserted *p*, *q*, *r*, '*p* and *q*', '*q* and *r*', and so on, while he has *assessably* asserted '*p* and *q* and *r*'.

By 'non-assessable' I do not mean that we could not assess the truth value of the above assertion of *p*. We could call it true if *p* is true, false if *p* is false. But we do not, simply because we do not *count* the (non-assessable) assertion of *p* made in the course of making the *one* assertion '*p* and *q* and *r*' as an assertion made by the speaker. We count it as part of an assertion. But it is a kind of assertion. Thus there is a need for a distinction which I mark with 'assessable' and 'non-assessable', while warning against possible misleading overtones of the term 'non-assessable'.

My doctrines about assertion and predication have the consequence that the number of non-assessable assertions is drastically increased, since besides ordinary compounds my rules will include the results of general predications of truth or falsity such as 'Every Cretan assertion is false', which will make many non-assessable assertions on my account. But these non-assessable assertions are treated exactly as they are in the already accepted cases, as necessary but not sufficient conditions of the truth of the assertion of which they are a part.

An adequate description of what is said, what is asserted (as an assessable assertion), from the standpoint of assigning a truth value, must describe all the non-assessable assertions that the assessable assertion made. This fact is of fundamental importance in dealing with the semantic paradoxes.

I have accepted the idea that most acts of predication made by a general assertion do not belong to the content of the assertion, to what is said, though they do contribute to the truth conditions of what is said. This is a common view, though it is not the view implicit in the semantics for modern quantification theory. For example, it would commonly be granted that whether Bill and Mary Jones have children or remain childless will make no difference to what is said in asserting 'All men are mortal'. That is, the proposition asserted is the same in either case, though its truth value would be affected if Bill and Mary had an immortal child. However, a translation of 'All men are mortal' into '(x) (man$(x) \rightarrow$ mortal $(x))$' could approximate the meaning of the original only with a domain specified as range for the quantifier. The domain would either include children of Bill and Mary or not, and thus whether they were credited with children or not would change the claim made. In the semantics for modern modal logic a closer approximation to the common idea of a proposition can be made.

Whether it should be made is another matter. But I grant the common view except for the case in which the predicate in the act of predication is truth (or falsity). Predicating truth is asserting. What is said in saying 'Every Cretan assertion is false' is not known until every Cretan assertion is known. We may know enough to determine truth or falsity without knowing what is said. But this will require at least knowing something of what is said.

Someone who asserts that every Cretan assertion is false is asserting the denial of each Cretan assertion. But to believe that every Cretan assertion is false does not entail believing the denial of every Cretan assertion. Thus we are brought to cases in which the relation between the object of belief and the object of assertion is not the straightforward one I stressed so strongly in the cases I called primary. To say that someone asserts (or believes) that every Cretan assertion is false may fail to give an account of his assessable assertion which he made in making the non-assessable assertion that every Cretan assertion is false. To believe that every Cretan assertion is false is to believe that the assertion that every Cretan assertion is false, is true. This can be done even by someone who does not know what is asserted (assessably) in asserting that every Cretan assertion is false. This divergence between what is asserted and what is believed is due to the dependence of generality in belief upon subscribing to the working of formal devices even when the believer does not know all that has been done by the working of the devices.

This view is no doubt paradoxical in the sense of being contrary to popular opinion. But it is this popular opinion that is responsible for real paradox – the semantic paradoxes. Before demonstrating this, it will be necessary to characterize the semantic paradoxes and comment on some of the main responses that have been made to them.

7
Semantic paradoxes

80   Consider the following two assumptions:

  (1) A sentence is true if and only if what it says is true.
  (2) What the sentence
    (A) A is not true
  says is that the sentence A is not true.

From (1) it follows that

  (3) The sentence A is true if and only if what the sentence A says is true,
and from (2) and (3) it follows that

  (4) The sentence A is true if and only if, that the sentence A is not true, is true.

We then add to (1) and (2) the assumption

  (5) That the sentence A is not true, is true if and only if the sentence A is not true.

From (4) and (5) follows the contradiction
  (6) The sentence A is true if and only if the sentence A is not true.

This means that either (1) or (2) or (5) must be false. Some who have written on this topic have doubted (1), and their view must be considered. But my own view is that (2) is false, and that (5) must be modified in light of this. My main concern will be with explaining why (2) is false, and with setting out the true answer to the question as to what, if anything, it is that the sentence A says.

This enterprise, of making clear what, if anything, A says, must be extended to apply also to a great variety of other sentences which share with A the property that the most natural assumptions about what it is they say are inconsistent with self-evident principles. These sentences are known collectively as *semantic paradoxes*. Since they arise in sentences of every form, accounting for the meaning of all of them requires the formulation of general principles of meaning, and thus poses a semantic problem of fairly considerable scope. At the same time, it is worth stressing that the search for these general principles falls under the restricted conception of semantics which is based on the question of what is said. When I ask for the meaning of a sentence, I mean the proposition it expresses to a given audience in particular circumstances. This is not what 'meaning' usually means, though it has been what some important philosophers have meant. Those who say that when we assert a sentence, we are not asserting its meaning, may well be speaking truly, depending on what they mean.

Saying what is said is so often a trivial matter that we may be lulled to sleep by accounts such as 'What the sentence "All men are mortal" says is that all men are mortal'. But this casual style will not do for semantic paradoxes. Applying it to sentences like A leads to contradictions. The trivial style of answering proves to be false for such cases. Finding the proper account of what is said for such cases is not trivial.

It is worth stressing that it is not A itself that has led to a contradiction. A was not a premise at all. The premise (2) was that what A says is that A is not true. This is a plausible premise, so that it is paradoxical that it should lead to a contradiction. And the fact that this premise does lead to a contradiction makes A very different from an ordinary contradiction. As a premise, 'All men are mortal and some men live forever' leads to a contradiction. But the premise that what this sentence says is that all men are mortal and some men live forever does not lead to a contradiction at all – it is simply true. Semantic paradoxes arise from assumptions as to what a given expression says, and not from the expressions by themselves.

81   In this work we will be concerned with paradoxes arising out of trying to say what it is that some sentence says, and we will also consider cases of saying what a person has used a sentence to say. However, there are thought to be paradoxes formulated in terms of other propositional attitudes than asserting by people or saying by sentences. For example, there is Prior's case in which James fears that every proposition which James fears to be true is in fact false, and happens to fear nothing else (1958). We might call this the *Angst*-Liar. It would seem that this proposition which James fears to be true must be false, since it is self-refuting, but then this must

mean that there is some other proposition which James fears to be true which is true, and it is thought paradoxical that it should be *a priori* true that James cannot fear only the one proposition to be true and no other.

For another example, suppose that Jones believes that every proposition which Smith believes concerning him (Jones) is false, and this is the only belief Jones has concerning Smith. Further suppose that Smith believes that every proposition that Jones believes concerning him (Smith) is true, and this is his only belief concerning Jones. Now it seems that the truth of Jones' belief entails its own falsity, and similarly for Smith's. So both are false. But then it seems that the falsity of Jones' belief entails that Smith believes something about Jones which is true, so that it seems that our assumption that Jones and Smith each had only one belief about the other is *a priori* false. And that this should be *a priori* false is thought to be para-doxical.

Just as we can prove that A can't express the proposition that A is not true, we can prove that there cannot be such a belief as the following: Jones believes that the belief before his mind at noon on July 4 is (or was?) false, and it turns out that *this* is the belief that was before Jones' mind at noon on July 4.

The question is whether the fact that there cannot be such a belief goes against intuitions which are as respectable as those disturbed by A. I think that the answer is no.

What does it mean to say that Jones believes that the belief before his mind at noon on July 4 is false? Does he watch some sentence printed on a screen in his mind or hear it over an internal loud-speaker? It must be something like this, because behavioral criteria are going to be sadly lacking, except for the possibility that he is disposed to *say* the 'belief' was false. If he has the sentence before his mind, what is the tense of the sentence? If it read 'The belief before my mind at noon on July 4 was false', then the belief can be false simply enough: Jones is wrong in thinking that it *was* noon July 4 – it *is* noon July 4.

On the other hand, if the sentence before Jones' mind at noon is 'The belief presently before my mind is false', then we have a right to ask this question: 'Does Jones believe that this is the belief presently before his mind or does he not believe it is?' If Jones believes it is, then it is not the only belief before his mind. Similarly if he believes it is not. If it is replied (that is, specified) that Jones is without opinions on the matter, then I ask: what makes you think Jones *believes* the sentence before his mind? Just visualizing a sentence is not believing what it says. But if Jones does believe that the belief present to his mind is false and does believe that this is *the* belief present to his mind, then he is wrong, because another belief is present to his mind as well. And if he believes it is *not* the belief present to his mind, then it isn't present to his mind, or at least it isn't *the* belief present to his mind.

Even though it is probably not true, it is not altogether implausible to hold that no one could assert or believe a very simple contradiction. However, it is clear that a *sentence* can *express* a very simple contradiction, and there is no plausibility at all in thinking otherwise. Thus a sentence can express a proposition even though a speaker or writer might find it difficult to use the sentence in such a way as to get credited with asserting or believing that proposition. From the standpoint of logic, sentences and what they express are more important than people and what they say and believe, even though people and saying are obviously more fundamental from the genetic point of view. As an answer to the problems posed by A, 'No one could assert A' is a poor answer. But as an answer to the problems posed by 'The belief presently before my mind is false', 'No one could believe that' is a good answer.

Now let us return to the case in which Jones believes that everything Smith believes about him (Jones) is false. We were asked to believe that this was Jones' *only* belief about Smith, and then to be puzzled by a proof that this could not be so, given a certain belief of Smith's. But suppose that we ask Jones what his opinion is on the question whether or not Smith believes that every proposition Jones believes about him is true. Is it surprising that it is absurd to think that Jones will have no opinion on this? If Jones is sure that every proposition Smith believes about him is false, then surely he is sure that Smith does not believe that every proposition Jones believes about him (Smith) is true. If he doubted this, then he would doubt that every proposition Smith believes about him is false.

It may be suggested that perhaps Jones is very stupid or that after all it is possible to believe even a simple contradiction. But what basis do we have for holding that Jones believes that every proposition which Smith believes about him is false? That he says he does? Then how do we know that he knows what he is saying? If he also says that he is without an opinion as to whether Smith believes that every proposition which Jones believes about him is true, then Jones doesn't understand the situation very well. If someone *says* he believes it is raining but says he has no opinion as to whether it is wet outside we may (in an ordinary case) wonder just what he *does* have in mind, just what he *does* believe.

Of course Jones may believe *both* that every proposition Smith believes about him is false *and* that Smith believes about him that every proposition he (Jones) believes about him (Smith) is true. But these two beliefs will not exist in a vacuum either. If we can make sense of saying that Jones has these two beliefs, then surely he believes that Smith's belief is false, and thus believes that he (Jones) believes something false.

It may be objected that this is assuming that if someone believes *p*, and *p* sufficiently obviously entails *q*, then he believes *q*. In its general form, I would question this formula as much as anybody. But with the particular beliefs which we have ascribed to Jones, I think it is reasonable to ask just how we can ascribe *those* beliefs while finding it *obvious* that they do not involve having others. It was supposed to be a *paradox* that Jones could not simply believe that every proposition Smith believes about him is false and Smith believe that every proposition Jones believes about him is true *without having any other beliefs about each other*. But I do not find the proofs of this paradoxical. They are, rather, good warnings against a naïve approach to the notion of belief. The approach I mean is that according to which believing a proposition is like having some thing set down on a stage before the mind, so that it is easy to suppose that the stage could be occupied by just one proposition. The fact is that even when one is *concentrating*, this isn't how it is. The closest I can come to the picture is to recite a sentence over to myself, or perhaps to visualize one written on a board. But this isn't believing.

Similar considerations apply to James' fear that every proposition which he fears to be true is in fact false. If he does fear this, then he must fear to be true something which is in fact true. I suggest as a candidate for such a fear the fear that James' fears are likely to be very silly. But other candidates will be available in any case. The idea that James could fear *only* that every proposition which he fears to be true is in fact false, is just based on a uselessly rarified notion of fearing. Suppose we decide that James fears that everything Jones said in his speech was true. Perhaps this does not mean that James knows of some dire prediction which Jones made in his speech. Perhaps it does not mean that James fears that by telling the truth to the crowd, Jones will get them on his side and turn them against James. Perhaps I cannot cite *a priori* anything else which James must also fear (though I think I could). The fact remains that it would be absurd to suppose that we could ever have reason to think that James had *only* the one fear and was untroubled about *any other* proposition.

Thus I do not think that the Liar family paradoxes as formulated for 'propositional attitudes' other than saying by sentences (and also, perhaps, asserting by people) should be considered to pose special *logical* problems.

82   Previously I have focused on the proposition as the thought, the object of actual or possible belief. However, there are propositions which no one has ever believed and perhaps propositions which no one could believe. This was a difficulty for the Russellian notion of a proposition because he treated the proposition as a 'supplemented' sentence and the only kind of supplementation he described was believing. It is plausible to say that such a sentence as 'Two plus one makes seven' expresses a necessarily false proposition whether or not anyone would ever believe or assert it. It is obvious that this fact about what the sentence expresses is in some way a fact about how people of a certain language community would behave, but the details are not easy to provide.

Since people of different language communities might take the same sentence, as a series of marks, to say different things, saying what a sentence says should always be relative to persons in the sense that the reference class of language users should be kept in consideration. In this sense what is said by a sentence depends on persons. It would be a bad mistake to move from this to the idea that if someone sincerely says that a given sentence does not express a proposition to him, or that it does express some proposition which he specifies, then he must be right. A dispute over whether such sentences as 'The Absolute is the world process' or 'The Nothing nothings itself' express propositions cannot be settled by saying that they express propositions to those that think they do and do not express propositions to those that think they do not. Such disputes are not likely to be settled at all, but that is another matter.

The question whether 'All John's children are asleep' entails that

John has children, or 'The King of France is wise' entails that there is a King of France, can be viewed as questions about what a sentence by itself says. Of course they require some 'supplementation', but it is not necessary that they be used to make assertions in order to say something. The answer that 'The King of France is wise' says that the King of France is wise, though a true claim, is not adequate for answering that question about entailment. The adequacy of an account of what is said depends on the question it is needed for.

My answer was that the sentence 'All John's children are asleep' cannot be taken to express a proposition by itself, because it could be used to express a proposition that entailed John had children and could also be used to express a proposition that did not entail this. So a dispute over whether the sentence by itself expressed one or the other sort of proposition would be based on the error of ignoring these two possibilities. Still, it is perfectly natural, for purposes of a logical discussion, to specify one of the possible interpretations without having to imagine a use of the sentence by some person. Similarly, 'This sentence contains more than twenty letters' can be treated as expressing a syntactically self-referential claim while ignoring the fact that 'This sentence' will be 'The sentence I see there' for a great variety of people. We naturally ignore the variation in tokens of this sentence as well as the various interpretations different people would give even the same token of it if they took it as expressing an actual judgement made by them.

With 'The King of France is wise', I argued that there is no proposition to the effect that the King of France is wise that does not entail that there is a King. My argument relied heavily on claims about what someone using such a sentence to make a sincere assertion would actually be thinking. But even for purposes of a logical discussion, where ontological and other metaphysical considerations can be idealized away, one cannot pretend that a sentence expresses a proposition unless there is such a proposition. One could, I suppose, use 'The King of France is wise' to mark merely the act of predicating being wise of the King, as long as care is taken not to confuse an act of predication or attempt at one with a proposition.

It is important to recognize that a sentence's expressing a proposition depends on the responses of people, and that it is only by acquiring a grasp of our language as a whole that we apprehend propositions and properties. And yet it is not true that questions about what is said by a given sentence can always be resolved by describing our responses and other linguistic practices. On the one hand, we have to stress that a sentence expresses a proposition only to a given person and not absolutely. On the other, we must bear in mind that a sentence expresses a proposition to a person because of the language system which he understands. And someone may understand a language without grasping all the properties and propositions which this system makes it ideally possible for him to grasp, if only he had the intelligence and persistence. We might say that a sentence expresses a proposition relative to a person *qua* suitably intelligent, persistent, and lucky user of a certain language.

83 A nominalist could not accept our formulation of the problem posed by semantic paradoxes, since he does not allow that there is such a thing as the proposition expressed by a sentence. As realists, we speak of what a sentence says as something distinct from the sentence. The nominalist refuses to recognize such entities. Accordingly, the nominalist cannot acknowledge our fundamental principle (1). He must either call it false or meaningless or must reconstrue it as the redundant and insignificant tautology, 'A sentence is true if and only if it is true', on the grounds that to say that what a sentence says is true can only be a roundabout way of saying that the sentence is true, which is acceptable in ordinary speech only because it really doesn't refer to any 'abstract entities'.

Perhaps there is some other way of reconstruing our presentation of the paradox so that it is acceptable to a nominalist. (Not the paradox, of course, but that the derivation constitutes a problem from the nominalistic standpoint.) But anyway, nominalists admit that the semantic paradoxes are a problem from their point of view, and have versions of them which do not involve a realist terminology.

Here we must distinguish varying degrees of nominalism. Some nominalists not only deny the existence of propositions, but also attempt to avoid sentence types, since they too are a bit too 'abstract'. For these extreme (or thorough-going) nominalists, we could set out the premises

(i) Sentence tokens like 'A is not true' are true if and only if A is not true,

(ii) Sentence tokens like the token in quotes in premise (i) are true if and only if A is not true, and

(iii) A is a sentence token like the token in quotes in premise (i).

These premises yield the contradiction

(iv) A is true if and only if A is not true,

which is the same conclusion as our (6) (since in (6) 'the sentence A' refers to the sentence token and not the type).

In these premises, we mean by 'like' something which would require some fairly tedious clarification, if done in the nominalist's own terms. But in our terms, a token is like A if it is a token of the same type as A and the 'A' in it has the same designation as the 'A' in A (namely the token A). Furthermore, we must understand that the token of 'A is not true' which occurs in (i) is like A, that is, that the 'A' in it refers to A. With this understanding, the premises (i), (ii) and (iii) have enough plausibility, taken separately, that we may consider the situation a paradox.

Thorough-going nominalists and realists are alike in predicating truth of sentence tokens rather than sentence types (though for the realist the ultimate bearer of truth or falsity is the proposition, while for the thorough-going nominalist the token is ultimate). However, casual nominalists such as Tarski and Quine often predicate truth of sentence types. This may be because they are used to dealing with formal systems in which it is impossible for two tokens of the same expression type to be used differently if they are both used as expressions of the formal system. The English sentence 'This won't do', for example, is such that one token of it can be used to say one thing and another token to say something quite different (and even the same written token might be used at different times to say different things), so that it would be impossible to make sense of calling the sentence type true or false. But sentences of fully interpreted formal systems are not allowed to behave in this way.

At any rate, a sentence such as A would not do for someone who wanted to ascribe truth values to sentence types. The letter 'A' has been used to refer to many sentences on different occasions. The sentence type 'A is not true' could not be assigned a truth value for this reason. Some tokens of it are true, some false. Some may be neither true nor false, or true sometimes and not others.

However, it is possible to formulate pretty genuine semantic paradoxes in which sentence types are called true or false. For example, consider the premises:

(v) 'Does not apply truly to itself' does not apply truly to itself if and only if ' "Does not apply truly to itself" does not apply truly to itself' is not true,

and

(vi) ' "Does not apply truly to itself" does not apply truly to itself' is true if and only if 'Does not apply truly to itself' does not apply truly to itself.

These two premises are obviously inconsistent, and yet both have high individual plausibility. It is a genuine problem to explain what is wrong with them.

84 Semantic paradoxes are very commonly regarded by philosophers as trifling problems. Of course they are taken seriously by logicians, but most philosophers are not logicians, and to this majority, the paradoxes are ranked intellectually about on a par with party games or newspaper 'brain teasers'. Handed a card with 'The statement on the other side is false' on one side and 'The statement on the other side is true' on the other, even an intellectually serious person may consider an amused smile an appropriate response.

One way of getting the problems treated as serious is to treat them mathematically. The introduction of formal symbolism tends to have a sobering effect, and since it is not generally understood, it makes it less embarrassing to be overheard discussing these problems.

However, logic is supposed to be concerned with all inferences in whatever language the premises may be stated, and no matter how silly or insignificant their specific content may sound. And when an argument or statement is difficult to assess logically, that is all the more reason to focus attention upon it.

The 'solution' to the paradoxes most popular with those who do not take them seriously is to dismiss the paradox sentences as nonsense. From the standpoint of realism, this would be to reject premise (2) on the grounds that A does not express a proposition.

Paul Ziff advocates a policy of this sort, though he would not put his point in realist terms. In his discussion of a paradox which he sets out as '(10): (10) is false' he says: 'The following is a regularity to be found in connection with English: if u is uttered by way of making a statement, then generally that statement does not lead to a contradiction' (1960, p. 138). This is Ziff's basis for classifying (10) as 'semantically deviant'. Ziff says that when he finds a contradiction in a formal system he 'crosses out the system', but when he finds a contradiction in English he 'crosses out the contradiction'.

Ziff does not explain what it is to 'cross out' a contradiction. The significance of simply drawing a line through a contradictory sentence is hard to see, since it could just as well be done with any sentence. And he does not actually show that (10) 'leads to a contradiction'.

In the case of (10), and our A, it is usually not shown that they lead to a contradiction. In the deductions I know, they are not *premises* in the derivation of a contradiction. They are objects talked about in premises, the subjects of premises. But perhaps it could be shown that as premises they lead to contradictions. If so, I shall argue that crossing them out would not have any significance for any logical problems posed by them.

A. H. Basson says:

> We can of course eliminate paradoxical expressions from the English language: the only objection to this procedure is that in doing so we shall inevitably lose many (an infinite number) of perfectly sensible and useful expressions. I mean there would be occasions when we should lack the means to assert even some straightforward matter of fact. We should only be able to hint at it in a mystical kind of way. Furthermore, the functions which have paradoxical values are useful too, and we could not eliminate them without similar loss. We could not even talk about truth and paradox and other things of that kind. (1960, p. 32)

Basson may mean, for example, that banishing the expression type 'A is not true', ruling that it is never to be used and no equivalent substitute is either, would deprive us. It certainly would. But ruling that the token named 'A' in this text is nonsense only deprives us of a paradox sentence. If *I* say 'A is not true', then I am speaking truly. It may be surprising that the token I use is true while the token named 'A' is nonsense, and I shall argue that this consequence of the simple 'crossing out' policy is indeed unacceptable. But it would be a mistake to hold that the reason the policy is unacceptable is that it deprives us of many non-paradoxical expressions. Ruling that A is nonsense deprives us of nothing but A, and if the ruling is right, then this isn't to be *deprived* of anything.

With 'No token of this sentence is true' we have a Liar family paradox which is a contradiction between a meaning assumption and firm logical principles, though the principles are not exactly the same as those which were involved with A. But at any rate, if I rule that this sentence is nonsense, does not express a proposition, the most natural way would be to rule that every token of the sentence is nonsense. So I will 'lose' a whole type in this case rather than a token. But the 'loss' is still negligible, since the only purpose the 'excluded' type served was trouble-making.

With the Heterological paradoxes, I will 'lose' not only a whole type class but a range of type classes. That is, I will say that 'does not apply truly to itself' does not apply truly or falsely to 'does not apply truly to itself'. So it will be nonsense to say 'Saying that "does not apply truly to itself" applies truly to itself is never true', since this would most naturally be taken as self-referring. But in expelling this self-referring use, we are not depriving ourselves at all. We just have to be careful to use quotation marks to keep ourselves out of the harmful self-reference.

The best known Heterological paradox is the one where the word 'heterological' is allegedly *defined* to stand for the property of standing for a property while not having the property. The 'cross out' approach here would involve denying that such a definition is possible. This is unsatisfactory in the same way as the 'cross out' approach to A. No explanation is given as to *why* the word 'heterological' cannot stand for the alleged property, other than the fact that the assumption is involved in the derivation of a contradiction. And after all, other assumptions are also involved in the derivation. However, though it is unsatisfactory, the 'cross out' approach does not 'cross out' anything other than paradox sentences.

Basson could point out that, on this attitude, the question as to whether or not something is meaningful would not be straightforward, since we can make up expressions for which it isn't easy to determine whether they are referring to themselves. This is a good point. Furthermore, as Basson shows, there is no effective test (in the technical sense of 'effective') for determining whether the assumption that a given expression expresses a certain proposition leads to contradiction. And there are simpler cases as well, which show even more clearly that if we adopt a 'cross out paradox' attitude, meaning assessments will cease to be straightforward. For example, given something like 'The first sentence on page 1 is false' we will have to wait until we see what is written on page 1 before we can even decide what 'The first sentence on page 1 is false' means, if it means anything at all.

This is an obstacle to the attitude that determining the meaning of an expression should be straightforward in some strong sense. This attitude would involve holding either that 'The first sentence on page 1 is false' can be seen at a glance to express 'the proposition that the first sentence on page 1 is false' or that it can be seen at a glance that 'The first sentence on page 1 is false' is meaningless, or more precisely, that it does not express a proposition. This latter approach would usually also involve holding that when something *is* meaningful the meaning will be easy to determine straightaway.

Basson is right in holding that 'crossing out' paradoxes will, if taken as our sole protection against them, leave us unable to always make straightforward assessments of the meaning of a given expression. It might be thought that it is obvious that we can't always make straightforward assessments, since everyone sometimes has to consult a dictionary to look up a word. But in discussing the view that meaning assessments should be 'straightforward', this will be considered irrelevant. It will be assumed that we are concerned with someone who knows the language of the expression perfectly, knows all the words. Such a person would still not find 'The first sentence on page 1 is false' straightforwardly assessable if we are following the 'crossing out' policy.

Basson's valuable observation that a policy of 'crossing out' paradoxes will make it impossible to straightforwardly determine meanings should not mislead us into thinking that such a policy would involve giving up perfectly good ways of speaking. He may have been thinking of avoiding paradoxes by some *general* procedure, which would find some general feature of paradox sentences, such as self-reference, and then give up all sentences having that feature. This would indeed involve also giving up many untroublesome sentences. But 'crossing out' paradoxes when we find them does not have this consequence. It only has the consequence that we cannot always be sure, just by reading a sentence, whether it says some definite thing.

Just what is it to 'cross out' a paradox sentence, on this account?

It is to treat it as not saying anything. But what sort of treatment is this? Classifying a sentence as 'nonsense' is notoriously vague and subjective. Saying that it 'says nothing' is not much clearer. I cannot give a *definition* of 'expresses a proposition'. But it may help to describe what, for our purposes, is involved in treating a sentence as if it does not express a proposition.

A thing which expresses a proposition, expresses it to a person. Such a thing might be a rock or stick displayed in accordance with a previous arrangement. But some sentences of a language will express the same proposition to so many people, with so little pre-arrangement, that we can simply say the sentence expresses that proposition. Examples of things which express propositions in this way, relative to persons of the sort who might read this, are such things as 'All men are mortal', or 'Eisenhower was president of the US in 1957'. Examples of things which do not are sticks and stones, the expression 'bxklil', the sentence 'Thoobles pleble ardronomosly', the sentence 'The Absolute is the world process', and the sentence 'Someone is standing there'.

Any of this latter group of things could express a proposition. But only 'Someone is standing there' is well suited to expressing a proposition and tokens of it only require a specific context of reference in order to express propositions.

Things which do not express propositions may fail to do so for a variety of reasons. But the case of a grammatical sentence which does not express a proposition is one where there is considerable risk of confusion and failure to recognize that nothing is said.

The basic rule about a nonsense expression is that while the expression itself may be discussed, the expression cannot be used to convey anything without ceasing to be nonsensical. Thus if I side with those who regard 'The Absolute is the world process' as nonsense, I should not say 'It is not the case that the Absolute is the world process', because this would imply that the negation of a nonsense expression was true. But a nonsensical expression does not even have a real negation, grammatical appearances to the contrary notwithstanding.

A nonsense expression has no place in a logical argument, and so it can pose no problem of logical assessment. This fundamental point is often overlooked by philosophers who say that some expression is nonsensical *on the grounds* that a contradiction can be deduced from it. This leaves unaccounted for those logical powers which make such a deduction possible. A nonsense expression has no logical powers; and for our purposes, that is the significance of labeling it 'nonsense'.

Consider: 'The Absolute is the world process; the world process is red; therefore, the Absolute is red.' Syntactically, this is similar to a valid argument. But it should not even be said to be *of* a valid form. For how do we know there is no equivocation, or rather, that like terms are used in like senses? In fact some of the terms are not used with any sense at all. If the above were a valid argument, then we could equally well present 'Either the Absolute is the world process or it is not the case that the Absolute is the world process' as valid. And then we should wonder which disjunct is true, and be liable to many other confusions as well.

Some similar confusions could arise in treating 'Someone is standing there' as a subject for logical inference. However, many tokens of this type could have complete meanings and figure in arguments, and generalizations can be made as to some sorts of valid argument such tokens could appear in. Thus 'Someone is standing there, therefore, someone is there' is not a valid argument, but tokens of it will be in a suitable context of reference.

All this might seem to make it quite simple to employ the 'crossing out' approach and to rule that A is nonsense. For this would only involve dropping a sentence token (or class of tokens). And to keep A out of logical arguments should be easy, since any work it could do as a premise could be done by some other token of the same type (one not named 'A').

However, this very replaceability of A by other tokens of the same type makes the 'crossing out' policy extremely implausible. Note that, unlike 'Someone is standing there', 'A is not true' has, in this writing, a perfectly complete context of reference. That is, the reference of 'A' can be located by anyone who has read this far.

What then, is it for a sentence to say something? If it is for people naturally and properly, on the basis of their language ability, to take the sentence to say that thing, then if that the sentence A is not true is something which can be said, most people would naturally and properly regard A as saying it just as well as any other sentence (such as 'The sentence A is not true', or some other token of the same type as A). And this would mean that A does say this thing, according to this very account of what it is for a sentence to say something.

Suppose that someone reads A and learns that it is A. Then we have him read it again, with the 'A' covered up. He mistakenly takes it to be another token of the same type as A. How can this make any difference in his estimate of what is said, *if* that A is not true is something which can be said? This point may be reinforced by considering a different paradox sentence:

(B) The proposition which Bill, on first reading, takes the sentence B to express, is not true.

Now, *if* there is such a proposition as the proposition that the proposition which Bill, on first reading, takes the sentence B to express, is not true, and Bill could take some other token of the type of B to express it, then why can't Bill take B to express this proposition? But the assumption that there is such a proposition *P*, which Bill takes B to express, leads to a contradiction. It is not enough to say that B does not express a proposition. Just the assumption that Bill *takes* B to express *P* leads to a contradiction.

The trouble with 'crossing out' paradoxes is that this leaves unanswered the question whether it can be said at all, by any sentence, that A is not true. And it thus fails to go on to the question, 'If not, why not?' The basic idea, of giving up premise (2), is sound enough. But without attempting to explain the trouble with premise (2), we are left with only a shallow treatment of the questions raised by the paradoxes.

On my view as to what it is for a sentence to say something, we must, as was just shown, conclude that either (a) there is no such thing as the proposition that A is not true, or (b) there is such a proposition but it cannot be said or asserted by A, and there will be similar propositions that cannot even be taken as said.

Tarski and Russell have set forth theories about truth which entail (a) or (b), though since neither is a thorough-going realist, they might not accept the way they are worded. At any rate, both reject unqualified uses of the word 'true' and require instead a more refined terminology.

85 Quine endorses Tarski's approach to the semantic paradoxes. His presentation has two parts. First, he makes the following observation:

Strictly, the notions of the theory of reference and ... the theory of meaning ... are relative always to a language; the language figures, albeit tacitly, as a parameter . . . a statement, thought of as a string of letters or sounds, is never simply true, but true in language L for appropriate L. This is not a philosophical doctrine of the relativity of all fact to language; the point is much more superficial. The point is merely that a given string of letters or sounds could constitute at once a statement, say, of English and a statement (different in meaning, to borrow a phrase) of Frisian, and it might happen in its English meaning to be true and in its Frisian meaning to be false. (1953, pp. 134–5)

One kind of example which might be cited by Quine is as follows: suppose I say to Heinrich, 'Can you tell me how many planets there are?' He replies by producing a sound. I know that Heinrich often lapses into German, so I have to ask him further, 'Heinrich, was your sentence meant as a sentence of German or as a sentence of English?', in order to determine whether he has told me there are nine planets or that he cannot tell how many planets there are. The sound Heinrich produced is the oral form both of a German one-word sentence and an English one-word sentence. And while I cannot think of any actual written examples, it is easy to imagine some such coincidence with a written sentence.

However, as Quine says, the difference between a sentence as a sentence of one language and the same sentence in another language is primarily a difference in meaning. That is, it is a difference in the range of things the sentence is suitable for use in saying. It is not primarily a difference in what is said. For a sentence may be used to say different things even in one language. And while this latter point may seem uninterestingly obvious, Quine seems not to give it enough emphasis.

For example, he says of the form '"——" is true if and only if ——' that 'it holds when any one statement is written in the two blanks' (1953, p. 134). On the same page he speaks of 'a statement, thought of as a string of letters or sounds'. This, combined with the fact that he speaks of putting one 'statement' in the two blanks (which rules out sentence tokens) must mean that he is speaking of sentence types. But the claim that putting two tokens of the same sentence type into the two blanks will always yield a true statement about the sentence type is false.

Quine's recognition that the same sentence may belong to two different languages leads him to qualify this claim. He adds the requirement that the form be in the same language as the sentence which is put into the blanks and that instead of just 'true' we put 'true-in-L', where L is that language. For example, he would accept as true '"Snow is white" is true-in-English if and only if snow is white'.

This qualification spares us some extremely slight risks. Just in case the sentence 'Snow is white' is a sentence of Frisian with a very different meaning from the sentence as an English sentence, we do not call the sentence type true. We merely call the sentence type, regarded as a sentence of English, true. We put this by calling it 'true-in-English'.

But this qualification does nothing for the real trouble with the form. For even as a sentence of English, the sentence type 'Snow is white' cannot be said to be true (or false). Someone may say truly 'In Pittsburgh, snow is black'. 'Snow is white' is true only when understood in a certain way. And it may be understood in different ways while yet being understood as an English sentence.

It may seem that this is merely perverse nagging. If instead of 'Snow is white' we had considered 'Snow, in its pure state, is white', wouldn't the criticism have been avoided? Perhaps so. Perhaps there are sentences sufficiently independent of context that the sentence type alone, taken as a sentence of a particular language such as English, says something. But even so, there are lots of sentences which are not so independent of context. And it may be a very fundamental feature of language that there are such sentences, not just an irritating flaw which can be avoided by restricting oneself to context-independent sentences.

I do not know just what Quine would say about this. One possibility would be to restrict the applicability of his formal criterion to sentences which are context-independent. This would be natural in view of the fact that 'sentences' of formalized 'languages' are context-independent.

Another possibility is that it might be said that a sentence which is used to say different things is automatically being used in different languages. This would mean, for example, that when two different people say 'I am hungry' they speak different languages. This obviously is to use the term 'language' in an unusual way. But it is not an incomprehensible way. There is nothing wrong with this conception of 'a language'. It is just that there is a more familiar notion of 'a language' such that a language of the familiar sort helps in making up languages of the other sort. And there is some indication that Tarski and Quine sometimes have 'languages' of the new sort in mind.

However, Tarski and Quine call 'languages' systems even more different from natural languages than this. For example, they would speak of systems such as that of Russell's *Principia Mathematica* or Quine's *Mathematical Logic* as 'languages'. These systems differ sharply from natural languages in that they have axioms, rules of inference, and theorems. In a natural language, we can carry on a debate as to whether the law of excluded middle is true, however misguided it may be to question such a law. But a language which has the law as a theorem or axiom would make the position of opponents of the law untenable in a much more obvious way.

We can distinguish between the axioms of a formalized language and the language itself, as the medium in which the axioms are expressed. But Tarski does not draw this distinction. He says, 'Our everyday language is certainly not one with an exactly specified structure. We do not know precisely which expressions are sentences and we know even to a smaller degree which sentences are to be taken as assertible' (1944, p. 349). Thus Tarski considers it a matter for dissatisfaction with 'everyday language' that it is so unclear what sentences of it are 'assertible', that is, axioms or theorems. Axioms and theorems are part of the 'structure' of a language, and the structure is not 'exactly specified' until the axioms and theorems are 'exactly specified'.

To say that a sentence is 'assertible' is rather ambiguous. The sentence 'Anyone who can count his toes is fit to govern the United States' is assertible in the sense that someone could assert it. But Tarski clearly does not mean this by 'assertible'.

There are two other ways in which a sentence could be assertible. We could mean that asserting it has the sanction of some authority, or we could mean that the sentence is true. We can say 'From the standpoint of so-and-so, it is assertible that . . .', meaning that this assertion is part of so-and-so's position. Or we can say that a sentence is assertible as opposed to not being assertible except on pain of speaking falsely.

On neither of these interpretations of 'assertible' is it any failing of natural language that it is 'unclear' what sentences are assertible in them. It is not up to a language to show us which of its sentences are true. And a language is not an authority, which can endorse some assertions or veto others.

However, Tarski must have in mind formalized languages, in which axioms and theorems ('assertible sentences') can be identified with some precision. So his complaint about natural languages must be that it is not clear what their axioms and theorems are, rather than that it is not clear what sentences are true. He must think that formalized languages are better than natural languages because it is clearer what their axioms and theorems are. But this is absurd. Men make up formalized languages, and choose what their axioms are. And there is nothing whatsoever to prevent someone choosing as an axiom something false. It will not be any less an axiom for being false. So there is no virtue simply in having axioms. This is just to have sentences taken as true without proof by someone. Natural languages cannot be said to have such sentences because there is no 'someone' with the appropriate relation to them (that of formulator of the language) such that his assuming of a sentence without proof qualifies it as an axiom of the natural language (as opposed to some axiomatic system formulated in the natural language).

It is a virtue in a natural language that it is able to express some proposition, and a defect if it is not able to do so. It is a virtue of a natural language to be able to express both some proposition and its contradictory. But it is not up to the language to see to it that the sentences, the one expressing the proposition, and the other expressing its contradictory, are not both true. Nothing could make two such sentences true. If the language can express this fact it can express at least in part the law of non-contradiction. But whether this law should be an axiom or not, is up to the mind that confronts it and not up to any language.

The idea that axioms are part of a language rather than something which can be expressed in a language or denied (however wrongly) in it may be reinforced by the idea that axioms provide 'implicit' definitions for some terms of the language. Thus it might be said that the various apparently incompatible set theories are not incompatible but just different 'languages' because they each give a different meaning to the word 'set' by setting out different postulates involving this word. This attitude would not fit very well with the practice of speaking of 'standard' and 'non-standard' models of the various formalized set theories since this talk presupposes that the word 'set' has a meaning which is not completely determined by the axioms involving it.

If the meanings of words are not independent of axioms then translation from one 'language' to another can be extremely difficult, to say the least. Finding out what a sentence in a 'language' says would involve understanding the axioms as well. Nothing could be translated in isolation. And if your 'language' has axioms too, the problems would be even more formidable.

At any rate, if we regard Tarski and Quine as using the term 'language' so that a language is, roughly, a precisely delineated (though not necessarily finite) collection of sentences each with a fixed meaning,[1] with identifiable axioms and rules of proof for determining theorems, it may help us to understand them. Pieces of English discourse, such as published papers, could be made out as 'English sublanguages', if we note that the sentences in the paper all have precise and fixed meaning and that some of them are assumed without proof and others are proved from the assumptions.

86   Keeping this in mind makes the second part of Quine's solution to the paradoxes, as well as Tarski's solution, easier to understand.

Quine says, 'it turns out that the semantical paradoxes . . . do not arise if we take these two precautions': the first is to qualify 'true' to 'true-in-L' where L is the language you are using; the second is to 'banish such terms as "true-in-L", "true-in-L-of", and "names-in-L" from the language L itself' (1953, p. 136).

Now who would have the power to banish any word from English? It is easier to understand just refraining from using the word in 'your' language. This also helps in understanding Tarski's answer to the Liar paradox. He states:

> (I) We have implicitly assumed that the language in which the antinomy is constructed contains, in addition to its expressions, also the names of these expressions, as well as semantic terms such as the term 'true' referring to sentences of this language; we have also assumed that all sentences which determine the adequate usage of this term can be asserted in the language. A language with these properties will be called '*semantically closed*'.

---

[1] Here, to say that a sentence has a fixed meaning means that it says just one thing and is not used (as a sentence of this language) to say anything else. In the broader sense of meaning with which we are not concerned, a sentence may have just one meaning and yet not have a fixed meaning in our present sense.

(II) We have assumed that in this language the ordinary laws of logic hold.

. . .

Since every language which satisfies both of these assumptions is inconsistent, we must reject at least one of them.

. . .

We . . . consider only the possibility of rejecting the assumption (I). Accordingly, we decide *not to use any language which is semantically closed in the sense given.* (1944, pp. 348–9)

Assumption (I) is the assumption that the language in which the antinomy is constructed is semantically closed. To reject it would be to suppose that the language in which the antinomy is constructed is not semantically closed. However, Tarski says 'every language which satisfies both of these assumptions is inconsistent', as if there were semantically closed languages. He says 'we decide not to use any language which is semantically closed', as if there were such languages for us to consider 'using'. And this doesn't fit the familiar notion of 'language' at all. It must be something like our new notion of language which is meant in these remarks.

If we construct 'languages' in accordance with the advice of Tarski and Quine, we will doubtless avoid formulating any semantic paradoxes, being deprived of the terminology for doing so. But this is an unsatisfactory reply to the paradoxes which have been formulated, as may be brought out by generalizing our original formulation of a semantic paradox. We have

(1*) A sentence of a language L is true-in-L if and only if what it says as a sentence of L is true,

and

(2*) There is a language L in which there is a sentence A* such that what A* says as a sentence of L is that A* is not true-in-L.

From these two assumptions it follows that

(3*) The sentence A* is true-in-L if and only if what the sentence A* says as a sentence of L is true,

and from (2*) and (3*) it follows that

(4*) The sentence A* is true-in-L if and only if, that the sentence A* is not true-in-L, is true.

We then add the assumption

(5*) That the sentence A* is not true-in-L, is true if and only if the sentence A* is not true-in-L.

From (4*) and (5*) follows the contradiction

(6*) The sentence A* is true-in-L if and only if the sentence A* is not true-in-L.

Since (1*) and (5*) are true, this shows that (2*) is false. There could not be a language L with a sentence which says of itself that it is not true-in-L.

Of course this is denied by Quine and Tarski. They would observe that premises (1*) and (5*), just like (1) and (5), violate their advice about using 'true' only relative to a language. But (1*) and (5*) follow this advice as far as it is reasonable to do so. They do not attribute truth *simpliciter* to sentences but only truth-in-L. They only attribute truth *simpliciter* to what is said by sentences, that is, to propositions. After all, what Quine said was that 'a string of letters or sounds, is never simply true, but true in language L for appropriate L' (1953, p. 134). And we have accepted this ruling. The sentence 'All men are mortal', for example, is not simply true, we admit, but only true-in-English (or, if need be, some restricted part of English). But the proposition that all men are mortal is simply true. That all men are mortal has nothing to do with any language whatsoever. To say that it is 'true-in-English' makes no sense. The English language has a lot to do with the truth of 'All men are mortal', but it has nothing (at least nothing relevant here) to do with the mortality of men.

There are two ways that Quine and Tarski could reject this. They could say: 'That all men are mortal is only true-in-L for appropriate L, none of this "just plain true" business for us.' Or they could say that they do not recognize the existence of such things as the proposition that all men are mortal, but only recognize such things as the sentence 'All men are mortal'. This latter is the likely reply. Their doctrines depend for their plausibility on nominalism.

However, even if our proof that there could not be a language L of any sort which contained a sentence A* which said as a sentence of L that A* is not true-in-L is rejected, it is still difficult to make sense of the claim that there could be a 'language' that was inconsistent because a semantic paradox could be formulated in it. For example, in Tarski's presentation of the Liar paradox, he derives the contradiction '(3) "s" is true if and only if "s" is not true' (1944, p. 348). Let us suppose that this contradiction is derived in some language L, so that 'true' in (3) might be replaced with 'true-in-L'. Now is this latter sentence true-in-L? According to Tarski part of the trouble with L, part of what makes it possible to formulate the Liar paradox in it, is that 'all sentences which determine the adequate usage of this term ["true"] can be asserted in the language'. So for L we have all instances of the form ' "——" is true if and only if ——', for which we put a sentence of L in the blanks. So by putting the sentence (3) in the blanks and using the fact that (3) is assertible in L, we can prove in L that (3) is true-in-L. But it is a pretty poor kind of truth that is possessed by contradictions.

So it might be said that (3) is not really true-in-L after all and that while it is possible to prove in L that (3) is true-in-L this is just because L is inconsistent. But if it is not true-in-L then what is wrong with those 'sentences which determine the adequate usage of this term ["true"]' by which (3) comes out true-in-L?

Or it might be said, 'I do not care to comment on whether the sentence (3) is "true-in-L" or not. Considering the state L is in, I'd rather not have terms like "true-in-L" in my language, so the question does not arise for me.' But then how can you say that the Liar paradox arises in L?

Consider a 'language' L with the following properties:

(1) Every sentence of the form ' "——" is a sentence containing exactly twenty-five letters if and only if ——', which is obtained by substituting the same sentence of L in each blank of the form, is an 'assertible sentence' (theorem) of L.
(2) There is a sentence S of L which runs 'S is not a sentence containing exactly twenty-five letters'.
(3) S is known in L by the name 'S'.
(4) The usual laws of logic are also axioms of L.

This 'language' L is just as much a language as the one Tarski describes as allowing the Liar paradox to arise. And it is inconsistent in exactly the same way, since it is possible to derive in L, given assumptions (1)–(4), the contradiction 'S is a sentence containing exactly twenty-five letters if and only if S is not a sentence containing exactly twenty-five letters'. The only difference is that this language has an obviously false assumption involving the property of containing exactly twenty-five letters while the language of Tarski's version of the Liar paradox has a not so obviously false assumption involving the property of truth. But this difference disappears if you refuse to recognize 'truth-in-L' as a kind of truth. That is, if you proceed without saying what it is that the predicates mean, there is no basis for saying that semantic paradoxes, as opposed to mere trivially false contradictions, arise in the language. There is no basis for Tarski's remark about his formulation of the Liar paradox: 'In my judgment, it would be quite wrong and dangerous from the standpoint of scientific progress to depreciate the importance of this and other antinomies, and to treat them as jokes or sophistries' (1944, p. 348). For if the Liar paradox does not arise in the language Tarski himself 'uses', how does he know that it arises in some other language?

To summarize: either the language has 'all sentences which determine the adequate usage of the term "*true*"' and this term 'true' really corresponds to the semantic property, truth, or not. If so, then such a contradiction as Tarski's (3) must be said to be true (in some language), which is absurd; if not, if the term does not really correspond to the semantic property of truth, then there is no point in speaking of a semantic paradox arising in the language and no point in suggesting that there is a genuine problem and not just a 'language' which, through a bad choice of assumptions, has turned out inconsistent.

Admittedly, to speak of 'corresponding to the semantic property, truth' is again to lapse into realism. But there are facts about the intertranslatability of languages which the nominalist must accommodate in some way, and these facts are enough to make the suggestion that the Liar paradox could arise in some languages but not others completely obscure. Recall Quine's claim that 'the notions of the theory of reference ... are relative always to a language'. He said, 'The point is merely that a given string of letters or sounds could constitute at once a statement, say, of English and a statement (different in meaning, to borrow a phrase) of Frisian' (1953, pp. 134–5). This phrase is borrowed from realism. And to continue the convenient realist way of speaking, the point is that to say that a sentence is true-in-L is to say that what it means in L is true *simpliciter*. This latter point may perhaps be translatable into the clumsy and tedious vocabulary of nominalism. But in any case it is a point which proves it is wrong to say that semantic paradoxes can be formulated in any language whatsoever.

This criticism is not meant to suggest that the problem of avoiding inconsistency in a formal language is not a genuine and important one. The point is just that *no* sentence in *any* language could be both 'true' and 'false' in any sense corresponding to truth and falsity. It may very well be true, in fact I think it is true, that the languages constructed by Tarski, in which 'true' is restricted to 'true in-L' and no sentence containing 'true-in-L' is a sentence of L, can be languages in which *some* of the facts about truth are expressed; specifically, in which any sentence that is 'true-in-L' where sentences containing 'true-in-L' are not allowed in L is in fact a sentence that expresses something true. But in *none* of the languages meeting Tarski's restriction on allowing 'true-in-L' to be a term of L is it possible to say that no sentence in any language is both true and false (or true-in-L and false-in-L). But this, which cannot be said in any of Tarski's languages, is a fundamental truth about truth. So Tarski's restrictions are too severe. Furthermore, Tarski writes so as to at least strongly imply that there could be some defective language L in which some sentence was both true-in-L and false in-L, where truth-in-L is a kind of truth. And this is a fundamental falsehood about truth.

Rejecting this falsehood has been the primary aim of this section. And Tarski's position could easily accommodate this because it is not an essential part of his position. However, I also reject that aspect of his position that would leave unsaid and unsayable the fundamental truth that no sentence in any language is both true and false. And this is a central feature of his position.

This is not to accept the possibility of 'semantically closed' languages. To be semantically closed a language has to have (1) names for expressions in the language and semantic terms such as 'true' which can be applied to sentences of the language, and (2) have as 'assertible' all sentences which 'determine the adequate usage of the term "*true*"' where, for Tarski, this is to have as assertible all the so-called 'T sentences' for that language. For a language L, a T sentence would be one resulting from the form '—— is true-in-L if and only if ——' being filled first with a quotation name of a sentence of L and in the second blank with that sentence of L. Thus for a language to contain all its T sentences would be for there to be a translation of that blank form in the language and for all its appropriate substitution instances to be sentences of the language. Requirement (2) is then that all those T sentences must not only be sentences of the language (this much of the requirement is satisfied by English) but must also be assertible theorems of the language. Tarski proposes to shun semantically closed languages. But actually he does something much more severe. To avoid semantically closed languages is to avoid any language which meets *both* (1) and (2). But Tarski proposes banning from science languages which meet *either* (1) *or* (2).

My position is that failing to meet (1) just means that the language is not adequate for saying all that can be said truly. On the other hand, Tarski is quite right that a language which meets (2) is defective, given that it also meets (1). But this is just because (2) is a mistaken requirement for languages that meet (1). For example, English satisfies (1), and in English there are 'T sentences' that are clearly false – one of them is our sentence A. The sentence '"A is not true' is true if and only if A is not true" is *not* a sentence which plays any part in 'determining the adequate usage' of 'true', other than a negative one. It isn't just that this sentence is not a theorem of English because English doesn't have theorems, though that is certainly true; it should not be made a theorem in some deductive theory couched in English, because it is a false claim about the English sentence type 'A is not true' which occurs in it. The 'adequate usage' of 'true' is determined in a much more complicated way, if indeed it is 'determined' at all.

87 Russell's approach to the semantic paradoxes is similar to that of Tarski and Quine in that neither allow sentènces to say of themselves that they are true or false. But there are profound differences. Russell would not allow that semantic paradoxes could be formulated in some language. He would agree that there is no sentence in any language which says of itself that it is false. Rather than Quine's suggested 'precaution' of 'banishing' such terms as 'true-in-L' from the language L itself, Russell maintains that something like this 'precaution' is built into the nature of language, so that it could not possibly be overlooked. For example, he says:

> Thus when a man says 'I am lying', we must interpret him as meaning: 'There is a proposition of order n, which I affirm and which is false.' This is a proposition of order n + 1; hence the man is not affirming any proposition of order n; hence his statement is

false, and yet its falsehood does not imply, as that of 'I am lying' appeared to do, that he is making a true statement. This solves the liar.   (1908, p. 79)

Russell says that we *must* take the speaker to mean something about a proposition of order *n*. This is not a 'precaution' to keep our 'language' free of contradiction. It is the only meaning the speaker's words could have. Quine and Tarski speak as if a sentence which affirms its own falsity is just a sentence which it is inadvisable to have around, while Russell says that there simply could not be any such sentence.

On Russell's view, the ordinary English use of 'true' and 'false' is not in any danger from paradoxes, it is just loose and inaccurate – a misleading way of saying what, when put precisely, is immune from trouble with semantic paradoxes. When I say 'What Bill said is false', I do not make clear, in my choice of words, that what I say has an 'order' which is one higher than what Bill said; and yet this has to be how it is.

In *Principia Mathematica* (1913), Russell sets out a formalized language which, it seems, he meant would exhibit in a precise way the features he held to be present, but not so easy to make out, in a natural language. Besides this feature of making explicit such things as the level a statement has, the 'language' is like those of Tarski and Quine in having axioms and rules of inference. However, it seems likely that Russell would agree to the distinction between the language of *Principia* and the axioms expressed by means of it. Even if the axiomatic system of *Principia* is not one in which all mathematical truths can be proved, it remains open to question whether the language of *Principia* is one in which anything which can be said at all can be said.

Specifically of interest to us is Russell's view as to what it is that a sentence like our A *does* say. Russell agrees with us that A cannot say that A is not true. Our reason is that the contrary assumption leads to contradiction with indubitable principles. Russell's reasons are none too clear, but they include the doctrine that was just quoted as set forth with reference to 'I am lying'. That is: we cannot adequately speak of being 'true' or 'false'. We must instead use 'true$_n$' and 'false$_n$,' where *n* designates some specific number. And any statement containing the term 'true$_n$' or 'false$_n$' is neither true$_n$ nor false$_n$ but is of a type level higher than *n*.

One difficulty with this view is the implausibility of the claim that distinctions of order may really be read into the statements of ordinary language. Russell appears to be actually committed to the view that if I say 'What Bill said is false', then there really are two numbers, n and $n+1$, such that my statement is of level $n+1$, and Bill's statement, if he made one, is of level n. It is just that it is hard to figure out specifically what the numbers are.

This seems pretty implausible, especially if we consider a case in which I say 'What Bill said is false' where I don't even know what Bill said but am just expressing the opinion that whatever it was, was false. I won't even know what 'level' my use of 'false' is at until I know what Bill said. And I cannot say that something is false at level n, unless that thing has level $n-1$. I may try, for example, saying 'What Bill said is false$_n$'. But whether I have said anything is false$_n$ or not is not up to me, but to the thing I am talking about.

Russell says:

> the word 'false' is ambiguous, and . . . in order to make it unambiguous, we must specify the order of falsehood, or, what comes to the same thing, the order of the proposition to which falsehood is ascribed . . . if p is a proposition of the nth order, a proposition in which p occurs as an apparent variable is not of the nth order, but of a higher order.
>
> (Whitehead and Russell 1913, p. 62)

It is not good of Russell to speak of *p* as an *n*th order proposition and also an apparent variable. And it is only with respect to a system of symbolic notation that he could say that specifying the order of falsehood 'comes to the same thing' as specifying the order of the proposition to which falsehood is ascribed. When I say 'What Bill said is false' it is very different to say that the type level of what I say is for *me* to specify, and to say, on the other hand, that the type level of what I say is determined by what Bill said. The former does not require knowing what Bill said, the latter does.

Russell wants, for his idealized language, straightforward meaning assessment. The natural interpretation of Tarski's recommendations, if applied to a natural language, would allow this straightforwardness. One should be able to tell by looking at a sentence to what language (or languages) it belongs, though of course freakish languages could be imagined for which this was not possible. If I say

'The sentence on the board is true-in-L', then I am *wrong* if the sentence on the board is not a sentence of L. This should not alter the question as to what language my sentence belongs. But in applying Russell's theory, we would have to know about the sentence on the board before we could determine the type level of my remark about it. Thus, if we consider the theories as they might apply to natural languages, Russell's would be a 'stratified' theory of truth and Tarski's would not. Of course it fits Tarski's approach to set out a series of 'languages', each one a metalanguage to the one preceding it. But still, Tarski's theory does not appear to be *necessarily* hierarchical in the way Russell's is.

The exact determination of the type of a sentence is a difficult matter to relate to a natural language such as English, and is not a special concern to us anyway. For our purposes, a much more fundamental difficulty with Russell's theory is that it requires us to regard as meaningless what are in fact self-evident truths, namely the laws of logic. As Russell says:

> The first difficulty that confronts us is as to the fundamental prin-
> ciples of logic ... 'All propositions are either true or false', for
> example, has become meaningless. If it were significant, it would
> be a proposition, and would come under its own scope. Neverthe-
> less, some substitute must be found, or all general accounts of
> deduction become impossible. (1908, pp. 63–4)

This is a good occasion to remember the difference between Russell's use of 'proposition' and mine, and to recall the difficulties discussed earlier (in section 2) surrounding Russell's notion that a sentence is an 'incomplete symbol' requiring 'supplementation' in order to acquire a 'complete meaning' – that is, to be a proposition in Russell's sense.

The chief problem concerning this idea that sentences 'have no meaning in isolation', and require 'supplementation' to acquire a complete meaning, is that it threatens to deprive Russell's claim that '"All propositions are either true or false"' ... has become meaning-less' of significance. For if Russell is speaking just of the *sentence* 'All propositions are either true or false', it is not surprising that it should be meaningless, on his view, because he has declared that *no* sentence, by itself, is meaningful.

The distinction between 'All propositions are either true or false' and other sentences is probably that this sentence *cannot* be given the 'necessary supplementation', given an understanding of the term 'proposition' and the quantification of the sentence.

With this in mind, we can set out Russell's claim about the sentence 'All propositions are true or false'. If this sentence (as understood by us) were true or false, it would be a proposition. But if it were a proposition, it would 'come under its own scope'. This means in this case that it would attribute to itself the property of being either true or false. But this is impossible according to Russell's theory, because if a proposition x attributes the property of being true or false to a proposition y, then x must be one level higher than y. So x and y could not be the same proposition and thus such self-attributions are impossible.

Before examining this ruling, it is worth discussing Russell's attempt to mitigate its harshness. He says:

> the fundamental laws of logic can be stated concerning *any* proposition, though we cannot significantly say that they hold of *all* propositions. These laws have, so to speak, a particular enunciation but no general enunciation. There is no one proposition which *is* the law of contradiction (say); there are only the various instances of the law. Of any proposition p, we can say: 'p and not-p cannot both be true'; but there is no such proposition as: 'Every proposition p is such that p and not-p cannot both be true'. (1908, p. 68)

However, this is only helpful to Russell himself, for purposes of formulating his theory. For while he is allowing us to say, of any proposition *p*, 'p and not-p cannot both be true', we cannot say, according to Russell, 'we can say, of any proposition *p*, that *p* and not-p cannot both be true'. In other words, Russell holds that the sentence (as understood by us)

(vii) For any proposition *p*, it is speaking truly to say '*p* and not-*p* cannot both be true'

is true, while the sentence

(viii) For any proposition *p*, it is speaking truly to say that *p* and not-*p* cannot both be true.

is neither true nor false, that is, for him, meaningless. For it is clear that Russell's argument, 'If it were a proposition, it would come under its own scope' applies just as well to (viii) as it does to Russell's own example.

How is it that (vii) does not also fall under Russell's argument? It is a proposition, and does it not say something about every proposition? Specifically, does it not fall under its own scope just as much as (viii) would if it were a proposition?

There are at least two ways that (vii) could be understood. It could be treated as like

(vii†) For any proposition, it is speaking truly to say, with reference to it, 'It and its negation cannot both be true'

or, on the other hand, as like

(vii‡) Whatever proposition is put into the blanks of the form '"____" and the negation of "____" cannot both be true', the result is a true proposition.

In either case, it is just as true to say that 'if this is a proposition, then it falls under its own scope' as it is to say this of Russell's own example. It would be just as easy to formulate the Epimenides paradox in the style of (vii) as of (viii). If Epimenides had said 'For any proposition *p*, we can say: "If *p* is asserted by a Cretan, then *p* is false"', it would have raised just as much a problem as if he had said 'For any proposition *p*, we can say that if *p* is asserted by a Cretan then *p* is false'.

Of course, if by 'proposition' Russell had meant a sentence token, then (vii*) could not 'fall under its own scope'. But Russell does not mean this. And this approach, involving a thorough-going nominalism, would be too restrictive in its own way.

This means that Russell's gesture towards allowing us to state the laws of logic is an empty one. His theory cannot allow us to state these laws concerning '*any* proposition' any more than they can allow us to state them concerning '*all* propositions'.

An illusion to the contrary may be created by the fact that his distinction between 'any' and 'all' does help in presenting the formal language of *Principia Mathematica*. For example, Russell wants to have as an axiom (or rather, a theorem) 'No level *n* proposition is such that both it and its negation are true' for every level *n*. However he cannot achieve this by taking as an axiom 'For every level *n*, no level *n* proposition . . .', because this axiom violates the rules of his theory. But he can take as axioms all the propositions which result from putting an integer in the blank of 'No level ——— proposition is both true and false'. And this is essentially what he does.

Now what is the difference between taking as axioms all propositions of the form 'No level ——— proposition is both true and false', on the one hand, and saying, on the other hand, that all such propositions are true? Should not doing the former entail doing the latter? It should. But at least, once he has the infinity of axioms (or theorems), Russell has available the laws of logic without violating his rule about levels within the axiomatic system. It is only in the presentation of the system that he goes against his own rule. It is possible to have a formal axiomatic system such that, in that system, it is possible to prove $P(n)$, for every integer n, and yet not possible to prove 'For every n, $P(n)$'. But such a system is just as much committed to this latter assertion as a system in which it is derivable.

This is not to adopt the view that a generalization is an infinite conjunction. The notion of an infinite conjunction is obscure. The point is that if the presentation of an axiomatic system presents to the mind that apprehends it the doctrine that $P(n)$ holds for each integer n, then it presents a generalization about integers, even if the mode of presentation is such that the generalization itself is not actually derivable, in the limited technical sense, within the system. If I can learn that according to this system $P(n)$ is a theorem for every integer n, then the system is presenting me with a generalization about integers, whatever the mathematical differences between this system and one in which the generalization is provable in the technical sense may be.

This problem could be avoided ('dodged' is a better word) by saying that you are speaking in a language which is somehow a 'metalanguage' to the language of *Principia*, and saying something like 'For every proposition p formulable within the language of *Principia*, we can say, in that language, "p and not-p cannot both be true"'. This is like the approach of Tarski and Quine which has already been criticized, and would have the defects of their program. Russell's intentions are clearly different from anything like this. He would say that as far as the law of non-contradiction, for example, can be stated at all, it can be stated in the language of *Principia*.

The language of *Principia* is not a natural language, but a formalized one, and it seems that the way in which such a language can be used to say anything at all is quite different from the sense in which a natural language can be used to say things. One of the admirable things about Russell's treatment of the paradoxes is that he was concerned with language in general. However he may have overestimated the possibilities of formalized languages, he tried to base the one he developed on considerations about language that would apply to any language whatsoever, formalized or not. This makes his rulings about the paradoxes more interesting than the pragmatic approaches taken by some developers of formalized languages in order to keep their mathematical exercises free of 'contradictions'. The formalized language of *Principia Mathematica* could be presented easily (for a mathematician) as an uninterpreted formal system. But Russell's laudable effort to say what his symbolism means brings out that his views as to the limits on language are too restrictive.

The situation is like the following one. Consider sentences of the form 'The integer n has the property P'. (Property P might be, for example, the property of being the number of a level such that no proposition of that level is both true and false, if there is such a property.) Now suppose that someone proposes to set out a deductive system which has as axioms every sentence obtainable from the form by replacing 'n' with a numeral. As far as putting together a deductive system is concerned, he is under no obligation at all to go ahead and add, in addition, the axiom 'For every integer n, n has the property P.' But if he tells us that all his axioms are true, he will have told us exactly the same thing whether or not he has this latter for an axiom. And if he does not think that his axioms are true, then he is just exercising his wits in the performance of his deductions. It must be conceded that he may also discover some truths *about* formal deductive systems like his, and these truths may fascinate mathematicians. But they will not be helpful in solving the problems posed by the semantic paradoxes – that is, problems such as that of explaining what, if anything, the sentence A says.

It is possible to say 'All these sentences are my axioms' without being willing to say 'and they are, of course, all true'. You may be merely exploring the consequences of making such assumptions. But then the question of their truth is still comfortably present during the proceedings. It is when the question of their being true is set aside as somehow out of place that the study ceases to be logic and becomes at best the study of some mathematical structure which needn't be regarded as language at all.

Russell was quite right to worry about pronouncing the 'fundamental principles of logic' to be meaningless. But his principle about order commits him to doing this. No proposition is both true and false, and that includes this proposition itself. To say that this is not a proposition but a rule of language and that rules of language are neither true nor false would be a pointless maneuver, because the semantic paradoxes could then be put in terms of rules and paradoxical inconsistencies would arise as before.

That no proposition is both true and false is at least as clear as that no proposition of order n (for some particular integer n) is both true and false, or that no proposition of some particular language L is both true and false. This is the basic reason why Russell's attitude towards the semantic paradoxes, as well as the attitude of Quine and Tarski, must be rejected.

88   So far we have not, strictly speaking, considered any answers to the question as to what is said by our sentence A. But this is only due to the nicety that the two responses to the Liar paradox we have considered do not subscribe to our realist way of speaking, which distinguishes between the sentence and what it says. Otherwise we could summarize by saying that Tarski implied that A does say that A is not true, so that we really do get a contradiction, and went on to say that in good languages we should not permit sentences to say what A says or even permit any sentence about the truth or falsity of any sentence in the language. And Russell said similarly that no sentence could say something about any other sentence of the same *level* (rather than 'language'), but he put this as a necessary fact about languages rather than as a desirable feature. And his positive account, according to which sentences using 'true' and 'false' really mean 'true$_n$' and 'false$_n$', would probably force him to hold that A does not say anything at all, since it can't be of higher level than itself. And other tokens of the same type as A which were like A, that is, referred to A, would be true at some level, because the token A itself is not true (or false).

Both these theories were rejected primarily because there must be sentences which speak of their own truth and falsity if the laws of logic are to be stated in full generality.

The apparent rationale for Tarski's theory is that it is the way to avoid inconsistent languages. If his theory were necessary to avoid inconsistency, this would be a strong recommendation for it. But it is not necessary, as has been observed.

Russell offers as a rationale for his theory a principle according to which the sort of self-reference involved in the paradoxes is impossible. This is not like Tarski's suggestion that such self-reference is bad because it leads to inconsistencies. Rather, it is supposed to show that it is not possible to have such self-reference. The principle intended to support this idea is known as 'the vicious-circle principle'. Russell says:

> An analysis of the paradoxes to be avoided shows that they all result from a certain kind of vicious circle. The vicious circles in question arise from supposing that a collection of objects may contain members which can only be defined by means of the collection as a whole. Thus, for example, the collection of *propositions* will be supposed to contain a proposition stating that 'all propositions are either true or false'. It would seem, however, that such a statement could not be legitimate unless 'all propositions' referred to some already definite collection, which it cannot do if new propositions are created by statements about 'all propositions'. We shall, therefore, have to say that statements about 'all propositions' are meaningless. More generally, given any set of objects such that, if we suppose the set to have a total, it will contain members which presuppose this total, then such a set cannot have a total. By saying that a set has 'no total', we mean, primarily, that no significant statement can be made about 'all its members'. Propositions, as the above illustration shows, must be a set having no total.   (Whitehead and Russell 1913, p. 37)

(This is a strange way for a 'no-class' theorist to speak, considering that it presents the vicious-circle principle as a doctrine about classes, as the basis for a doctrine about propositions. But I will ignore this.)

A frequently noted drawback of this rationale of Russell's is that, as he writes about it in English, he often violates his own ruling. For example, to say of the set of propositions, 'no significant statement can be made about "all its members"', is to make a universally quantified statement about 'significant statements', which should be a set 'having no total'. Russell's pretense to get around this difficulty in expressing his theory has already been criticized.

Consider, in the above quotation, Russell's claim about 'All propositions are either true or false'. He says 'such a statement could not be legitimate unless "all propositions" referred to some already definite collection, which it cannot do if new propositions are created by statements about "all propositions"'. For this reason, he throws out 'All propositions are either true or false' as meaningless.

Now, either 'New propositions are created by statements about "all propositions"' is true or it is not. If it is true, then Russell's theory is wrong. If it is not true, then as Russell himself observes, it follows that propositions do form an 'already definite collection'. So why can't 'all propositions' refer to this collection, contrary to Russell's claim?

The point is this. Russell claims there are no propositions with the phrase 'all propositions' as subject. (Whether this ruling is consistent with the theory of types may be ignored for now.) He makes a pretense of giving a reason for this claim, by implying that 'all propositions' cannot refer to some already definite totality. But this is not a reason, but rather the same claim reworded. A proposition couldn't be about all propositions without being about itself, and Russell doesn't allow that a proposition can refer to itself. But the requirement that there be a 'definite totality' for legitimate reference is not an argument for this claim. It is just another version of the claim.

Russell can, of course, say that new propositions are created by statements about 'all propositions' in the sense that there will be a new proposition of higher type. That is, each time I say 'All propositions are either true or false' what I say is a 'new proposition' of one type higher than the propositions I was talking about. But this is not to be giving a reason for regarding 'All propositions are either true or false' as meaningless. This is to treat it as typically ambiguous, usable to make an ever ascending series of legitimate statements. And this is to leave the ordinary, unambiguous interpretation of the sentence out of the discussion. It is not to give reasons for thinking there can be no such interpretation.

89   Russell supports his theory of types with his objections to self-reference. Some philosophers approach the paradoxes with objections to self-reference, with no further developments such as the theory of types. One such philosopher is Ryle.

Ryle says:

When we say 'The current statement is false' we are pretending *either* that no namely-rider is to be asked for *or* that the namely-rider is '. . . Namely that the present statement is false'. If no namely-rider is to be asked for, then 'The current statement' does not refer to any statement. It is like saying 'He is asthmatic' while disallowing the question 'Who?'. If alternatively, it is pretended that there is indeed the namely-rider, '. . . namely, that the present statement is false', the promise is met by an echo of that promise. If unpacked, our pretended assertion would run 'The current statement (namely, that the current statement, namely, that the current statement . . .'. The brackets are never closed; no verb is ever reached; no statement of which we can even ask whether it is true or false is ever adduced. (1954a, p. 52)

This view has a long tradition but Ryle sets it forth in a particularly lucid way. Langford presents a similar view, but his version is marred by old-fashioned mistakes about the use of quotes (Lewis and Langford, 1959, chap. 13). Langford would say, for example of A, that attempts to replace the 'defined symbol' 'A' with its value lead to an infinite regress. But the value of the symbol 'A' is just a sentence and it is forthcoming with no regress. Ryle makes it clear that the sentence won't be enough to satisfy him, and makes clear why.

However, Ryle's namely-rider test won't do to justify his remark that 'inattention to grammar is the source of such paradoxes as the "Liar"', if we take the 'Liar', not as A, but as the Epimenides, which deserves the name just as well. How do we apply the namely-rider test to 'Every statement made by a Cretan is false'? Cretans might go on making statements until the end of time. It could hardly be fair to expect Epimenides to produce them all, and he might very well be able to produce quite a number of false ones. The fact that he did this would not help us with the paradox.

For that matter, Ryle's test doesn't really apply at all well to A. Ryle's example is 'The current statement is false', which is like 'The proposition this sentence expresses is false'. A, on the other hand, is like 'This sentence does not express a true proposition'. Ryle's test is to ask what proposition it is, but in the case of A this seems altogether out of place.

As it stands, Ryle's objection would even seem to apply to my statement-candidate 'The sentence John uttered at noon yesterday expressed a false proposition', if John had asked a question at noon yesterday. On learning that John had uttered 'What time is it?' I would say that I was wrong, that what I said was false, but Ryle could complain of my remark about John that 'no statement of which we can even ask whether it is true or false is ever adduced', and thus he might say that what I said wasn't even a statement.

Of course there is a difference between 'What I am saying is false' and 'The sentence John uttered at noon yesterday expressed a false proposition', assuming that John asked a question rather than saying something that sets up a Liar family paradox. In each case, we ask, 'Namely, what proposition?' But when we bring forward John's sentence it does not invite further questions, while producing this paradox sentence does. Also, John's sentence does not even make a grammatical namely-rider expansion possible. Suppose he said, 'What time is it?' Then 'The sentence John uttered at noon yester-day expressed a false proposition, namely the proposition that what time is it' isn't even good grammar (in the traditional sense of 'grammar'). But 'I am asserting a false proposition, namely, the proposition that I am asserting a false proposition' is all right from a grammatical standpoint.

So there are two different ways in which a statement-candidate could fail to satisfy us when asked the 'Namely?' question. It might be *just* that 'no statement of which we can even ask whether it is true or false is ever adduced', or it might be *further*, that the 'Namely?' question generates an infinite regress – a *grammatical* infinite regress.

This might be exploited as a way of improving Ryle's theory. A statement-candidate will be rejected only if the 'Namely?' question leads to an infinite regress of grammatically correct expansions of the original statement-candidate. Otherwise, we are still free to call it false even if it isn't possible to produce a satisfactory answer to the 'Namely?' question.

This notion of 'grammatically correct expansion' would call for some clarification. For example, if John had uttered 'Bill' at noon yesterday in response to the question 'Who won the race?', then we would normally agree that John had made a statement. But if I say 'The sentence John uttered at noon yesterday expressed a false proposition', I can't reply to the question 'Namely, what proposi-tion?', 'Namely, that Bill'. However, we can allow for ellipsis, but we mustn't think it is a trivial matter, because it is important that the 'namely . . .' should stick to the words which were said if our notion of a namely-rider expansion is to be a purely grammatical matter. And it must be a purely grammatical matter if we are to distinguish between the case in which 'no statement of which we can even ask whether it is true or false' is forthcoming and the words which are produced do not even invite a grammatical regress and the case in which no statement is forthcoming but the words which are produced do invite a grammatical regress.

The use of the notion of a grammatical regress serves to spare innocent remarks such as 'What John said at noon yesterday is false' from Ryle's theory. There remain two main objections: first, that the theory's treatment of things like A is unjustified, and second, that the theory does not apply generally enough to cover, for example, the Epimenides.

An attempt to answer the first of these might begin with the idea that 'A is not true' might be true in two different ways. It might be that A does not express a proposition, or it might be that A expresses a proposition which is not true (and thus false). So we could treat A as like the disjunction 'Either A does not express a proposition or A expresses a false proposition'. And then the 'namely-rider' test could fairly be applied to the second disjunct, which would fail the test.

On the other hand, there is no basis for applying the 'namely-rider' test to the first disjunct. The best course is to rule that 'This sentence expresses a proposition' is true, while 'This sentence does not express a proposition' (which of course is not the negation of the former) is false. Then whether the first disjunct is true or false depends on what we say about a disjunction with a meaningless disjunct (where we mean by 'disjunct', 'disjunct in the grammatical sense').

If we say that a disjunction with a meaningless disjunct says nothing, then the first disjunct is true. If we say that such a disjunction just says what the meaningful disjunct says, then the first disjunct is false. In this latter case, the disjunction would thus be classed as false, while in the former, it would say nothing and thus would have no truth value. This second course fits Ryle's assessment of paradox sentences.

There is a serious difficulty with this approach to applying the namely-rider test to A. A is not a disjunction, and if it is meaningless, as the account says, then it is not logically equivalent to a disjunction either. So then what basis is there for saying that A fails the namely-rider test just because a disjunction such as 'Either this sentence does not express a proposition or it expresses a proposition which is not true' fails the test? If being meaningless doesn't keep a sentence out of logical relations, then being meaningless will not eliminate the sentence as a logical trouble-maker.

Another objection to applying the namely-rider test to A is that if, as the test says, A doesn't express a proposition, then it would seem to follow that A doesn't express a *true* proposition. But this, which seems to follow from the test's ruling, fails the test in the same way A does.

However, even if Ryle's namely-rider test could provide a good account of A, it does not apply to the Epimenides, and if it is extended to apply to it, the theory then becomes too restrictive in the same way Russell's is.

The way to extend Ryle's theory to the paradoxes involving quantifiers would be to bring in the additional notions of 'for example' riders and 'e.g.' riders. Thus of 'Every proposition of kind *k* is false' we can ask 'For example?', and we can rule that the only propositions which can fall within the range of the quantifier are those which can be cited in response to 'For example?' without generating a grammatical infinite regress. Similarly, with 'Some proposition of kind *k* is false', we can ask 'e.g.?', and rule that the only things which could be accepted as true or false answers must be such as to avoid a grammatical infinite regress.

The Epimenides paradox fails this 'for example' test, but so do the laws of logic. No proposition is both true and false, and that includes the proposition that no proposition is both true and false. Thus it is only by being left undeveloped that Ryle's theory avoids being just as objectionably restrictive as the theories of Russell and Tarski. And Ryle's theory is worse than Russell's in that Russell at least offers an explanation why, if it is possible to say that A is not true, then A itself does not say it. He denies that it is possible to say, *simpliciter*, that A is not true. But Ryle does not take up the question at all of explaining why A does not say that A is not true, if other sentences do say this.

90 Strawson (1949) makes remarks which suggest a line of solution to the paradoxes which I shall call the 'performatory theory'. It is suggested by such remarks as:

The paradoxes arise on the assumption that the words 'true' and 'false' can be used to make first-order assertions. They are formally solved by the declaration that these words can be used to make only second-order assertions. Both paradoxes and solution disappear on the more radical assumption that they are not used to make assertions of any order, are not used to make assertions at all.   (p. 271)

To complete the analysis, then, of the entire sentence (3) 'What the policeman said is true', we have to add, to the existential meta-assertion, a phrase which is not assertive, but (if I may borrow Mr. Austin's word) performatory. We might, e.g., offer, as a complete analysis of one case, the expression: 'The policeman made a statement. I confirm it.'; where, in uttering the words 'I confirm it', I am not describing something I do, but *doing* something.   (pp. 272–3)

To say that the performatory theory is 'suggested' by these remarks is no understatement. A good deal of development will be necessary before the theory can be evaluated in its strongest form.

Strawson regards his essay as developing ideas of Ramsey (1931, 'Facts and Propositions'), specifically Ramsey's theory of truth, according to which the terms 'true' and 'false' are eliminable. Of course if they are eliminable, they are introducible too, but Ramsey's idea was to show that they are conceptually dispensable and thus show that 'there is no separate problem of truth'. This project bogged down in Ramsey's generally rejected analysis of generality. But at any rate, Ramsey never intended it as a line of solution to the paradoxes. His own solution was basically similar to Russell's.

To see how useless the eliminability of 'true' and 'false' is, we have only to consider the Epimenides. One version would be to have Epimenides (a Cretan) assert 'Every proposition asserted by a Cretan is false'. Applying Ramsey's method to eliminate 'false' from this sentence would give 'For every proposition p, if p is asserted by a Cretan, then not-p'. Whether or not this method of Ramsey's is acceptable is not of concern here. The main point is that any logical trouble posed by the original is posed equally by the version without 'false'. So insofar as Strawson's theory really does follow Ramsey's, it does not tend to make the paradoxes 'disappear'.

Strawson has said 'I reject the thesis that the phrase "is true" is logically superfluous' (1950a, p. 147), but he is so using 'logically' that this claim would be consistent with holding that the phrase 'is true' is logically superfluous. That is, Strawson's remark is not intended to make the claim that there could not be a general theory such as Ramsey's, which told us how, for any statement containing 'is true', to construct a logically equivalent statement from which 'is true' was non-trivially absent.[2] Rather he is saying that these logical equivalents might lack some of the contextual nuances possessed by the ones containing 'is true'.

For example, Strawson says of 'true' and 'not true' that 'In using them, we are not *just* asserting that X is Y or that X is not Y ... we may also be granting, denying, confirming, etc.' (1950a, p. 147). However, in my exposition of the performatory theory, 'granting that', 'asserting that', and the like, will be run together in a very coarse way.

What I find most interesting in Strawson's remarks is the suggestion that something like:

THE STATEMENT WRITTEN BELOW THIS IS FALSE
ALL MEN ARE MORTAL

might be treated as accomplishing the same thing as

THE STATEMENT WRITTEN BELOW THIS IS HEREBY DENIED
ALL MEN ARE MORTAL

Now if we find:

THE STATEMENT WRITTEN BELOW THIS IS FALSE
THE STATEMENT WRITTEN ABOVE THIS IS TRUE

and we stick to the above interpretation, it will cause no more trouble than:

THE STATEMENT WRITTEN BELOW THIS IS HEREBY DENIED
THE STATEMENT WRITTEN ABOVE THIS IS HEREBY AFFIRMED

and it seems plausible to write these off as empty gestures – one an affirmation which comes to nothing, the other a denial which comes to nothing.

One objection which might be raised is that 'The statement written below is hereby denied' can't be equivalent to 'The state-

[2] By 'non-trivially absent' I mean that the equivalences would not be achieved merely by replacing 'true' with some trivial equivalent such as 'corresponds to reality'.

ment written below is false', since the former claims that something is denied while the latter makes no such claim, not even a claim that something is called false. But we are interested in what is accomplished by the latter expression, what performance it amounts to, and we say that the former does whatever the latter does. If someone says 'I say it is raining', he may be taken to report that he says it is raining, or to report that it is raining, or to report both these things. The first of these seems plainly not what is usually meant by someone who says 'I say it is raining'. However, cases could be imagined in which it does mean this, say if the speaker were pointing to a place where, in writing, he says it is raining.

Strawson clearly favors the second interpretation. Recall his remark that 'in uttering the words "I confirm it", I am not describing something I do, but *doing* something' (1949, p. 273). However, in uttering any words I am doing something, but this is not incompatible with my also describing what I do. When, after I say 'I confirm it', someone says of me, 'He confirms it', then he is not confirming, but only reporting my confirming. But why cannot I be *both* confirming and reporting my confirming? What is there about confirming and reporting to preclude this?

Suppose that several people all say 'It's true' referring to the same assertion. The traditional view is that they have all made the same assertion. This could be denied by claiming that each has made a *different* assertion ('I, Jones, confirm it', 'I, Smith, confirm it', 'I, Brown, confirm it', etc.). It is a further step to claim that Jones, Smith, Brown, *et al.*, weren't saying anything and were only indicating their confirmation.

At any rate, if I say, for example, 'What Bill said is true', then if someone says 'You're wrong', he certainly is not concerned to deny that I have affirmed what Bill said. It is my affirmation he will be disagreeing with. It is the main thing about my performance.

The idea that affirmations and denials do not create propositions over and above those denied or affirmed is supposed to help with the paradoxes. This is our main concern. But the idea needs clarification first.

Another objection to the performatory theory might be that 'p is false' is not synonymous with 'p is hereby denied'. But the theory need not deny this. It is obvious that the two expressions do not have the same use, and this will be even more obvious in the case of other pairs of expressions to be compared later on. In saying 'p is hereby denied', you might not even succeed in denying *p*, since in many contexts this expression would hardly be understood, as it is not a phrase in common ordinary use. But all this does not mean that in saying '*p* is false' you aren't denying *p*, any more than the fact that 'Jones is a scoundrel' doesn't mean the same as 'Jones is hereby condemned' should lead us to deny that to say 'Jones is a scoundrel' is usually to condemn Jones. In comparing '*p* is false' with '*p* is hereby denied' we are seeking to better understand the *function* of the expression '*p* is false' in order to see why such an expression, though it has many normal uses, does not work in such a way as to make a genuine paradox.

Let us return to:

THE STATEMENT WRITTEN BELOW THIS IS FALSE
ALL MEN ARE MORTAL

The first of these is the sort of expression from which Liar family paradoxes are made. It refers to another statement. The performatory theory might better be named the 'parsimony of meaning theory', since it tells us the first expression involves fewer propositions than we usually think. Our usual intuitions, the ones which are challenged by the paradoxes, tell us that the two expressions each express a proposition. The second expresses the proposition that all men are mortal, the first expresses 'the proposition that the statement written below it is false'. But the performatory theory tells us that there is just one proposition involved among the pair of expressions: the proposition that all men are mortal.

It is not clear whether Strawson would mean his claim that the first of the two above expressions is not an assertion to have the consequence that this expression does not constitute a false statement. Of course saying it is a false statement would just be our denial of it and all that, but is it something which can be denied? Can we affirm and deny affirmations and denials, or is this only possible with propositions?

It might be said that when I disagree with someone's denial, I should not say 'What you say is false', but rather, 'You're wrong', or some such. This sort of question is best postponed until we are actually attempting to apply the theory to the paradoxes. Strawson says that the terms 'true' and 'false' are not used to make assertions, and I am taking this as the claim that the concepts of truth and falsity do not figure as constituents in any *asserted* propositions, that, for example, there is no *assertion* of the form '*p* is false'. Let us call such expressions as '*p* is false', *performatory* vehicles.

The following comparisons are intended to show how performatory vehicles may be distinguished from propositional vehicles:

ALL THE STATEMENTS WRITTEN BELOW THIS ARE FALSE
ALL MEN ARE MORTAL
LOTS OF CANDY IS GOOD FOR CHILDREN
GRASS IS GREEN

is to be compared with:

ALL THE STATEMENTS WRITTEN BELOW THIS ARE HEREBY DENIED
ALL MEN ARE MORTAL
LOTS OF CANDY IS GOOD FOR CHILDREN
GRASS IS GREEN

or alternatively, with:

A DENIAL OF ANY STATEMENT WRITTEN BELOW THIS IS HEREBY OFFERED
ALL MEN ARE MORTAL
LOTS OF CANDY IS GOOD FOR CHILDREN
GRASS IS GREEN

In each of these three lists only three propositions are expressed, though there are four statements, two true and two false.

SOME STATEMENT WRITTEN BELOW THIS IS FALSE
ALL MEN ARE MORTAL
LOTS OF CANDY IS GOOD FOR CHILDREN
GRASS IS GREEN

is to be compared with:

A DENIAL OF SOME STATEMENT WRITTEN BELOW THIS IS HEREBY OFFERED
ALL MEN ARE MORTAL
LOTS OF CANDY IS GOOD FOR CHILDREN
GRASS IS GREEN

In each of these lists there are three propositions and four statements, three true and one false.

The offer of a denial in the last list is like a bartender who says 'I hereby offer to give someone in the house a free drink'. No person in the house is offered a free drink, but the bartender is nonetheless committed to giving someone a free drink. In this way an offer of a denial or affirmation differs from a denial or affirmation. That is, the difference is revealed by contrasting 'I hereby offer to deny some statement . . .' with 'I hereby deny some statement . . .'. When a denial of a specific statement is offered, the performance is the same as that of just denying it. If someone offers to call you a fool, with sincerity, it is just as insulting as if he went ahead and called you a fool. That is, it is just as insulting if it is understood that what is being offered is a *sincere* insult, made without changing present attitudes. It might not be insulting to say 'I admire you immensely, but if you should want me to sincerely call you a fool, I would then take the drugs necessary to enable me to do such a terrible thing'. But this is not the sort of offering here meant.

This treatment of general propositions can be extended to apply to things like 'All men are mortal' rather than just to things of the form 'All (some) propositions of kind K are true (false)' and other forms which serve to deny or affirm some or all of a class of propositions.

If this were done, the only propositions remaining expressed in assertions would bè atomic and relational ones, plus compounds of these. The result might bear some resemblance to Ramsey's analysis of generality, which made an assertion of, for example, $(x)Fx$ into an assertion of an infinite conjunction consisting of the values of Fx. However, there is the crucial difference that such a 'conjunctive proposition' is an unusually long one, and our theory would have no proposition at all corresponding to $(x)Fx$ over and above the propositions which are expressed by instances of the form Fx.

Against Ramsey's analysis it might be objected that saying 'All the Straws are happy' couldn't be the same as saying 'Jack Straw is happy and Mary Straw is happy and Billy Straw is happy', even if that were all the Straws, since the latter would be consistent with 'There is one Straw who isn't happy' while the former would not be. The complaint against Ramsey's analysis into a conjunction would be that we have left out the crucial 'And that's all the Straws there are', which could not be built into the conjunction without making Ramsey's analysis circular.

This objection would not apply to the performatory theory. For the performatory theory, 'Every proposition of kind K is false' is the form of a performatory vehicle serving to deny every proposition of kind *K*. And to do this requires no *proposition* to the effect that every proposition of kind *K* is false. Such a proposition is of no use to the performance or to determining the truth value of the performance.

'Every proposition of kind *K* is false' could be compared with the performance of a politician who says 'I hereby congratulate anyone who succeeds in the oil venture out west'. No one may succeed; or people may succeed, and thus fall under the congratulation, whom the politician may wish hadn't fallen under it. But everyone who succeeds falls under it, and this is seen to by the performatory vehicle, not by a proposition.

It should be noted that in giving performatory accounts of quantified statements, quantificational expressions are used freely. For example, 'Some men are mortal' is held to be an offer to affirm mortality of some man. But there is no circularity here. The idea is not to find an original proposition equivalent to some other, as in Ramsey's theory. Rather, the theory holds that what was thought to involve a proposition, really involves only an act of offering.

P COULD BE FALSE

is to be compared with:

A DENIAL OF P RELATIVE TO SOME SPECIFICATION OF A POSSIBLE WORLD IS HEREBY OFFERED

and

P IS NECESSARILY FALSE

is to be compared with:

P IS HEREBY DENIED UNRESTRICTEDLY WITH REGARD TO ANY SPECIFICATION OF A POSSIBLE WORLD

Other comparisons for modal statements should be suggested by these two. In '*p* could be false', the main point is that *p* is the only proposition involved.

Comparisons such as the above should make clear why the performatory theory could be regarded as a 'parsimony of meaning' theory. The theory holds that affirming or asserting, and denying, are performances which do not *create* propositions. To say that *p* is false is to deny *p*, and this performance is accomplished by a performatory vehicle, and not by any new proposition.

An important qualification for the performatory theory is to stress the word *assertion* in the claim that 'true' and 'false' do not serve to make assertions. The theory claims that *asserting* that every proposition of kind K is true is just to affirm every proposition of kind K. It would be foolish to hold that *believing* that every proposition of kind K is true is to believe every proposition of kind K. The 'proposition that every proposition of kind K is true' is only eliminated from assertions, not necessarily from beliefs.

Asserting 'Every proposition of kind K is true' is to commit yourself to the truth of each proposition of kind K. It is like wagering that each proposition of kind K is true. Your money may be at risk on propositions you do not know of.

Since the 'belief' formulations of the paradoxes were set aside in section 81, the fact that the performatory theory does not deal with belief cases does not disqualify it as an approach to the semantic paradoxes.

We must now ask how the performatory theory affects the laws of logic, and the premises (1), (2) and (5) set out in section 80. We certainly don't want to interpret 'Every proposition is either true or false' as like 'Every proposition is either affirmed or denied'.

One course would be to regard the laws of logic as *performance nouns*. The law of non-contradiction could be treated as like 'No proposition should be both affirmed and denied' and the law of excluded middle as like 'Every proposition should be either affirmed or denied'. These laws would be addressed to the individual thinker.

This interpretation of the law of excluded middle makes the law sound very implausible. The interpretation could be reserved for an Intuitionist faction among performatory theorists, but it would not do for those who respect the law. So it seems best to try a different course – resolutely side-stepping the question.

The performatory theory is only obliged to show that there is no asserting truth and no asserting falsity, of things. It could be said that this does not require that there be no asserting truth-or-falsity. It could be held that claiming a thing has a truth value is not the same as claiming it is true or claiming it is false. Similarly, the theory can leave the 'true' in 'If P is true, then Q' undisturbed, since it is not asserted of P.

(On my own theory of assertion in section 79, asserting that P is either true or false entails that you have either asserted P or denied

P, though you may be unable to find out which you have done. You will have asserted *P* if it is true, denied it if it is false. But this is of course perfectly compatible with the above denial that asserting *P* is either true or false is not the same as asserting *P* or denying *P*. The difference is just that, on my theory, there is such a property as being true, and further, the assertion or denial of *p* will be of the kind I have called 'non-assessable'.)

Premise (1) could be left unchanged for the same reasons. Or it could be interpreted as saying that to affirm a sentence is to affirm what it says. Premise (2) will be discussed later. Premise (5) is an instance of the general rule 'The proposition that *p*, is true if and only if *p*'. Perhaps this could be taken to mean, for example, just that to say that 'the proposition that all men are mortal is true' is the same as to say that 'all men are mortal'.

Ramsey's method for eliminating 'true' and 'false' works equally well in belief contexts, logical laws, and within unasserted parts of compounds. This serves to show up the difference between Ramsey's view and the performatory theory. The important difference is that the performatory theory is concerned with affirming and denying, and applies just as well to the sentences from which 'true' and 'false' are eliminated by Ramsey's method as it does to the originals. Thus if I say 'Everything Bill said is true', I give a blanket endorsement of every proposition Bill asserted and those are the only propositions involved. But if I say 'For every proposition *p*, if *p* was asserted by Bill, then *p*' I give exactly the same performance – a blanket endorsement of the propositions asserted by Bill, and no other proposition is involved. The performatory theory doesn't just trade in 'It's false' in favor of 'It's not the case'. It holds that in either case the only proposition involved is the one (if any) denoted by 'it' and the two sentences are performatory vehicles serving in 'its' denial.

I hope that this discussion, sketchy as it is, suffices to show that the performatory theory represents a view about truth and related matters, which, though radical, is not lightly refutable. This doesn't make it true, of course, and I would be among the first to reject it if that were the question. We need to know if the theory explains the paradoxes. Strawson did not make clear *why* 'the paradoxes disappear on the radical assumption that 'true' and 'false' are not used to make assertions'. He did not, in fact, even work out the radical assumption to show it was feasible. But having at least begun this, we are still left with the question, from our standpoint, of 'So what?'

What can the performatory theory contribute to the problem of paradoxes? In further elaborating the theory, we must relate it to the paradoxes.

It would seem to be Strawson's intention to have it that A says nothing, and is just an empty gesture of denial, or a device for use in making denials which is not in a working role.

This raises a question which should be familiar by now. What if *we* want to conclude that the sentence A is not true, in the same way that we might want to say that 'bxklil' is not true? Isn't this a judgement of fact, not a denial? And for that matter, why couldn't A be interpreted in the same way? This would restore the original problem.

If we were studying the performatory theory itself, with no interest in applying it to paradoxes, we could allow it to set aside things like ' "bxklil" isn't true' as 'non-standard' uses of 'true' which really don't involve affirming. But that would leave unanswered the difficulty about A.

Here the only course is for the theory to hold that

'BXKLIL' IS NOT TRUE

is to be compared with

'BXKLIL' DOES NOT SAY ANYTHING WHICH IS HEREBY AFFIRMED

Applying this to A leaves us with something like 'A does not say anything which is hereby affirmed'. To follow the course of regarding this as purely performatory would require counting it as just a case of ostentatiously refraining from affirming. And it would be an empty gesture, like a no-confidence vote cast by someone who mistakenly thinks there is a government when in fact he has been deceived, and there is none.

This account rejects premise (2) and offers an explanation for doing so. And other tokens of the same type as A would get the same treatment. There would be no problem for the performatory theory in explaining why A can't say something other tokens of the same type can.

For all that, the assessment of A as a performance can still be a bit of a teaser. Refraining from trying to affirm what A says might be praised as very judicious, considering that A doesn't say anything. So we might regard A and other tokens of its type as making a wise gesture. Similarly, if the man who cast his no-confidence vote had done so by saying 'We do not have a government in which I place my confidence', this might be regarded as a very appropriate gesture in a case where we have no government at all. On the other hand, if we regard him as intending to hurt the government's feelings, his gesture is pretty empty. Similarly, if we interpret A's gesture as an attempt to slight A, the performance does not seem so felicitous. But these do not seem to be very formidable questions for logic.

So it seems that the performatory theory does at least give an internally coherent account of a paradox such as A. This leaves two major questions. First, how does the theory do with the other semantic paradoxes? And second, at what cost has the theory been able to avoid logical difficulty over A?

Let us consider the Epimenides. If Epimenides the Cretan says that every proposition asserted by a Cretan is false, then on the performatory theory he has not even made a self-referring statement. He has just given a blanket denial of propositions asserted by Cretans, and not asserted any new proposition in the process.

Suppose now that we try to upgrade the problem by having Epimenides try to include Cretan performatory gestures under his denial. Here again we have our earlier question. Can we affirm and deny affirmations and denials?

Suppose we rule that affirmations can only be çalled 'right' or 'wrong', not 'true' or 'false'. This doesn't help avoid paradox. Suppose Epimenides says 'No performatory gesture made by a Cretan is right'. Is not calling a gesture 'right' or 'wrong' as much a performatory gesture as calling an assertion 'right' or 'wrong'? So suppose that it happens that Epimenides' gesture is the only one ever made by a Cretan. Is it right or not? Here is a familiar Liar paradox situation for which the performatory theory seems unhelpful.

If, instead of saying that calling a performatory gesture 'right' or 'wrong' is itself a gesture, we said instead that it is to make an assertion, to attribute the property of being right or the property of being wrong, we would then have some pretty powerful technical equipment for dealing with paradoxes, equipment reminiscent of that found in some formal set theories. If Epimenides said 'No Cretan gesture is right', that would be an assertion and not a gesture. And if he said 'No Cretan assertion is true', that would be a gesture and not an assertion. But to allow the asserting of wrongness but not the asserting of falsity would be to arbitrarily fabricate a distinction (in a way also reminiscent of formal set theories) where there is none in reality.

However, there is another possible response to the Epimenides which might be suggested on behalf of the performatory theory, which is worth discussing. It might be said that Epimenides' utterance of 'No Cretan gesture is right' cannot be a gesture applying to itself on the grounds that gestures can't apply to themselves. This sort of suggestion amounts to grafting on to the performatory theory an objection to self-reference which has no essential connection with it. My main objection to banning self-reference is that such logical laws as 'no proposition is both true and false' clearly apply to themselves. The performatory theory's suspicious treatment of logical laws has so far been tolerated for the sake of discussion. But suppose I say 'No gesture which affirms a contradiction is right'. Even if we tolerate having to regard this as just a gesture of mine, a blanket denial by me of affirmations of contradictions, it is intolerable to me that I should not be able to regard my gesture itself as one which would be wrong if it were the affirmation of a contradiction. So the gesture does fall under itself, and even if the performatory theory were true, it would not entail denying this. The rejection of self-reference, besides being mistaken, would be an ad hoc 'anti-paradox' clause grafted on to the performatory theory.

This brings me back to the comment at the beginning of this section: Ramsey's theory of truth was never intended as a solution to the paradoxes. It was also wrong, but even if it had been right, it wouldn't have helped with the paradoxes, and Ramsey knew this perfectly well. It is possible to have a theory of truth, even a right one, without thus getting an explanation for the paradoxes which will supplement the crossing out approach with some further rationale. But there is a tendency for philosophers to think, every time some new idea about logical classification comes up, that this must somehow 'cause the paradoxes to disappear'. For example, Strawson's distinction between sentence and statement has been thought to 'solve' the paradoxes. (In this work this distinction has been ignored, and the formulations of the paradoxes given here should serve to show its irrelevance.) Even Hare's neustic-phrastic distinction has been thought to cull out the paradoxes from our language.

The tendency is understandable, because a 'solution' to the

paradoxes over and above 'crossing out' will be a theory about how language works. It's just that not even all theories about how 'true' and 'false' work are solutions to the paradoxes. A theory may explain some things without its following that it explains everything.

91 There are 'non-stratified' theories of truth which also preserve straightforwardness of meaning assessment. One is outlined by Bochenski (1970, pp. 249–51) and attributed to Paul of Venice. As Bochenski presents it, the solution involves giving up the principle

(1.1) If A signifies *P*, then A is true if and only if *P* (which is essentially our premise (1)), and replacing it with the principle

(1.2) If A signifies *P*, then A is true if and only if (i) A is true, and (ii) *P*.

The effect of this change is to replace a principle which tells us that 'All men are mortal' is true *if and only if* all men are mortal, with one which tells us that 'All men are mortal' is true only if (i) 'All men are mortal' is true and (ii) all men are mortal. In other words, (1.2) involves just giving up stating sufficient conditions for the truth of a sentence in terms of what it says. We can use (1.2) to prove A is not true, but we cannot go on to prove A true, because we have no principle stating conditions for the truth of any sentence in terms of what it says.

Furthermore, contenting ourselves with adopting (1.2) as answer to the paradoxes would involve holding that A is not true while refusing to credit A as true for saying precisely that. But if the proposition that A is not true is a true proposition, and A expresses only it, we get the result that A is not true even though the proposition it expresses is true. And this is a strange idea.

This latter objection to the Paul of Venice solution would also hold against any such strategy as altering premise (1) to

(1.3) A sentence is true if and only if
    (i) The proposition it expresses is true, and
    (ii) The assumption that the sentence expresses that proposition does not lead to a contradiction by premise (i).

In other words, (1.3) would also lead to calling A not true while it expresses only a true proposition.

Jean Buridan (1966) discussed a solution based on ruling that any propositional vehicle conveys the proposition that it is itself true, whatever else it may convey. This makes A into a harmless contradiction. Working in terms of a meaning postulate rather than an alteration in premise (1) avoids the second objection raised against Paul's solution which was that the alteration leaves A expressing only a true proposition and yet classes A as not true. The Buridan solution has A expressing two propositions which contradict each other, so that it escapes this objection. But the first objection to Paul's solution still applies. What makes 'All men are mortal' true if it isn't that all men *are* mortal? We can't verify ' "All men are mortal" is true' if to do so always involves first verifying ' "All men are mortal" is true'. Besides, 'All men are mortal' clearly *doesn't* say of itself that it is true – which is why Buridan himself rejected this theory.

Buridan sets forth an answer to one semantic paradox which does involve giving up premise (1). He says, 'it does not suffice for a proposition to be true that it is as it signifies . . . Rather, it is required that it is as signified by the consequent which was virtually implied' (1966, p. 195). It would seem that this answer is open to the second objection raised against Paul. However, Buridan is a nominalist and his term 'proposition' is not used in the sense followed here. I do not propose to take up the evaluation of this answer in detail.

92 The idea that the truth of a sentence should be determined, not just by what it says, but by some of the *consequences* of what it says, is in my opinion, unsatisfactory. But it is a very suggestive idea.

One important kind of 'consequence' a sentence may have is not a 'logical consequence', but the result of *expanding* the sentence with a namely-rider. For example, consider

(x1) What x2 says is false.
(x2) All men are mortal.
(x3) What x2 says, namely that all men are mortal, is false.

Ordinarily it would not be held that x1 entails x3. For x2 might have been some other sentence than 'All men are mortal'. Or it might be said that x1 is *ambiguous*, and if 'what x2 says' is taken 'purely referentially', then x3 follows from x1. But otherwise, it

Semantic Paradoxes 281

would be held that other premises would be required in order for x3 to follow. In any case, there is an important sense in which x3, being a namely-rider expansion of x1, could be called a consequence of x1. This relation of consequence holds between sentences. Nominalist logicians would similarly hold that logical consequence is a relation between sentences, holding because of the form of the sentences. In my opinion, logical consequence holds between what is said by sentences, though the form of the sentences may be one important criterion for determining whether such a relation holds. 'Namely-rider' consequences are rather consequences of attempting to specify what is said. Ryle held that since there is an infinite regressive series generated by the namely-rider consequences of trying to say what is said by a given Liar-type paradox, such paradox sentences are nonsense. It has already been observed that this reason, if generalized to apply to all the semantic paradoxes, would effect the laws of logic as well, so that it is not a good reason for holding semantic paradoxes to be nonsensical. There is another objection as well. If a namely-rider expansion is supposed to be presenting the proposition the assertion is about, there is no reason to think that merely inserting the words of the sentence the assertion is about will automatically name the proposition the assertion is about.

It is not a correct account of what A says to say that it says that A is not true. Nor is it a correct account of the truth conditions of A to say that A is true if and only if A is not true. It is correct to say that 'All men are mortal' is true if and only if all men are mortal and that 'All men are mortal' expresses the proposition that all men are mortal. Someone who thinks that this trivial style of answer, which works fine for 'All men are mortal', is somehow an essential feature of any adequate account of truth conditions is bound to go wrong in dealing with the semantic paradoxes.

This fact must not be overlooked, but it is interesting to note what happens when we do uncritically form namely-rider expansions in the way Ryle (1954a) does. For example, consider the sentence 'This sentence is false', which is an easier example to start with than A. In order to apply Ryle's notion of a namely-rider, as opposed to the inaccurately formulated version of Langford, we must regard this sentence as elliptical for 'What this sentence says is false'. For we do not want 'This sentence, namely "this sentence..."'. Rather, we have, as the first namely-rider expansion, 'What this sentence says, namely, that what this sentence says is false, is false'. What is interesting is that, besides the infinite regress of which Ryle complains, this first namely-rider expansion is inconsistent with the original sentence.

A is a more complex case, because, as was observed earlier, if we regard it as elliptical for 'A does not express a true proposition', it seems obviously wrong to ask, 'Namely, what proposition?' But unlike Ryle, who holds A is nonsense, our theory can treat A as equivalent to the disjunction 'Either A expresses a proposition which is not true or A does not express a proposition'. But we reject the second disjunct as false and so it is fair to apply the 'Namely?' question to the first disjunct. And the 'namely-rider' expansion of this first disjunct, namely 'A expresses a proposition which is not true, namely, that A is not true', is inconsistent with A.

'Every proposition of kind K is false' does not have a namely-rider expansion, but an example of a 'for example' expansion would be if 'All men are mortal' happened to be a proposition of kind K: 'Every proposition of kind K, for example, the proposition that all men are mortal, is false'. Here again we may note that Epimenides' statement 'Every Cretan statement is false' has as one of its 'for example' expansions, 'Every Cretan statement, for example the statement that every Cretan statement is false, is false'. Epimenides' statement is inconsistent with one of its 'for example' expansions.

A statement of the form 'Some statement of kind K is false' would not invite either a namely-rider or a 'for example' expansion. Sometimes such a statement invites an 'e.g.' expansion. For example, we might say 'Some statement of kind K, e.g. the statement that some men live forever, is false'.

Let us consider the Policeman paradox. The policeman deposes that some statement deposed by the prisoner is false and deposes nothing else, and the prisoner deposes that something deposed by the policeman is true, and deposes nothing else. Since the only thing the prisoner uttered is 'Some statement deposed by the policeman is true', it seems fair to say that the 'e.g.' expansion of the policeman's statement must be[3] 'Some statement deposed by the prisoner, e.g. the statement that some statement deposed by the policeman is true, is false'. This is the *first expansion* of the policeman's statement. The

---

[3] When a particular 'e.g.' expansion is the only such expansion that is available, or any other 'e.g.' expansion is false I shall say it is an *unavoidable* 'e.g.' expansion.

second expansion will be what is obtained by expanding the 'Some statement deposed by the policeman is true' which occurs in the first expansion. Thus the second expansion of the policeman's statement will be the result of following the words of the prisoner which occur in the first expansion of the policeman's statement by citing the words of the policeman's statement. The second expansion of the policeman's statement is thus: 'Some statement deposed by the prisoner, e.g., the statement that some statement deposed by the policeman, e.g., the statement that some statement deposed by the prisoner is false, is true, is false'. The interest of this is that the policeman's statement is inconsistent with its second 'e.g.' expansion.

The significance of this fact that a large class of semantic paradoxes (though not all of them) have formally inconsistent sentences among their 'namely-rider' Rylean expansions is limited by the consideration that the Rylean expansions are unwarranted anyway. But in spite of this limitation, this rule is a truth about truth:

(1.4) A sentence is true if and only if every namely-rider expansion of it (or every 'for example' rider expansion of it, or every *unavoidable* 'e.g.' rider expansion of it) is true.

However (1.4), unlike (1.2) and (1.3), is not meant to replace (1). Rather (1.4) states a separate, though logically equivalent, condition for the truth of a sentence. Since we accept this logical equivalence, we must give up (2). If we accept (1.4) as a substitute for (1), and do not give up (2), then the objection applying to (1.2) and (1.3) applies here as well. And to this objection can be added another that is even more serious. Remember our earlier example,

(B) What Bill, on first reading, takes B to say is not true.

The assumption that B could even be taken by Bill to say that what Bill takes B to say is not true leads to a contradiction. Bill can't even mistakenly think that B says such a thing. These rulings about what is said and what a sentence can be taken to say are supported by considerations of consistency. But they can also be explained and justified independently by the theory of predication set forth earlier, a theory not developed as an ad hoc response to paradoxes but as an account of predication and assertion. This is the theoretical requirement posed by the paradoxes and not a theory which tampers with the notion of truth and the laws of logic.

93 The adequacy of an account of what is said must be judged relative to the purpose of the account. If our purpose is to know what is said, then no adequate account is possible for semantic paradoxes, because accounts will always be circular. But our not being able to know in full what is said does not mean that nothing is said. Furthermore, we may be able to give a semantically adequate account of what is said even if it does not constitute a full account. On my theory, no one knows a full account of what is said in asserting 'Every true proposition is true', since asserting this is to assert every true proposition. To say that this assertion is to the effect that every true proposition is true does not fully indicate what has been asserted. Yet it is a semantically adequate gloss of what is said because it is enough to allow us to determine that what is said is true.

To say that A says that A is not true is neither a full account nor a semantically adequate account. On the other hand, to say that A says that A is not true and that it is not true that A is not true, though not a full account of what A says, is semantically adequate, because it brings out that A is contradictory and thus false. The solution to the paradoxical move from A's not being true to its qualifying as true for that very reason is that A is not only committed to A's not being true – it is also committed to its not being true that A is not true. There is thus no more difficulty in determining its truth value than there is for someone who says 'What I am saying is both true and false'. This is a contradiction (ignoring possible but irrelevant figurative uses and the like) and thus false, and the fact that one thing asserted is the true claim that it is false does not affect this assignment of falsity.

It may be objected that the paradox arises from the fact that the claim that what A says is not true is identical with the claim that what A says, namely that what A says is not true, is not true. And yet the first of these 'identical' claims is true and the second false! Well, someone who regards this as plausible will indeed have a paradox on his hands, but it will not be one to justify a stratified theory of truth which rejects the unrestricted generality of the laws of logic! The fact is that neither of these characterizations of what is allegedly the same claim adequately characterize any claim. But they do bring out that if anything is being said by A, it is also being denied, and that is to be contradictory. If A says anything, it says what it says is not true. But it also says what it says, and this is the same as saying what it says is true. So even without a non-circular characterization of what A says, which we will never have, we can see that if A says anything it is something contradictory, which we have no reason to count as true and thus no source of conflict in our principles for assigning truth values.

It may then be asked why I do not just go along with Ryle and others and say that A says nothing? Well, I am certainly not concerned to show that A says something. The primary problem is to explain why A does not say that A is not true even though this is something we can say. My answer to this is that if A says that A is not true it can only be in what I earlier called the 'non-assessable' sense of 'assert'. A may predicate non-truth of what A says, but it also says what A says and thus predicates truth of it. Thus if we ask what proposition A expresses, and we mean by this to ask what is the assessable assertion it makes, 'the proposition that A is not true' will not do for an answer. On the other hand, when we say that A is not true we are not both asserting and denying that which A asserts. If A asserts anything (assessably), we are denying that thing. So is A, but it is also asserting it.

The fact that we cannot give a non-circular description of what A says is not a sufficient reason for denying that it says anything. The same sort of circularity arises with 'Every proposition is either true or false'. One proposition which is either true or false is the proposition that every proposition is either true or false. Any attempt to specify what propositions the law of excluded middle is about will never avoid circularity. But the law is still a fundamental truth about truth. Of course the laws of logic have applications, uses, in a way that A does not. Still, I prefer to dismiss A as a trivial contradiction rather than as saying nothing, but I do not regard this choice as essential.

Someone could claim that A expresses the proposition that A is not true, which is, on the foregoing assumption, the proposition that the sentence A either does not express a proposition at all or the proposition it expresses is false. This proposition, which someone could claim that A expresses, is a true proposition, which can naturally and properly be expressed by using the same words as A. If lots of people claimed that A expressed this proposition, and were sincere, then would it not follow that relative to this class of people, A expressed that proposition?

This would not follow. People sincerely making such a claim

would not understand what they were claiming. They would be making a simple conceptual mistake in failing to see that what they are claiming as the assessable assertion made by A could not possibly be all that A says. A does say what they say it does, but only non-assessably, as part of what it says.

Someone (Jones) could of course see the sentence A without knowing it to be A. Just one possibility of this sort is one in which Jones sees A with the name covered and takes it to be saying something about some other sentence which is somehow named 'A'. There need be no conceptual mistake in this as long as Jones recognizes that he does not know in full what is said by the sentence he is considering. He should recognize that what is said by the sentence he is considering depends on what is said by the sentence A.

Similarly with B, if Bill sincerely utters the words 'It seems to me, on first reading, that what the sentence B says is that what I, on first reading, take it to say, is not true', he merely exhibits a conceptual confusion and does not identify any proposition at all, not even one B does not express, and so does not connect B with any proposition, even mistakenly. According to Bill, B predicates non-truth of what he takes B to say, where that predication is what he takes B to say. But then Bill ought to have said that B predicates non-truth of that predicating. That is, he ought equally well to have said this, but it won't do either. Bill's utterance, though sincere, would be nonsense. The sincerity would consist in his believing that he was saying something true. Though there is a great logical difference between the two cases, Bill's situation would in one respect resemble that of someone who sincerely uttered the words 'That sentence expresses the proposition that her dog is ill' with reference to a token of 'Her dog is ill' in a situation where there is no thought of woman or dog in the case. Such an utterance sounds natural and like one that expresses a proposition, but it does not.

If I were to assert 'What Bill, on first reading, takes B to say is not true' (in a case with a real Bill), I would be making a false statement because my included claim that there is something Bill takes B to say, is false. This false proposition is one Bill could not even think that B expresses. For Bill's use of similar words in an attempt to express a thought would not express any thought. This claim does not rest merely on the ground that it is the assumption required to avoid inconsistency. That is, of course, quite a firm ground, but has no explanatory value. The claim is also justified by my account of asserting and certain considerations about believing. When I speak of 'what Bill takes B to say' (of course I do not thus actually speak of anything, since there is no such thing) I need have no thought whatever of what it is that Bill takes B to say. I may only express the view that there is something he takes it to say, though I have no idea what. But Bill is using the same words in a performance purporting both to report something which is said about what he takes B to say and to say what he takes B to say. And this performance, due to the assertoric force of its components, comes to nothing. If the report of what is said were right, the report of what is said about it would have to be wrong, and conversely, if the report of what is said about what is allegedly said were right, then the report of what is said must be wrong. Thus Bill's attempt to report what is said would be a failure to report anything.

If we suppose that the truth about A is recorded in a sentence which is a token of the same type as A, and we then confront the two sentences with their names covered up or cut away, then it may seem absurd to wonder which of the two sentences expresses the contradiction and which the truth about it. But this is only because it is a matter of indifference which sentence is assigned which role from the standpoint of a logical problem. It is absurd to care which of the tokens was in fact named 'A'. But to understand the different roles is important.

It is possible that Bill is suffering from amnesia and does not know that he is Bill. In that case he could sincerely assert 'What Bill takes B to say is not true', without conceptual error. He might just think that there is someone named 'Bill' and a sentence named 'B' and so on. He would then be in the same position I was in in the foregoing paragraph. There would not be any proposition that Bill takes B to express, so his claim would be false.

Now suppose that Bill, thinking that there is somewhere a sentence named 'B' and man named 'Bill' who takes it to express some proposition which happens to be a false proposition, is writing a letter and wishes to convey this thought to his addressee. He notices the sentence token which has been cut out and left lying on the table, with its name gone, and he decides to save himself writing out his thought by just pasting that sentence into his letter. Surely he is now using the sentence B to express a certain proposition? No. For if he were asserting a proposition, in the assessable sense, that could be characterized in those terms, he would also, however unbeknownst to him, be predicating falsity of it, which would show that it was not what he was assessably asserting after all. Bill and I might both think quite sincerely and with no conceptual error that he was expressing the same proposition with the sentence he was using that I was with the sentence I was using, which could be a token of the same type or even the same token. But we would be mistaken because we did not know that the token Bill was using was in fact B. If we knew this, and knew of Bill that he was Bill, then persisting would involve conceptual confusion. (To say exactly what thought we would be persisting in is possible, but unnecessary and tedious.)

Since it is possible for me to use the same words as B to assert a false proposition it may be asked why I could not equally well take B to express that proposition. There would seem to be nothing contradictory in such an assumption. It is just the assumption that Bill takes B to say that that leads to trouble. There would be a paradox involved in this, in the sense that there would be the highly surprising consequence that everyone but Bill would be able to take B to say a certain thing! Bill could say 'So many people can't be wrong about what B says! I wish I were allowed to agree with them – it's hard being cut off from the truth this way!' But there would be no trouble for logic.

If this attitude towards B were adopted, the resulting situation would resemble those that arise with paradoxes of the 'Knower' family. Consider

(C) Bill does not know that C is true.

On the usual account, the assumption that C is false leads to a contradiction by having the consequence that Bill knows that C is true. So C is proven true by *reductio ad absurdum*, and yet poor Bill, no matter how acute he may be at following proofs, must not qualify as knowing this! This is not a logical contradiction, but it is paradoxical in the broad sense. Furthermore, our attitude towards Bill should be very sympathetic when we remember that he is a variable who ranges over us. This is brought out in the Knower paradox that goes 'No one knows that this statement is true'. And a similar general relative could easily be produced for B.

I once held that these Knower paradoxes were just a branch of the Liar family, giving what trouble they give because being known entails being true. I pointed out that each Knower paradox can be recast to fit the form of a Liar family paradox. For example, the point of C can also be made with

(C′) Either C′ is false or C′ is true without Bill's knowing it

which is a case of the disjunct-liar, 'Either this statement is false or *p*', which, like the implication-liar, makes it seem possible to prove any proposition put in as value of *p*.

However, this fact does not establish my claim, because even though each Knower paradox can be converted to a Liar form, my solution to the problem posed by that Liar form does not solve the problem posed by the Knower. For example, my answer to the implication-liar is that such a sentence asserts the truth of its consequent, because it makes itself its own antecedent. Thus if we put a false proposition for *p* in 'If this statement is true, then *p*', we get a falsehood as a result, on my account, rather than a paradoxical proof of *p* which can be made a logical paradox by choosing a logically false proposition for *p*. This is a perfect answer to the implication-liar, but if we cast C in this form the puzzle about Bill's knowledge will just be pushed into the consequent of the resulting conditional. So my theory of predication, which solves the Liar paradoxes, makes no difference to the Knower paradoxes.

Another reason for rejecting my former idea that the Knowers are subsumable under the Liars is that while knowing does indeed entail truth, paradoxes very similar to the Knowers can be produced using notions which do not entail truth. For example, there is

(D) Bill does not have good reasons for concluding that D is true.

Having good reasons for concluding true, unlike knowing, does not entail truth. And yet the assumption that D is false seems to entail that Bill has good reasons for concluding it is true. And while this is not a contradiction, for a suitable Bill it is very dubious indeed. And this makes it seem that the more dubious D becomes to Bill the more likely it is to be true. This, like the Knowers, is no logical paradox, but it is intellectually unwholesome, and clearly has similarities to the Knowers. So I was wrong to say that the Knowers belong in the Liar family. In fact, these paradoxes shade off into cases such as the 'surprise test' paradox, which raises problems which can be put in a case that does not involve any self-referring statements at all. I have discussed these problems elsewhere and will not go into them now. However, those features of the Knowers which relate to what they are taken to say are worth taking up here.

First let us return to B, where the remaining puzzle was that we seem to be able to take B to express a false proposition that Bill is barred from taking it to express. This is made unduly mysterious by thinking of the proposition in physical terms, as if it were a physical object that we can pick up but which magically recedes from Bill's attempts to grasp it. Similarly, someone might note that it is logically possible for him to assert 'Every Cretan assertion is false' and be speaking truly, while this is not logically possible for someone who remains a Cretan, and then wonder why he has access to this proposition while Cretans do not. Perhaps such puzzlement cannot be relieved – it depends on the person – but it should help to consider that due to facts about predication and assertion, a Cretan who asserts 'Every Cretan assertion is false' is asserting a different proposition from one asserted by a non-Cretan.

Epimenides may not know he is a Cretan. Both he and some non-Cretan may sincerely believe that in asserting 'Every Cretan assertion is false' they are making the same assertion; perhaps they may be issuing what they think is a joint statement about Cretans. They have the same opinion about the words they utter, but the words convey a different assertion for each. Until they know more about what predications they are performing, neither knows what he is saying.

If Bob uses the sentence B to make a false statement and neither he nor Bill know it is B that Bob used, they may naturally assume Bill takes the sentence Bob used, to say just what Bob used it to say. But neither of them knows what Bob has said. To know that, they would have to know what proposition it is, if any, Bob has denied the truth of. This requires finding out what sentence B is, and who Bob is. This 'knowing what' and 'knowing who' is not, in this context, satisfied by such answers as 'the sentence Bill asserted'. When Bill and Bob do find out that the sentence B is the one Bob used to make his statement they will, if they reason correctly about assertion and predication, see that no proposition can be adequately described as being taken by Bill to have been expressed by B. They can also both see that if Bob's use of B came to anything at all, it said something that entailed that there is a proposition which Bill takes B to express. This latter being false, they have reason to conclude that if Bob's use of B expressed a proposition, it was a false one.

If this reason is followed up, then we have the paradoxical result already mentioned, with Bob using B to express a false proposition which Bill is for some mysterious reason unable to take B to express. (I am assuming that Bill and Bob are ideally rational agents, doing the best possible with the case. A case in which Bill mistakenly takes B to say something such as that all men are mortal or even just that there is a proposition he takes B to express, with the attribution of falsity overlooked, is not important.)

However, it is not necessary to accept this idea. It is reasonable to reject the assumption on which it depends – that Bob has used B to make a statement. There is such a thing as claiming that Bill takes B to say something which is false. But there is also reason to deny that this claim can be made by using B itself. Bill cannot follow through an enquiry into what B says and get a consistent answer. For if he attempts to answer, his words will necessarily leave out an important predication that, it will be plain to Bill, is equally well entitled to be part of what is said by B. Bob appears to be better off, but he can recognize that taking a sentence to express a proposition is not a private activity. It is somehow a matter of how properly trained readers or hearers respond due to their overall grasp of the language of the sentence. In this respect B differs radically from other tokens of its type, because of the role it plays, which a suitable agent will have to understand in the course of a properly conducted enquiry into what B says. If 'Bill' in B were replaced by 'any rational user of the language of this sentence', Bill's situation would be shared by everyone else. It seems to me perfectly reasonable to hold that, due to its being B, that particular token cannot be taken to express a false proposition in the same way that other tokens of it can.

This is not a decisive answer to the residual paradox but it must be stressed that this paradox is not a logical contradiction. It is a question of how the notion of regarding a sentence to express a proposition should be applied. My theory of assertion and predication provides the basis for setting aside the premises that lead to contradiction. Plausible assumptions as to the universalizability of judgements about what a sentence says give a reason for saying that B does not say anything. If these reasons are rejected, then we get a peculiar result – Bill cut off from what B says. I will not press further the question which course should be followed.

The situation with C and D is similar in this respect: one must choose between accepting the strange conclusions they appear to make necessary, or else one must give up the idea that certain descriptions of what they say are satisfactory. How could C possibly not be known true by an ideally rational agent like Bill who has studied it carefully, except by not being true? If C were taken to advance its not being true as reason for Bill's not knowing it to be true, then C would come out as contradictory and there would be no problem as to why it is not known to be true by Bill. Insofar as we do not regard C itself as being committed to explaining its denial of Bill's knowledge in terms of maintaining its own falsity, then we have Bill paradoxically cut off from the truth. And with 'No one knows this statement is true' all the rest of us will join Bill. This would make a grand-scale case of Moore's paradox – we would all be saying 'That statement is true but we don't know it is'! This is consistent, but it is also consistent to regard B as committing itself to its own falsity. And that avoids the paradox about our ignorance of the truth. Again I will not try to determine which course is right.

My distinction between assessable and non-assessable assertion is crucial to my treatment of the semantic paradoxes, so it is worth taking up a case in which the distinction is featured in a paradox sentence. Consider, for example,

(E) Some proposition asserted by E is false,

where it is understood that the proposition may be either assessably or non-assessably asserted by E. On the usual approach, E raises the same problem as A. On my account, for any proposition that is assessably or non-assessably asserted by E, E asserts the truth of that proposition. This is not the same as asserting that every proposition asserted by E is true, but it is materially equivalent to this assertion. So if C does make an assessable assertion it is a false one. I could assert that some proposition asserted by E is false without thereby asserting every proposition that is asserted by E, but E cannot. That dissolves the contradiction.

It is not so clear whether E says anything. If we took E as asserting that everything that it asserts is true, then it would straightforwardly express a contradiction. But it would not be correct in general to infer from a sentence's asserting the truth of every proposition it asserts to its asserting that every proposition it asserts is true. For that would make every sentence self-referential, in the way that one of Buridan's proposals would have done. 'All men are mortal' asserts the truth of whatever it asserts, but it does not assert anything about itself. We can only say that E does not assessably assert that some proposition it asserts is false. If it asserts that at all, it must assert something else. For if it were the only thing it asserted, then it also must predicate falsity of that thing, which means that 'that some proposition asserted by E is false' would not adequately describe what E said. E cannot say just the one thing, but there is no basis for determining what else it says. Thus it seems reasonable to conclude that E does not say anything. Here again, though, it must be stressed that this decision is not an essential part of my theory.

I have held that the principal problem posed by the semantic paradoxes is that of determining what is said by these sentences. Perhaps it would be more precise to say that the problem is to explain why it is that what cannot be said by these sentences or even taken to be said can be said by using other sentences which may in some cases even be tokens of the same type as the paradox sentence. And my answer is in terms of my theses concerning assertion and predication. Going beyond this to decide what is said or if anything is said by these sentences is a less strongly determined matter. There is a certain amount of freedom in how we interpret sentences taken by themselves. The degree of freedom should not be overestimated, but there is some.

For example, someone might argue as follows about the sentence E: E itself puts forward the idea that what it says can be described as 'that some proposition asserted by E is false'. If this were what E said, then E would predicate falsity of that proposition and thus would have said that it is false that some proposition asserted by E is false. Neither of these descriptions of what is said are free of circularity. They require following out to see what proposition could be one to satisfy the existential claim, and this can never be done without circularity (at best). But still we can see from these descriptions that a formal contradiction is involved. Perhaps they are not distinct contradictory propositions. There is clearly contradictory predication, and so E is a contradiction. Thus a semantically adequate account of what E says is that it says that there is a false proposition asserted by E and that it is false that there is a false proposition asserted by E.

I do not accept this because it is only if 'that some proposition asserted by E is false' described the only proposition asserted by E, that is, described the assessable assertion made by E, that it would follow that E predicated falsity of this proposition. But if E did predicate falsity of this proposition, then that description would surely not properly describe what is said by E, which is tacitly acknowledged in the above paragraph, since the final 'semantically adequate' description of what is said by E is phrased to indicate both a predication of falsity and a denial of that predication. But even if the argument for attributing to E that contradictory claim is not compelling, there is no inconsistency in assigning this claim to E. There is no inconsistency in returning to the consideration that lots of intelligent people might so interpret E, and using this as a consideration in favor of taking it to say something so describable.

I prefer to say that E does not say anything, which is for it to be what Russell calls nonsensical. Here it must be remembered that this is not because of attempted self-reference. *Anything can be predicated of anything.* But nothing can be predicated of nothing. It is not that E attempts to attribute a predicate to the wrong sort of subject. It attempts to attribute a predicate to something when there is no such thing. Thus even if my verdict about some of the semantic paradoxes is similar to Ryle's, the basis is altogether different.

This can be brought out further by considering

(F)   Every proposition asserted by F is false.

F is a contradiction, because 'the proposition that every proposition asserted by F is false' only needs to be non-assessably asserted by F for it to follow that F predicates falsity of it. This is because the universal generalization attributes its predicate to everything, or everything that satisfies the subject condition if the subject introduces a restriction, while the particular or existential and the singular subject-predicate statements attribute the predicate more restrictedly. E only predicates falsity of the proposition that some proposition asserted by E is false if that is the only proposition asserted by E (or if all others are false; but this clause in the account of existential predication does not apply in the case of E). But for F, or the Epimenides, that does not matter.

This is why the laws of logic are so clearly meaningful in spite of the fact that they are as self-referential as A is. It is the lack of generality of B and E (and indefinitely many others) that leads to their saying nothing, not their attempt at semantic self-reference.

(For that matter, they are not semantically self-referring at all, since they have no semantic selves to refer to.) Even A is a questionable case as far as saying something goes, but the Epimenides is all right. For a Cretan to assert that every Cretan assertion is false is for him to assert that, among other things, it is false that every Cretan assertion is false. We cannot state in full what Epimenides has said just because he has said so much at once. But it is easy to see that what he has said is contradictory and also to understand what kind of thing he has said. An account which tends to class general self-referential attempts at saying as successful (at saying something, not necessarily at being true) and particular or singular ones as unsuccessful, is going in a direction which preserves the laws of logic. (Here when I contrast 'general' with 'singular' I mean a distinction in terms of predication. 'The property of being a man is subsumed under the property of being a mortal' predicates being subsumed under the property of being a mortal in a singular way, of one thing which is introduced by an individuating condition. But it predicates the property of being mortal in a general way, of things that satisfy a general condition, just as 'Every man is mortal' does. The application of my claim here to semantic paradoxes thus depends on a distinction between general and singular that is only relative to the predicates that happen to be the important ones in the paradoxes, and not on any absolute distinction.)

'Some proposition is either true or false' does not predicate being either true or false of any proposition. It does predicate being true or false of everything subject to the condition that that thing is such that nothing but it is a proposition. But nothing satisfies this condition since there is more than one proposition. So there is no problem saying what it says. So it is not mere lack of generality combined with self-reference that tends to prevent a sentence from saying something. It is rather, *exclusive* self-reference of the sort exemplified by B and E. The words of E cannot be taken to describe just one thing said by E, because it would have to be just one thing (that is, non-assessable) rather than the only thing, and yet there is no basis for assigning it anything else to say, because it is only if it were the one thing that its predicate would apply to itself to produce some further claim. But because F uses universal predication, its words can be taken to describe a proposition which it non-assessably says. This proposition does not have to be the only thing F says in order for its predicate to apply to it, yielding another thing F says, which makes F contradictory. This additional thing F says is true, but being part of an overall contradictory performance, that does not help F qualify as true.

It has been observed how easy it is to give a theory explaining why A says nothing. But either the reasons given provide no basis for dealing with such semantic paradoxes as the Epimenides, or they are reasons which also rule out the general laws of logic. My account gives reasons for rejecting many of the singular paradox cases as meaningless while making the Epimenides clearly contradictory, without affecting the laws of logic at all.

It may be asked how I can say of a meaningless sentence that it is self-referring. The main answer is that by meaningless, I only mean that there is nothing which is what is said. There can still be a working referring expression and a predicate term which is meaningful in the sense of expressing a property. Then applying rules for predicating that property determined by the style of reference, we may find that nothing can qualify as what is said, so the referring expression will fail to refer and the predicate fail to be attributed. There is no stratification.

The rest of the Liar family paradoxes can be dealt with along the lines already set forth. The implication-liar, 'If this statement is true then two plus two is five' says that if a certain statement is true then two plus two is five and it says that that statement is true. So it says that two plus two is five and is thus false. Similarly for conjunction-liars and disjunction-liars. The quantified implication-liar, 'If every statement on this blackboard is true, then two plus two is five', says that if everything of a certain kind is true then two plus two is five and for everything of that certain kind, it says that it is true, so it says that two plus two is five.

The alethic modal versions of Liar paradoxes are dealt with on the assumption that all true modal assertions are necessarily true. Consider for example

(G) G is not necessarily true.

G is ambiguous. It could mean that the sentence G could express a false proposition. This is true, a case of a true syntactically self-referring sentence. On the other hand, G could be taken to represent an attempt to predicate possible falsity of what G says, or at least to deny that there is something which G says (in the assessable sense) which is necessarily true. On the usual approach, assuming that G says in the assessable sense that what G says is not necessarily true, we get a contradiction, since the assumption that G is false leads to a contradiction, which entails that it is necessarily true, which is inconsistent with what it allegedly says.

On my account, if what G says were just that what G says is not necessary, then G would deny the necessity of this as well. And to deny the necessity of a modal claim is inconsistent with that modal claim, so that G, being committed to both claims, would be a contradiction. My claim that G is not necessarily true would not be so committed, and is true, and thus necessarily true.

This approach is analogous to the one described earlier which makes E out to be false rather than saying nothing, and would have the same rationale, which I reject in this case for the same reason as before. I would say that G says nothing, for essentially the same reason that E does not. Other paradoxes based on alethic modality but universal with respect to the problematic property would escape this failure to say anything in the same way that F manages to outdo its relative E and earn itself a truth value, namely false. For example, there is the case of Epicautious the Discretan, who asserts 'Everything I say is contingent'. Without going into the obvious details of how this makes trouble on the usual account, on my account it involves predicating contingency of Epicautious' (non-assessable) assertion that everything he says is contingent, and is thus inconsistent.

Paradoxes based on phrases rather than full sentences may still belong to the Liar family. The phrases 'does not apply truly to itself' and 'yields a falsehood when appended to its own quotation' give paradox sentences which can be dealt with straightforwardly along lines already indicated. This is not the case with the Heterological paradox. It can be stated in various ways. First, the term 'heterological' is defined either by saying that a term is heterological if and only if it expresses a property of which it is not an instance, or by saying that it does not express a property of which it is an instance. (Whether 'red' is heterological when written in red ink depends on whether we are talking about tokens or talking about types. Furthermore, 'expresses' can be taken in more than one way. 'Being here' does not express a property as independently as 'heavy' does and 'heavy' does not express a property as independently as 'red' or 'weighing 180 pounds' does. Then 'red' may in some contexts express the property of being a communist, which is a rather

different sort of variation from context to context from that of
'here'. 'Being here' expresses a property relative to my assertion 'I like
being here', where by here I mean my farm. It does not express a
property by itself. On the other hand, 'red' does, in spite of having
its own kind of variations. To begin, then, it will be assumed that
'heterological' is concerned with expressing *simpliciter*, so that
'being here' is heterological by the second definition, because it does
not express a property, and not heterological by the first definition,
also because it does not express a property.)

My theses about assertion and predication have the consequence
that, by either definition, 'heterological' does not express a property.
When one says that 'verb' is heterological, one speaks truly. There
is nothing wrong with the definition of the term 'heterological'.
But what one does, in saying that the word 'verb' is heterological, is
to deny the property of being a verb of that word. For this saying is
equivalent to saying that some property is such that it is expressed
by the word 'verb' and not possessed by it. This is to say that every
property which is such that none besides it is expressed but not possessed by 'verb', is expressed but not possessed by 'verb'. The
property of being a verb satisfies the antecedent condition in this
generalization and so the predicate, being expressed but not possessed by 'verb' is predicated of it by the assertion that 'verb' is
heterological. And this is to deny the property of being a verb of
'verb'. Similar reasoning shows that asserting that 'obscene' is
heterological predicates not being obscene of 'obscene', with 'long',
not being long (for a word!), with 'pronounceable' not being pronounceable, and so on.

Thus on my account of predication, 'heterological' is like 'being
here' in that it does not, by itself, express any property at all. The
definition of 'heterological' is in perfectly good order. But 'here' is
definable too. A definition does not always supply a property. It
may, as in this case, supply a recipe for properties.

It might be thought that a different Heterological paradox could
be generated by working with the notion of expressing relative to a
given occasion of use rather than that of expressing *simpliciter*. This
is not so, but I will not take time to go over that point in detail.

This solution to the Heterological paradox provides a good case
for contrasting my theory with traditional ones. My doctrine that
asserting that some *A* is a *B* will involve predicating being a *B* in
cases where there is exactly one *A* or no *A*, is likely to be regarded as

radical. But it follows straightforwardly from the idea that asserting that every *A* is a *B* involves predicating being a *B* of each *A*, and this view has some traditional support. The contrary popular view, that the 'existential' assertion does not involve predicating being a *B*, but only 'claiming that this property has instances', is the principal source of trouble in the Heterological paradox, though the blame has usually been attributed everywhere else. The idea has been that one can say of a given word that there exists some property which it expresses and does not possess, without having to specify what property. And this is true. One can make an existential claim without being able to cite an instance. But it has also been assumed that for that reason no property is attributed to the word beyond the 'property' of expressing some property and not possessing it. And when this leads to trouble, the laws of classical logic are ravaged and the concept of truth mistreated, while this false assumption passes undisputed. The truth is, not that one cannot say of a given word that there exists a property which it expresses but does not possess, but that this is not to predicate the same thing no matter what the word. The traditional approach to the paradox regards the quantifier in 'such that there exists a property which it expresses and does not possess' as requiring restrictions on its range. It is not restrictions that are necessary, but rather, recognition of the unrestricted working of predication.

Just as there is no such property as being heterological, there is no property of being a property which does not have itself as an instance. Most properties do not have themselves as instances. But when I say of a property *F* that it is not an instance of *F*, I predicate being non-*F* of it. And when the property is *G*, I do something different, and so on.

Liar family paradoxes which involve a cycle of statements such as the Policeman, do not pose any problems, except that they can become complicated by their length. That is, a version of the Liar paradox featuring a million sentences passing along the fateful predication could be impossible to follow. But this is no problem for logic. If one member of a cycle such as the Policeman could escape to reflect on the cycle as we do when we report the truth about it, that might create problems, but that cannot happen, for if a member of the cycle were to step out of the inconsistency, it would no longer be a member of the cycle. If the policeman sought to have his words understood as a comment on the logical trouble the prisoner has gotten into with his statement, the prisoner would no longer be in any logical trouble, either. There would be no more cyclical paradox.

If we count semantic paradoxes as sentences such that the usual account of what they say leads to contradiction, there are infinitely many, and even if there were a recursive definition of the notion of a grammatical sentence in a natural language, there would be no recursive procedure for picking out paradox sentences. My answer to them certainly does not provide such procedures and my account is not complete in the technical sense. The stratified theories of truth achieve a kind of guarantee of completeness by ruling out all self-reference including the laws of logic. By rejecting this undiscriminating approach, I must confront semantic paradoxes as they arise. But I think I have covered a sufficiently varied sample of them to establish my claim that the paradoxes do not warrant restricting the universality of the laws of logic or denying that anything may be predicated of anything. Before closing I will discuss one semantic paradox which differs considerably from those covered so far, Richard's paradox, and elaborate further on the attitude towards the paradoxes of set theory which was described earlier.

94 Richard's paradox is standardly set forth as follows: let the series S of finite sequences of words (of English, we may suppose) which definitely describe a number (or define a number – the difference does not matter here) be put into alphabetical order. Then consider the following finite sequence of words: the number which is formed by writing first zero, then a decimal point, then a number which is obtained by adding one to the first number in the decimal part of the first number described in series S unless that first number is nine, in which case zero is written, and which is continued according to the rule that its nth decimal place is obtained by either adding one to the nth decimal place of the nth number described in series S, or writing zero if the nth decimal of the nth number is nine. If there is a series S, then this 'diagonal' description necessarily describes a number which is not determined by a description in series S. And yet the diagonal description is a finite sequence of English words and thus necessarily qualifies as a member of series S. Thus we have a contradiction.

This shows that there is no such thing as series S. However, it is objected that every finite sequence of words either determines a number or does not, so that the existence is unavoidable. This is not true. A sequence of words only determines a number to one or more persons and for some sequences then only with respect to a given temporal position. Trying to follow the directions of the diagonal definition leads to a contradiction. The directions cannot be followed through. For if the diagonal definition were in a series *S*, then it would occupy a position in the alphabetical ordering, say the *m*th place. But then to calculate the *m*th decimal place of the diagonal number, one would have to alter that very decimal place to follow the instructions of the diagonal definition! Relative to any series of number-determining sequences, to which it does not belong, the diagonal definition defines a number. But no series can both include it and be its referent. There is such a thing as a sequence which determines a number only relative to series to which it does not belong. There is no well-defined series consisting of sequences which determine a number *simpliciter*.

However, relative of course to the understanding of some group, there is an alphabetically ordered series of English sentences which are true and the series may be infinite, even though sentence types tend not to be true since some of their tokens will be false, some true. For example, 'This sentence is not in the series of true English sentences', if taken to make a claim about its own sentence type, is true, because no doubt some tokens of that type have been used to refer to other sentences entirely. It is possible to construct sentence types which avoid these possible variant token uses and refer unambiguously to themselves. This is done in a way rather like the device of Goedel numbers in mathematical logic. A sentence refers to the sentence which results from combining letters according to certain rules, where the rules are so chosen that it turns out that it is that very sentence which is constructed in that way. In this way the nuisance of having to deal only with tokens can be gotten round to a certain extent.

Anyway, a sentence which manages to say of itself that it is not in the series of true sentences will never say that in the assessable sense, and will be a contradiction just like A. But something analogous to the case of someone trying to construct a series of number-determining sequences arises when we consider the task of *constructing* a series of true sentences. That is, rather than speaking of the abstract series, we speak of the series some agent has set to work to produce, call him Jones. The infinite number of true sentences is a handicap to

Jones, but not the most serious one. The worst trouble is that such a sentence as 'This sentence is not on Jones' list', interpreted self-referentially, cannot be put on Jones' list without Jones' having failed to list only true sentences, and cannot be left off Jones' list without Jones' having failed to list all true sentences. The concept of all true sentences is consistent, but the instruction, to list all true sentences, cannot consistently be carried through. The 'concept' of all number-determining sequences is not all right, that is, there is no such concept – the notion is ill-defined, and the instruction to list all number-determining sequences cannot consistently be carried through.

Richard's paradox is sometimes cited as a purely semantic problem not involving set theory. I think that, on the contrary, it suggests a very important idea about classes. Richard's paradox brings in classes because it makes reference to a series which is a kind of collection or class. And it brings out that a class must be viewed as constructed by a rule, and that the rule must be one that could consistently be followed.

I would rather deny that there are such things as classes than grant that a class could be a member of itself. Why is that? There is no problem at all in a property's being an instance of itself. Why isn't the class of non-men a non-man? The difference between classes and properties becomes clear if we consider that a class is something that can be constructed while a property is not limited in that way. The instruction for forming the class of non-men is to find a thing, apprehend it, and determine whether it is a man, and then list its name on the class roster. If this instruction is not limited, is extended so you are to apply the rule to *everything*, it is contradictory. For if the class roster were completed (on an infinite sheet, or by writing diminishingly small) then and only then would the class be completed. But then and only then would the class be a thing, and thus require extending the list. A class cannot belong to itself because to be a candidate for membership it must be complete while as a thing still open to membership it cannot be complete.

This reasoning is a lot like the vicious-circle principle, except that it has no application to propositions and properties. Russell held that 'propositions are a set having no total' and took this to mean that there could not be a proposition about all propositions. This has already been criticized. But there is no need to make this step from valid considerations about the limits on construction of classes to false restrictions on the universality of laws of logic.

This does not involve the awful idea that sets are actual human constructions. Their having to be possible constructions would still leave their existence mind-independent. At any rate, I said earlier that I have no theory of sets to offer. I do not know of a satisfactory no-class theory, so my sympathy for the general idea of such a theory is of no importance. Perhaps a stratified set theory is acceptable after all, if it is clear that it does not require a general restriction on generality.

References

Anscombe, G. E. M. 1965. 'The Intentionality of Sensations', in R. J. Butler (ed.), *Analytical Philosophy* (2 vols., Barnes and Noble), 2

Austin, J. L. 1950. 'Truth', *Proceedings of the Aristotelean Society*, supp. 24

Basson, A. H., 1960. 'Propositional Functions', *Proceedings of the Aristotelean Society*, supp. 32

Bennett, Jonathan. 1966. *Kant's Analytic* (Cambridge University Press)

Bergson, Henri. 1944. *Creative Evolution*, trans. Arthur Mitchell (Modern Library)

Bernays, Paul. 1967. 'On Platonism in Mathematics', in Jean van Heijenoort (ed.), *From Frege to Godel* (Harvard University Press)

Bochenski, Innocenty M. 1970. *History of Formal Logic* (2nd edn, Chelsea Publishing Co.)

Buridan, Jean. 1966. *Sophisms on Meaning and Truth*, trans. Theodore K. Scott (Irvington)

Cargile, J. 1967. 'On Believing you Believe', *Analysis* 27 (6), pp. 177–83

—— 1969. 'The Sorites Paradox', *British Journal for the Philosophy of Science* 20, pp. 193–202

—— 1970. 'Davidson's Notion of Logical Form', *Inquiry* 13, pp. 129–39

Dedekind, Richard. 1901. *Essays on the Theory of Numbers*, trans. Wooster Woodruff Beman (Open Court)

Devitt, Michael. 1974. 'Singular Terms', *Journal of Philosophy* 71, pp. 183–205

Donnellan, K. 1966. 'Reference and Definite Descriptions', *Philosophical Review* 75, pp. 281–304

—— 1974. 'Speaking of Nothing', *Philosophical Review* 83, pp. 3–31

Dretske, Fred. 1972. 'Contrastive Statements', *Philosophical Review* 81, pp. 411–37

Dummett, Michael. 1974. *Frege: Philosophy of Language* (Harper Row)

Frege, Gottlob. 1893, 1903. *Grundgesetze der Arithmetik* (2 vols., H. Pohle)

—— 1952. *Translations from the Philosophical Writings of Gottlob Frege*, ed. Peter Geach and Max Black (Basil Blackwell)

—— 1956. 'The Thought', trans. A. M. and Marcelle Quinton, *Mind* 65 (259), pp. 289–311

—— 1968. *Foundations of Arithmetic: A Logico-Mathematical Enquiry into the Concept of Numbers*, trans. J. L. Austin (Northwestern University Press)

Geach, Peter T. 1962. *Reference and Generality* (Cornell University Press)

—— 1969. 'Quine's Syntactic Insights', in Donald Davidson and Jaako Hintikka (eds.), *Words and Objections* (Reidel)

Kant, Immanuel. 1972. *Critique of Pure Reason* (Dutton)

Kaplan, David. 1968. 'Quantifying In', *Synthese* 19, pp. 178–214

Katz, Jerrold J. 1965. 'The Relevance of Linguistics to Philosophy', *Journal of Philosophy* 62, pp. 590–602

Kenny, Antony. 1969. 'Descartes' Ontological Argument', in Joseph Margolis (ed.), *Fact and Existence* (University of Toronto Press)

Kripke, Saul. 1972. 'Naming and Necessity', in Gilbert Harman and Donald Davidson (eds.), *Semantics of Natural Language* (Humanities)

Lakoff, George. 1968. 'Counterparts, or the Problem of Reference in Transformational Grammar', presented at the Summer Meeting of the Linguistic Society of America, July 27, 1968

Lewis, Clarence I. and Langford, Cooper. 1959. *Symbolic Logic* (Dover)

Lockwood, Michael. 1975. 'On Predicating Proper Names', *Philosophical Review* 84, pp. 471–98

Malcolm, Norman. 1963. 'Knowledge and Belief', in *Knowledge and Certainty* (Prentice-Hall Inc.), pp. 58–72

Mayo, Bernard. 1962. 'The Open Future', *Mind* 71 (281), pp. 1–14

Meinong, Alexius. 1961. 'The Theory of Objects', in Roderick Chisholm (ed.), *Realism and the Background of Phenomenology* (Free Press), pp. 76–117

Mill, J. S. 1843. *A System of Logic* (Longman's)

Moore, G. E. 1944. 'Russell's "Theory of Descriptions"', in P.A. Schilpp (ed.), *The Philosophy of Bertrand Russell* (Harper Row)

Prior, A. N. 1958. 'Epimenides the Cretan', *Journal of Symbolic Logic* 23, pp. 261–6

Quine, Willard. 1940. *Mathematical Logic* (Harper Row)

—— 1953. *From a Logical Point of View* (Harper Row)

—— 1956. 'Quantifiers and Propositional Attitudes', *Journal of Philosophy* 53, pp. 177–87

—— 1969. *Set Theory and its Logic* (rev. edn, Harvard University Press)

—— 1975. 'On the Individuation of Attributes', in A. R. Anderson, R. B. Marcus and R. M. Martin (eds.), *The Logical Enterprise* (Yale University Press)

Ramsey, F. P. 1931. *The Foundations of Mathematics* (Routledge and Kegan Paul)

Russell, B. 1903. *The Principles of Mathematics* (2nd edn, Norton, 1964)

—— 1905. 'On Denoting', in Robert C. Marsh (ed.), *Logic and Knowledge* (Putnam, 1971)

—— 1908. 'Mathematical Logic as Based on the Theory of Types', in Robert C. Marsh (ed.), *Logic and Knowledge* (Putnam, 1971)

—— 1940. *Inquiry into Meaning and Truth* (Allen and Unwin)

Ryle, Gilbert. 1954. *Dilemmas* (Cambridge University Press)

—— 1954a. 'Heterologicality', in Margaret MacDonald (ed.), *Philosophy and Analysis* (Blackwell)

—— 1962. *The Concept of Mind* (Barnes and Noble)

Strawson, P. F. 1949. 'Truth', *Analysis* 9 (6), reprinted in Margaret MacDonald (ed.), *Philosophy and Analysis* (Blackwell, 1954), pp. 260–77

—— 1950. 'On Referring', *Mind* 59 (235), pp. 320–44

—— 1959. *Individuals* (Methuen)

Tarski, Alfred. 1944. 'The Semantic Conception of Truth', *Philosophy and Phenomenological Research* 4, pp. 341–75

Vendler, Zeno. 1967. *Linguistics in Philosophy* (Cornell University Press)

Whitehead, A. N. and Russell, B. 1913. *Principia Mathematica* (Cambridge University Press, 1962)

Williams, Bernard. 1969. 'Descartes' Ontological Argument: a Comment', in Joseph Margolis (ed.), *Fact and Existence* (University of Toronto Press)

Wittgenstein, L. 1973. *Philosophical Investigations*, ed. Kenneth Scott (3rd edn, Macmillan)

Wolterstorff, Nicholas. 1970. *On Universals: An Essay in Ontology* (University of Chicago Press)

Ziff, Paul. 1960. *Semantic Analysis* (Cornell University Press)

Index